August Euler & His Airplanes

1908 – 1920

Volume 2

A Centennial Perspective on Great War Airplanes

Michael Düsing

Translated by Dr. Hannes Täger

Great War Aviation Centennial Series #33

Notes

For our aviation books in print please see our website at: **www.aeronautbooks.com**
I am looking for photographs of the less well-known German aircraft of WWI for future titles. For questions or to help with photographs please contact me at **jherris@me.com**

ISBN: 978-1-935881-69-8

Design and layout: Jack Herris
Cover design: Aaron Weaver
Digital photo editing: Aaron Weaver & Jack Herris

Books for Enthusiasts by Enthusiasts
www.aeronautbooks.com

Table of Contents

Volume 1

Volume 2

14. The Treaty of Versailles – Demise and Restart of the German Aircraft Industry

The First World War was finished. Germany had to sign the armistice agreement on 11 November 1918 in the wood of Compiègne. Then already on 18 January 1919 the representatives of the victorious allied powers met in the mirror hall of the castle of Versailles for consultations about the peace conditions which were summarized in the equally called Treaty of Versailles.

32 nations participated in the conference but not the defeated middle powers, which were not allowed at all to the conference.[1] The most important decisions met the "Council of the Four", in which the heads of the governments of Great Britain, David Lloyd George, of France, Georges Clemençeau, and from Italy, Vittorio Orlando, as well as the American president Woodrow Wilson were represented.

The treaty aimed for a compensation for the war damages on one hand and should make sure at the same time that that Germany would have at her disposal only a very limited economic and military power for many years.

Its effects for Germany were far worse than commonly feared and expected by the directly involved German diplomats.

In his charge as leader of the Reichsluftamt August Euler did not feel integrated in the negotiations of the questions of the future aviation in Germany as he had wished. Several times he complained to senior places that the discussions about questions of the future German aviation did not happen with direct involvement of the Reichsluftamt or at least the aviation experts. When the negotiations began the Reichsluftamt was still subordinated to the Ministerium des Innern, this did not represent the interests of the German aviation in the necessary way on the ambassador's conferences in Euler's opinion.

Only a few days before the signing of the Treaty

Above: Scrapping of airplanes.

of Versailles by representatives of the German government Euler got the task in the Reichsluftamt to decide, based on available text of the conditions for a peace, if the aviation-related articles were "compliable" for Germany or if the text of the trety could result in risks of all kinds for Germany. According to a protocol of the meeting from 18 June 1919 Unterstaatssekretär Euler vehemently defended his postion that the content of the treaty was by far not fulfilling the expectations of the German aviation industry and the aviation in general but in the interest of peace the forced obligations (Art. 313 to 320) for the civil aviation had to be considered attainable with the following objections: "The satisfiability will be possible in bigger extent, also in the interest of international aviation, if we can keep the stationary means of aviation traffic, mentioned in paragraph III article 198–202.

If the opponent rejects the preservation of the stationary means of air traffic and if he is not granting the mutuality of air traffic, then this means heavy damage for German aviation. However, questions of civil aviation are not such questions of life that the conclusion of the treaty should be endangered therefore.

The Reichsluftamt became convinced after article 320 that pre-conditions for verbal negotiations of aviation questions are given in special measure."[2]

The Treaty of Versailles had to be signed as was to be expected under non-observance of all objections and doubts of Germany on 28 June 1919 and was brought into effect on 10 January 1920. It formally finished the World War between the German Empire and the powers of the Entente and associated powers.

The aspects of the German aviation were treated in two separate segments: While the articles 198 to 202 threated regulations about the military and naval aviation, the articles 313 to 320 concerned the civil aviation. Their text was:

Concerning Military Aviation:

Article 198.
The armed forces of Germany must not include any military or naval air forces.

Germany may, during a period not extending beyond 1 October 1919, maintain a maximum number of one hundred seaplanes or flying boats, which shall be exclusively employed in searching for submarine mines, shall be furnished with the necessary equipment for this purpose, and shall in no case carry arms, munitions, or bombs of any nature whatever.

In addition to the engines installed in the seaplanes or flying boats above mentioned, one spare engine may be provided for each engine of each of these craft.

No dirigible shall be kept.

Article 199.
Within two months from the coming into force of the present Treaty the personnel of air forces on the rolls of the German land and sea forces shall be demobilised. Up to 1 October 1919, however, Germany may keep and maintain a total number of one thousand men, including officers, for the whole of the cadres and personnel, flying and non-flying, of all formations and establishments.

Article 200.
Until the complete evacuation of German territory by the Allied and Associated troops, the aircraft of the Allied and Associated Powers shall enjoy in Germany freedom of passage through the air, freedom of transit, and of landing.

Article 201.
During the six months following the coming into force of the present Treaty, the manufacture and importation of aircraft, parts of aircraft, engines for aircraft, and parts of engines for aircraft, shall be forbidden in all German territory.

Article 202.
On the coming into force of the present Treaty, all military and naval aeronautical material, except the machines mentioned in the second and third paragraphs of Article 198, must be delivered to the Governments of the Principal Allied and Associated Powers.

Delivery must be effected at such places as the said Governments may select, and must be completed within three months.

In particular, this material will include all items under the following heads which are or have been in use or were designed for warlike purposes:

- Complete aeroplanes and seaplanes, as well as those being manufactured, repaired or assembled.
- Dirigibles able to take the air, being manufactured, repaired or assembled.
- Plant for the manufacture of hydrogen.
- Dirigible sheds and shelters of every kind for aircraft.
- Pending their delivery, dirigibles will, at the expense of Germany, be maintained inflated with hydrogen; the plant for the manufacture of hydrogen, as well as the sheds for dirigibles may at the discretion of the said Powers, be left to Germany until the time when the dirigibles are handed over.
- Engines for aircraft.

- Nacelles and fuselages.
- Armament (guns, machine guns, light machine guns, bomb-dropping apparatus, torpedo-dropping apparatus, synchronisation apparatus, aiming apparatus).
- Munitions (cartridges, shells, bombs loaded or unloaded, stocks of explosives or of material for their manufacture).
- Instruments for use on aircraft.
- Wireless apparatus and photographic or cinematograph apparatus for use on aircraft.
- Component parts of any of the items under the preceding heads. The material referred to above shall not be removed without special permission from the said Governments.

Article 210.
The Aeronautical Inter-Allied Commission of Control will represent the Governments of the Principal Allied and Associated Powers in dealing with the German Government in all matters concerning the execution of the air clauses.

In particular it will be its duty to make an inventory of the aeronautical material existing in German territory, to inspect aeroplane, balloon and motor manufactories, and factories producing arms, munitions and explosives capable of being used by aircraft, to visit all aerodromes, sheds, landing grounds, parks and depots, to authorise, where necessary, a removal of material and to take delivery of such material.

The German Government must furnish to the Aeronautical Inter-Allied Commission of Control all such information and legislative, administrative or other documents which the Commission may consider necessary to ensure the complete execution of the air clauses, and in particular a list of the personnel belonging to all the German Air Services, and of the existing material, as well as of that in process of manufacture or on order, and a list of all establishments working for aviation, of their positions, and of all sheds and landing grounds.

Concerning Civil Air Traffic:

Article 313.
The aircraft of the Allied and Associated Powers shall have full liberty of passage and landing over and in the territory and territorial waters of Germany, and shall enjoy the same privileges as German aircraft, particularly in case of distress by land or sea.

Article 314.
The aircraft of the Allied and Associated Powers shall, while in transit to any foreign country whatever, enjoy the right of flying over the territory and territorial waters of Germany without landing, subject always to any regulations which may be made by Germany, and which shall be applicable equally to the aircraft of Germany and to those of the Allied and Associated countries.

Article 315.
All aerodromes in Germany open to national public traffic shall be open for the aircraft of the Allied and Associated Powers, and in any such aerodrome such aircraft shall be treated on a footing of equality with German aircraft as regards charges of every description, including charges for landing and accommodation.

Article 316.
Subject to the present provisions, the rights of passage, transit and landing, provided for in Articles 313, 314 and 315, are subject to the observance of such regulations as Germany may consider it necessary to enact, but such regulations shall be applied without distinction to German aircraft and to those of the Allied and Associated countries.

Article 317.
Certificate of nationality, airworthiness, or competency, and licences, issued or recognised as valid by any of the Allied or Associated Powers, shall be recognised in Germany as valid and as equivalent to the certificates and licences issued by Germany.

Article 318.
As regards internal commercial air traffic, the aircraft of the Allied and Associated Powers shall enjoy in Germany most favored nation treatment.

Article 319.
Germany undertakes to enforce the necessary measures to ensure that all German aircraft flying over her territory shall comply with the Rules as to lights and signals, Rules of the Air and Rules for Air Traffic on and in the neighborhood of aerodromes, which have been laid down in the Convention relative to Aerial Navigation concluded between the Allied and Associated Powers.

Article 320.
The obligations imposed by the preceding provisions shall remain in force until 1 January 1923, unless before that date Germany shall have been admitted into the League of Nations or shall have been authorized, by consent of the Allied and Associated Powers, to adhere to the Convention relative to

Above: Aircraft cemetary.

Aerial Navigation concluded between those Powers.

The German government was obliged by article 201 of the Treaty of Versailles to adopt legal regulations at the latest six month after the treaty coming into operation, this means on 10 July 1920, that prohibit the production of air vehicles and the parts necessary for it. However, this was delayed by more than one year.

At first an implementation law for the peace treaty was published on 12 September 1919, after which everybody was punished with prison up to six months or with custody or with a fine up to 100,000 Mark, who manufactured air vehicles, engines for air vehicles, or parts of the latter within six months after the introduction of the peace treaty.[3] For the Implementation and control of this implementation law the "Interalliierte Luftfahrt-Überwachungs-Kommission" (Ilük), and on the German side the "Luftfahrt-Friedens-Kommission" (Luftfriko) were appointed on 27 September 1919. One of the most urgent tasks of this commission was the comprehensive stock-taking and supervision of the destruction of Germany's left airplanes, airplane engines and installations. According to the will of the ambassador's conference on 8 May 1920 especially all German airship hangars had to be destroyed. Another conference of the Allieds found out on 9 July 1920 in Boulogne that Germany did not fulfill the imposed aviation conditions. As a result a construction ban that was ending on the same day was decided on the part of the victorious powers to be kept, however, without to determine a new precise deadline. A little later (on 24 July 1920) the ambassadorial council decided that Germany had to break off all aircraft hangars and sheds that were left for the international traffic, also in the occupied areas and the neutral zone.[4]

At the same time as the introduction of the treaty of Versailles on 10 July 1920 came the formal construction ban for German airplanes and airplane engines for the next six months, also until 10 July 1920 at first. However, as mentioned already earlier the victorious powers judged the reduction and destruction of German war material as insufficient and decided on 22 June 1920 in Boulogne to extend the aircraft construction ban until three months after fulfilment of article 202 of the Treaty of Versailles. Two days later the Reichsschatzminister enacted a regulation about the delivery of aviation material. In spite of the renewed statement of the Allieds on a conference one day before the end of the original term of the construction ban (on 9 July 1920) the German government announced it would be disarmed and the construction ban would be lifted.

Several aircraft factores immediately begun with the development of new airplanes. Most of all Hugo Junkers was active in Dessau. Motivated by the sucesses of his airplane F 13, its maiden flight was a little bit more than a half year after the end of the war, on 25 June 1919, Hugo Junkers developed airplanes like the J 15 and K 16. In the Albatroswerken the L 58 was developed, Dornier developed the "Komet" and Rohrbach in Staaken a four-engined giant airplane.

However, the euphoria did not last long. Also the development of non-military aircraft was hampered by all sorts of obstacles. Suspicion ruled with the Allies. The "Interalliierte Luftfahrt-Überwachungs-Kommission" (Ilük) found out that the number of the founded aviation enterprises in the unoccupied areas did not decrease. The intention of the German government to equip the police with airplanes was countered with a ban. After 50 million Reichsmark had already been demanded on 25 August 1920 for allegedly 1,000 illegal exported (also "trafficked") airplanes and airpane engines, the Allieds demanded another 25 million again on 18 November 1920 because the numbers of the exported devices had been estimated too low (only 1,500 units). They did even go so far to claim that the erection of airports in the neutral zone would be preparations for a mobilization. On 7 April 1921 a completely new ban on all flying was imposed "to keep the safety of the occupation forces".[5] The total number of the newly founded, to the largest part very little aviation enterprises[6], was limited to 150 airplanes.

Finally, on 5 May 1921 a so called "London Ultimatum" came: Again a general construction ban was called for and Germany had to undergo a permanent supervision by the Entente.[7] The "Law about the restriction of the air vehicle construction" cam finally in force on 29 June 1921 after a resolution of the German Reichstag. According to this law "the production and import of air vehicles and parts of such" as well as of "air vehicle engines and parts of such" was forbidden. Furthermore "the Imperial government was authorised on 5 May 1921 to take those measures in the field of aviation that that were necessary to fulfill the obligations imposed on the German Empire by the Allied governments on 5 May 1921."

So the construction ban is brought into force

Right: Destruction of aircraft propellers.

once more. Therefore the remaining aircraft plants and their employees, as for example the factories of Junkers, Fokker, and others came into biggest economical harsship. A partial exodus of the German aviation industry to other countries began which continued at first until the repeal of the construction regulations in 1926: Dornier built in Pisa, Italy, Rohrbach in Copenhagen, Denmark, Junkers in Sweden and Russland.

That's why for the protection of the German aviation industry an additional paragraph was taken up in the "Law about the restrictions of the airplane construction", which said, that "for the damages, which arise for the aviation industry from this law, ... the Empire gives compensation".[8] And these "damages" were anything but neglectable because the London Ultimatum with its published criteria for the differentitation between military and civil air vehicles meant almost the decline of the civil German air traffic that was just in awakening and this was probably the intention.

Finally, Ilük confirmed on 5 February 1922 that the German side was disarmed in the air and the demands of article 202 of the treaty of Versailles was fulfilled. An end of the contruction ban was promised for 5 May 1922 if the criteria agreed by the allieds was followed. The so called "definitions", for its recognition the German government had comitted itself without any reservations, excelled in every respect the worst expectations of the aviation circles. The German government brought into force the following "9 rules" with the "Order about the airplane construction" on 5 May 1922.

Definitions of the Uppermost Council

(Rules for the differentiation of civil and military airplanes)

Airplanes Heavier Than Air

Rule No. 1: Every one-seater with more performance than 60 HP is seen as militarily and therefore a war device.

Rule No. 2: Every airplane that can fly without a pilot is seen as militarily and therefore a war device.

Rule No. 3: Every airplane with armor or any mean of protection or any device which allows to mount any armament on it: guns, free fall bomb, with sights for the earlier mentioend machines is seen as militarily and therefore a war device.

The following limitations are maximum values for airplanes heavier than air of all types. All, which exceed these limits, are seen as militarily and therefore a war device.

Rule No. 4: Highest ability to climb with full load 4000 m (an engine with a device that allows over-compresssion puts the airplane which is fitted with such a device in the military category).

Rule No. 5: Speed with full load and in a height of 2000 m: 170 km per hours. (engines with full load that develop maximum power as a result.)

Rule No. 6: The maximum amount of to be carried oil and fuel (best quality of aviation petrol) may not cross (800 x 170)/V gram for each horsepower and V means the speed of the machine with full load and highest performance in 2000 m altitude.

Rule No. 7: Every airplane which exceeds a pay load of more tan 600 kg, pilot, mechanic and instruments included, if it can achieve the maximum conditions of the rules 4, 5 and 6 at the same time, is seen as militarily and therefore a war device.

Dirigible Airships

If the volume of dirigible airships is exceeding the following numbers then they are seen as militarily and therefore a war device:

I. Rigid dirigible airships:	30,000 m^3
II. Half rigid dirigibles:	25,000 m^3
III. Non-rigid dirigible airships:	20,000 m^3

Rule No. 8: The factories which produce aviation devices must be reported. All airplanes and pilots or trainees must be enlisted under the conditions which were included in the convention form 13th October 1919. These lists are kept available for the guarantee comittee.

Rule No. 9: It is not allowed any more stocks of aircraft engines, loose parts, and engine parts then is deemed necessary to cover the need of civil aviation. These amounts are are determined by the guarantee committee.

Finally, it was determined that the present definitions of terms should be checked every two years to account for the respective state of technology. Nevertheless, it was clear to politicians and industrialists that is was not the intent of these conditions to secure the meanwhile established military inferiority of Germany, it was obvious that the development of German aviation should be hampered in all fields and therfore be made incompetetive.

Merely rule No 3 really concerned military issues and it would have been sufficient to prevent the new awakening of a war-ready air force. In the decisions of the disarmement conference in Washington (1922) it was stressed, under emphasis of all advantages of commercial aviation, to promote the development of the civil aviation in all directions and therefore not to hinder the reconstruction of the German economy.

The definitions of terms could not satisfy this

goal. A comparison with traffic airplanes in service at this time clearly proves that the definitions obliged on Germany stayed far behind the state of the international aviation technology. Thus for example the French Bréguet 18 T had a ceiling of 5,200 m, the postal airplane Potez P 14 more than 5,800 m, the de Havilland 18 4,900 m, the Handley-Page W 86 6,000 m and the newest american traffic airplane Lawson L-4 even more than 6,700 m ceiling. It was the same with the relations concerning speed. One finds speeds up to 200 kph for all foreign traffic airplanes. However, most sharply the disporoportion became visible for the pay load. The afore mentioned Bréguet 18 T could transport a pay load of 1,552 kg, the de Havilland about 1,120 kg, the Handley-Page W 86 about 1,960 kg, the Lawson L-4 even 4,060 kg."[9]

Nevertheless, these restrictions had also positive effects in the opinion of the author: Rule No. 1 (max. 60 HP engine power for one-seated air vehicles) obviously hindered at first the development of the German sports airplanes but on the other hand this led to the fact that Germany's designers like Messerschmitt, Klemm, Fieseler and others, developed airplane lightweight constructions to the state of perfection. The same is also valid for the development of the "gliding flight that was born from the state of emergency" and gliders itself. Till today no nation could challenge Germany's supremacy in this field.

The "definitions" served at first to order and legalize the airplane park of the German aviation companies. In the few still existing aircraft plants started developing projects had to be broken off and airplanes already in the making had to be destroyed.

On the 5 May 1922 Ilük finished its work. It was replaced by the Luftfahrt-Garantiekomitee.[10] On the German side the Luftfriko was replaced by the "Kommissar für Luftfahrzeugbau".[11] The long-desired end of the construction ban was achieved. Import and export of aviation devices were formally allowed for Germany within the scope of the definitions.

At that time the airplane types used in the German air traffic were mainly the following types:

Junkers F 13,
Fokker F II and F III,
Dornier Komet II and Komet III.

In the years 1924/25 the Dornier Merkur and for the first time a multi-engined airplane, the Junkers G 23 (with a 250 HP middle engine and two 100 HP side-engines) were added.[12] Other modern airplane types originated after abolition of the construction restrictions, for example:

Rohrbach Roland (3-engined),
Junkers G 31 (3-engined),
Dornier Superwal (2- and 4-engined),
Rohrbach Rocco (2-engined) and Romar (3-engined).

August Euler's influence as Unterstaatssekretär in the Reichsluftamt on the results of the negotiations in Versailles and later remained extremely low. Thought he was informed about the state of negotiations, even still in the time of his vacation, however, his requests concerning direct influence on the negotiations about the building ban as well as for the restrictions of the civil post-war aviation in Germany were not considered by both the Ministerium des Innern and the Verkehrsminister.

It must be emphasized that already since 1919 a big number of governments (without inclusion of Germany) had founded a state aviation convention, the so-called "Cina". The European air traffic companies united on 28 August 1919 in Den Haag under the active co-operation of Germany to the still today existing privaten umbrella organization of the airlines, the "International Air Traffic Association" (IATA).

After four years of practiced construction restrictions the restraints for the German aviation industry were loosened on 21 May 1926, nevertheless, it found no complete end, while the "Paris Aviation Agreements" were applied. These arrangements determined mainly the following:

- It is prohibited to built air vehicles, to keep them, to introduce them and to use them in traffic which are armor-plated or protected in any way or which are equipped with racks for the installation of war machines of any kind, as guns, machine guns, torpedoes, bombs or visor or bomb-dropping sights for such machines.
- The fact that the German government will promote the civil aviation only with the limitations of a normal development, the aid for the commercial aviation should be held in a suitable frame.
- The German government will make dependent from her special approval the construction or the import of airplanes which meet the technical characteristics of modern fighters concerning empty weight, ratio between empty weight and engine power, the arrangements of seats, the construction security, the climbing and air speed and the ceiling.
- The German government will give these special approvals exclusively for the participation in offically announced international competitions or offically supervised records as well as for the necessary preparations for the participation.

These preparations may not enclose excercises in aviation schools.

- The number of airplanes of this kind will be kept within the borders of the number of those civil airplanes of the same kind which are used in another country of Europe for the above mentioned purpose.
- The German government will take the suitable measures so that the number of pilots, who are allowed to fly such airplanes, is kept within the scope of the declared needs.
- The German government takes care that no public means are used to aid for the training and advanced training of pilots that exceed the needs of air traffic and factories. Cash prizes and organizational means for competitions should not have the character of aids and only be granted for approved competitions.
- Training and advanced training in military aviation is forbidden...

The German government arranges the keeping of lists about:

- factories, that produce air vehicles;
- finished or under construction air vebicles and aviation engines, whereby air vehicles and engines determined for export must be listed separately;
- the pilots and pilot trainees (pilots, who can pilot airplanes of kinds that are mentioned under standing number number 3,must be endorsed in a special list);
- the enterprises which pursue an airline;
- the associations, societies or individuals that do aviation or use air vebicles;
- the other owners of air vehicles.
- Pilotless airplanes are forbidden.
- For police officers are the same flight restrictions valid as for members fo the Reichswehr, ...

With the acceptance of these regulations by the German government the Luftfahrt-Garantiekomitee was dissolved on 30 August 1926.

The fact that this pleasing but not yet satisfying progress could be achieved, was especially owed to the fact that Germany had strictly sticked to the imposed obligations on the national level since the day of the introduction of the construction restrictions (5 May 1922).

Endnotes

1. Germany and her allied states in war.
2. BA Koblenz, estate Euler, signature N1103, Protokoll der Verhandlung über den Friedensvertrag vom 18.06.1919.
3. "Der Leidensweg unserer Luftfahrt", Novissima-Korrespondenz für Luftverkehr und Flugsport, vol. 5, issue 19, 15.2.1932.
4. Article V of the peace treaty said: Clearing of the areas on the left siede of the Rhine by the German armies. The areas on the left side of the Rhine are administered by the local authorities under supersvision of the occupying troops of the Allieds and the United States. The troops of the Allieds and the United States arrange the occupation by garrisons that dominate the most important Rhine crossings (Mainz, Koblenz, Köln) including a bridgehead of 30 km diameter on the right shore and moreover the stratigical points of the area. On the right Rhine shore a neutral zone is created. It runs between the river and a line which is drwan parallel to the bridgeheads and the river, in a width of 10 km from the Dutch up to the Swiss border. [...]
5. Interalliierte Rheinland-Oberkommission, Ordonnanz 80.
6. The huge number of 37 air transport companies melted away in 1922/23 and two bigger groups were formed: "Deutschen Aero Lloyd" and "Junkers Luftverkehrs-A.G."
7. France and Great Britain as well as Russia had united by contract to the Entente or Tripleentente.
8. On the basis of this law August Euler tried in vain to receive even compensations from the state because of not granted production of air vehicles. However, he had to take note that this law was not appliable to him because the Euler-Werke lay in the French occupied area and therefore beyond the area of application of this law.
9. ZFM, vol. 13 (1922), p 109, Curt Eppinger
10. 30 August 1926: Abolition of the Luftfahrt-Garantiekomitee.
11. 1 November 1926: Kommissar für Luftfahrzeugbau finished his work.
12. After the end of the construction restrictions built with stronger engines as G 24.

15. The Build-up of the German Aviation Administration

The Political Conditions at the End of World War I

The First World War approached recognizably its end. On 29 September 1918 Generalfeldmarschall Paul von Hindenburg and General Erich Ludendorff demanded from the government to immediately enter truce negotiations. Already on 3 October 1918 the last Reichskanzler, Prinz Max von Baden, who was appointed by Emperor Wilhelm II, formed a new government which included for the first time Reichstag deputies. Under the pressure of the Oberste Heeresleitung the government sent an armistice request to the American president Wilson in the night of 4 October. After weeks-long exchange of notes and tough negotiations the signing of the armistice agreement finished the fighting of the First World War on 11 November 1918.

In the interim the events in Germany had rushed. At the end of October the sailors in Wilhelmshaven refused to follow orders for the sailing of the ships. After the arrest of thousands of sailors it came to mass meetings. In Kiel the first soldiers' councils were founded. The opposition against the military leadership and the government grasped all of Germany wihin a few days. On 7 November the revolution in Munich has overthrown as first dynasty the Wittelsbacher. The ruling houses of the other German states fell during the next days. On 9 November 1918 the revolution arrived in Berlin. Hundred thousands demonstrated on the streets and demanded the end of the war and the resignation of the emperor. When the latter refused, Max von Baden announced the resignation of the emperor about midday of the 9 November on own responsibility.

Prince Max von Baden transferred his office as Chancellor of the Reich, without being legitimised constitutional-juridically, to Friedrich Ebert, the chairperson of the social democrats which formed the strongest faction in the Reichstag. The newly appointed Chancellor of the Reich had the intention to leave the decision on the future form of government to an elective National Assembly. However, this was ruined at first because the fellow party member of Ebert, Philipp Scheidemann, exclaimed the German Republic about 14.00 o'clock on a balcony of the Reichstag building. The political mess increased when the leader of the Spartacus group in the Reichstag, Karl Liebknecht, announced the socialist republic in front of the Berlin castle. However, all this could not prevent that still on 10 November 1918 the Rat der Volksbeauftragten was formed. Under the direction of Friedrich Ebert the provisional government began its work.

Under these completely unsettled relations of power the armistice between Germany and her opponents was signed on 11 November 1918 as already mentioned. According to this armistice the occupied areas and Alsace-Lorrain had to be left by German troops and the left shore of the Rhine within 30 days.

In the following peace negotiations which finally led to the Treaty of Versailles (on 28 June 1919), Germany was obliged to pay war reparations at the rate of 132 billion Goldmark. However, not only the high financial burden were in enormous strain for Germany and her industry in the following years. All areas were hit, the German aviation industry was concerned in an espcially big magnitude, what should be discussed in the next chapter in more detail. In this chapter the personal portion of Euler in the development of the German civil aviation and its management after the end of the First World War should be shown.

Right: Undersecretary of State August Euler.

The Reichsluftamt

The idea of a Kaiserliches Luftamt was not so new. With the inexorably growing number of airvehicles, whether aiships, balloons, gliders ,or powered airplanes, in particular since 1910, the German government was forced to create regulations for the then nearly exclusively civil aviation. For the German empire the creation of a "Luftamt" was considered which should work be instructed to work out an air traffic law. However, the Bundesrat and the Reichstag could not make final decisions because of the outbreak of the First World War. The foundation of an air office was not followed up. Nevertheless, during the war efforts went on to order the military and civil aviation. On 10 March 1917 a discussion about the regulation of air traffic under peace conditions took place in the Reichsamt des Inneren which was responsible for the regulation of air traffic.[1] The creation of a Reichsluftamt was already seen as indispensable now.

After the surrender the Ministerium des Innern under the lead of Staatssekretär Dammann prepared precise measures to establish an aviation office. On 21 November 1918 one demanded from the Deutsche Versuchsanstalt für Luftfahrt in Berlin to evaluate drafts for regulating orders of aviation. In the course of several negotiations with the war ministry and the Inspektion der Fliegertruppen one came to the decision to establish the already for 1914 planned "Deutsches Luftfahrtamt" as "Reichsluftamt" for the execution of these tasks. The necessary decree of the Rat der Volksbeauftragten was issued on 26 November 1918.[2]

The creation of legal regulations should especially help to organize and promote the civil air traffic with all its auxilliarly fields in Germany. The setup of an office fit for this work was an essential precondition and urgent task. The Ministerium des Innern that was assigned with the foundation of the new office by the Rat der Volksbeauftragten announced the foundation of the new office for 4 December 1918.[3] So the German aviation administration was established. The management of the office was given to Herr Unterstaatssekretär August Euler.

The Inspekteur der Fliegertruppen, Oberstleutnant Siegert, formulated at first the most important tasks of the Reichsluftamtes:[4]

1. Central, civil centralization and direction of all positions, authorities, associations and organizations that were involved in land-, sea- and colonial aviation, airship travel, the weather service, the airplane and airship radio telegraphy and the air mapping service until now.
2. The most economic exploitation of the material and personnel national wealth in cooperation with the Verwertungsamt [Utilization office].[5]
3. Surveillance and supervision of the whole air traffic in Germany and over its borders, including the acceptance and licensing of airplanes and flying staff.[6]
4. Expansion and standardization of the many by different places independendly and without connection established airmails and personal transports[7];
5. Participation in the preparation of laws, assignment of concessions (e.g. for airplines), patent affairs and the regulation of international questions.

The basis for the work of the Reichsluftamt was the "Act concerning the temporary regulation of the aviation laws"[8], which was announced on 7 December 1918.

The fact that not all proposals presented by Oberstleutnant Siegert were taken over as duties for the Reichsluftamt comes from the approach that not all ministerial duties of the ministry of the Interior should be transferred to an executive (subordinate) organ.

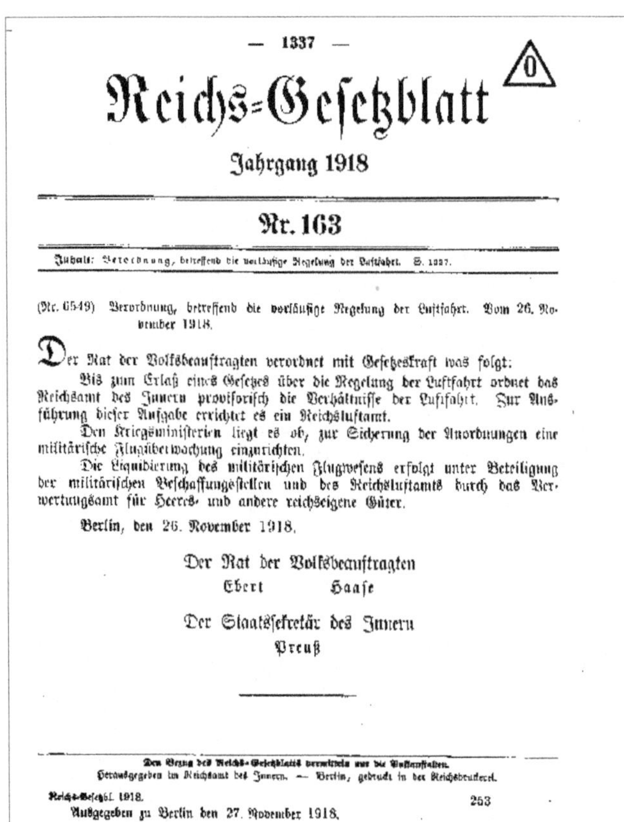

— 1337 —

Reichs-Gesetzblatt

Jahrgang 1918

Nr. 163

Inhalt: Verordnung, betreffend die vorläufige Regelung der Luftfahrt. S. 1337.

(Nr. 6549) Verordnung, betreffend die vorläufige Regelung der Luftfahrt. Vom 26. November 1918.

Der Rat der Volksbeauftragten verordnet mit Gesetzeskraft was folgt:

Bis zum Erlaß eines Gesetzes über die Regelung der Luftfahrt ordnet das Reichsamt des Innern provisorisch die Verhältnisse der Luftfahrt. Zur Ausführung dieser Aufgabe errichtet es ein Reichsluftamt.

Den Kriegsministerien liegt es ob, zur Sicherung der Anordnungen eine militärische Flugüberwachung einzurichten.

Die Liquidierung des militärischen Flugwesens erfolgt unter Beteiligung der militärischen Beschaffungsstellen und des Reichsluftamts durch das Verwertungsamt für Heeres- und andere reichseigene Güter.

Berlin, den 26. November 1918.

Der Rat der Volksbeauftragten
Ebert Haase

Der Staatssekretär des Innern
Preuß

Den Bezug des Reichs-Gesetzblatts vermitteln nur die Postanstalten.
Herausgegeben im Reichsamt des Innern. — Berlin, gedruckt in der Reichsdruckerei.

Reichs-Gesetzbl. 1918. 253
Ausgegeben zu Berlin den 27. November 1918.

Above: Decree from 26 November 1918.

Euler becomes Unterstaatssekretär

Euler's prominent achievements as undersecretary

— 1400 —

(Nr. 6569) Erlaß über die Errichtung des Reichsluftamts. Vom 4. Dezember 1918.

Auf Grund der Verordnung des Rates der Volksbeauftragten, betreffend die vorläufige Regelung der Luftfahrt, vom 26. November 1918 (Reichs-Gesetzbl. S. 1337) wird hiermit das

Reichsluftamt

errichtet. Die Leitung des Amtes wird Herrn August Euler aus Frankfurt a. M. übertragen, der den Titel „Unterstaatssekretär" führt. Das Reichsluftamt bearbeitet die Angelegenheiten der Luftfahrt selbständig mit der Maßgabe, daß das Luftfahrtrecht unter seiner Mitwirkung vom Reichsamt des Innern geordnet wird.

Berlin, den 4. Dezember 1918.

Der Staatssekretär des Innern
Dr. Preuß

Above: Decree of 4 December 1918.

and later state secretary should be appreciated in the following; also should be tried from today's perspective to explore and uncover the reasons and backgrounds for Euler's failure as leader of the Reichsluftamt and the later Reichsamt für Luft- und Kraftfahrwesen.

Why the council of the deputies of the nation decided itself for August Euler as leader of the office, presents itself in the review as follows:

At first the Ministery of Interior intended to make the (former) Inspekteur der Fliegertruppen, Oberstleutnant Siegert himself to the leader of the planned office. He noticed:[9] "...already on the 1st day of the revolution, the 10.11.18, 11^{40} a.m. I was handed over the following writing by a city council member:

"City council member Pätzel has the order of the worker- and soldier council to initiate the supervision of the whole aviation troop by Oberstlt. Siegert, Suarezstr. 31. This troop is under survey of the social-democratic party.

Sign. Otto Wels, M.d.R.
[M.d.R.=Member of the Reichstag]
The Executive of the Socialdemocratic Party of Germany"."

However, when Siegert rejectd this proposal, one remembered a man, who was well-known at this time in circles of aviators, economy and politics alike – August Euler. Euler could fall back on his experiences as aviator, flight instructor, and industrialist. Above all his pragmatism was known. Best references came for example from the aircraft industry and the Verein Deutscher Motorfahrzeug-Industrieller (VDMI), the lobby organization of the aviation industry.

Finally, on 16 November 1918 one got in contact with Euler by telephone and invited him to a discussion with the Inspection of the Aviation troops.

Euler himself writes: "On 19 November 1918 I got in Frankfurt a.M. ... a telegram of the council of the representatives of the Nation, with which I was asked to come to Berlin immediately. Therefore I drove – because an immediate opportunity for a journey with the railway was not possible in this revolutionary time, with a car in the same evening from Frankfurt a.M. to Berlin and arrived in the next morning, my 50th birthday, in Berlin." [10]

During a discussion with Unterstaatssekretär Göhre who was working in the Prussian war ministry at this time Euler got to know that the government intended to assign him the dealing with the aviation affairs. This proposal was supported by Inspektor der Fliegertruppen, Herr Oberstleutnant Siegert and other prestigious military leaders.

In another discussion Euler was prepared to take over the utilization of the empire's war planes as well. However, August Euler refused this order categorically with the reasoning that he as the first German pilot would not like to be the liquidator of the German aviation material. He said he had trained the first civil piots of the German Reich as well as the first officer pilots, as he had founded the first German airplane factory in Darmstadt in 1908."[11] Finally, this demand of Euler was taken into account.

At the end of the discussion Euler agreed to take over the management of the new office for aviation

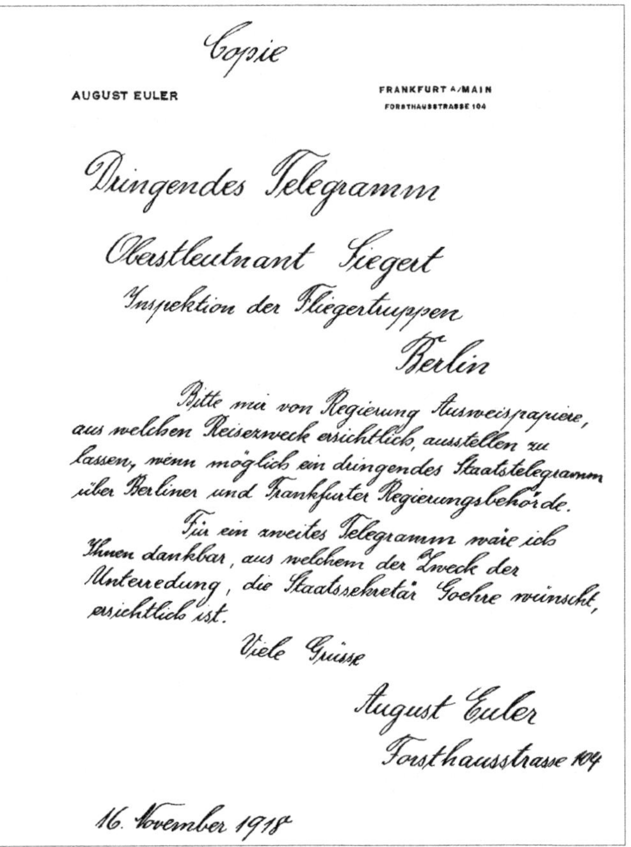

Copie

AUGUST EULER

FRANKFURT A/MAIN
FORSTHAUSSTRASSE 104

Dringendes Telegramm

Oberstleutnant Siegert
Inspektion der Fliegertruppen
Berlin

Bitte mir von Regierung Ausweispapiere, aus welchen Reisezweck ersichtlich, ausstellen zu lassen, wenn möglich ein dringendes Staatstelegramm über Berliner und Frankfurter Regierungsbehörde.

Für ein zweites Telegramm wäre ich Ihnen dankbar, aus welchem der Zweck der Unterredung, die Staatssekretär Goehre wünscht, ersichtlich ist.

Viele Grüsse

August Euler
Forsthausstrasse 104

16. November 1918

Above: Euler's telegram of 16 November 1918.

Above: Mosaic in the hall of the Reichsluftamt.

or to participate in the future development of the German civil aviation.

On 28 November 1918 Euler got the following telegram:[12]

"The council of the national deputies has just prescribed that the Reichsamt des Innern has to order the relations of aviation temporarily and to establish an Reichsluftamt for the implementation of tasks. The Reichsluftamt should deal with the air traffic and furthermore, so far as possible, participate in the buildup of the civil aviation and take over the liquidation of the military aviation, which after all becomes basically task of the Reichsverwertungsamt with the military procurement offices. I consider to entrust you with the management of the air office. Would be grateful for immediate arrival for the purpose of talk and telegraphic notification of the arrival.

Staatssekretär des Innern, Preuss", Oberstleutnant Siegert, who has had decisive influence for the choice Euler's for the management of the new Reichsluftamt, wrote on the same day to Euler, that he would be the "only possible "Civil-Dictator", who could bring "Order into this matter".

Last arrangements were made on 30 November in a final conversation with the Staatssekretär, Dr. Preuss, in Berlin.

The necessary decree of the council of national deputies "became known to me on the 4 December in the evening by the fact that I read it in Berlin, Unter den Linden, in the shop-window of the Lokalanzeiger, for the first time," August Euler remembered later.[13]

The Work of Unterstaatssekretär Euler

August Euler began his service as leader of the Reichsluftamt on 10 December 1918, after he had closed his aircraft factory in Frankfurt-Niederrad.[14] As offices several rooms were assigned to him in Berlin, Wilhelmstrasse 72. At first his staff involved only three secretaries.

The expactions regarding the new authority were very high. Equally big and manifold were the problems which undersecretary of state Euler faced. One of the most important tasks was the establishing of the workability of his "office". On one hand this meant the creation of a competent authority for this subject and – this was much more difficult – a clear separation of the fields of work. Up to now several civil and military authorities ruled on the interests of aviation. In his "fight" with the influence losing ministries Euler was supported by a formulation in the decree from 4 December 1918, after which the Reichsluftamt had to regulate the matters of aviation independently. His distinctive sense for authority helped him to get respect within a short time; however, it did not always got him new friends, which we will address later.

Already on 19 December 1918 a session was arranged with all ministries in question under the leadership of the Reichsamt des Innern. Among them were representatives of war ministry, justice ministry, and postal ministry as well as from the inspectionors of the signal troops, airship crew troops, and aviation troops and other offices. August Euler explained as lecturer his ideas about the tasks of the Reichsluftamt and its cooperation with Imperial, state and military offices. Support was assured to the Reichsluftamt from the owners of air vehicles, the ministry of war, and the Reichs-Marineamt. To all partners in this meeting it became clear that, although exact figures were not available, gigantic national wealth was to be administrated. On one hand the available air vehicles and immobile installations (airfields, hangars, etc.) had to be partially liquidated. On the other hand, however, the military offices, still absolutely unsuspecting, what would come up as cuts soon afterwards by the Treaty of Versailles, intended to reduce the strength and to reorganize the German air forces. Euler demanded with vigor a clear demarcation of competences. He

Above: Berlin, Wilhelmstrasse 72. The Reichsluftamt moved into the rooms main floor left.

represented the point of view that, emanating from the formulation of the decree about the foundation of the Reichsluftamt he alone had to regulate the civil aviation, but not the liquidation of the military units.

On 5 January 1919 Unterstaatssekretär August Euler signed the first licensing certificate for a German air traffic company – the Deutsche Luftreederei GmbH Berlin (D.L.R.). The beginning of a regular civil air traffic was created therefore. The certificate allowed at first only "..., to do air traffic from 10 January to the end of January 1919 for propaganda purposes."[15] At first for individually listed airplanes were only "day flights allowed which were leaving Berlin and ended on the same day without stopover in Berlin." Short time later, on 17 January 1919, the Reichsluftamt extended the sphere of activities of the D.L.R. for flights within the borders of Prussia; however with the specification that the airplanes might approach the areas occupied by the Allieds and the neutral zone only up to 20 km distance. The temporary limitation of the allowance was lifted on 28 January 1919.

With the end of these preparatory measures all preparations had been made until 5 February 1919 to establish the regular air traffic from Berlin to Weimar and back to support the National Assembly there. On 6 February at 7.12 a.m. the first LVG airplane started in in Berlin-Johannisthal with the destination Weimar.

In spite of the ruling raw material shortage that would reduce the necessary flights on an absolute minimum according to the imaginations of the Reichsluftamt, the military offices tried to establish an air courier's service from Weimar to Berlin, Dresden, Stuttgart, and Munich.[16] Euler opposed this request with all his power. On 25 February 1919 he sent an urgent state telegram with the following content to the National Assembly:[17]

"While civil air traffic is forming under the administration of the Reichsluftamt, the military authorities are creating an Reichsluftkurierdienst for the National Assembly, allegedly for military purposes. I think one must protest against this action in the most emphatic way in the national interest and point on the perishable results of such an air service. The military lacks all preconditions for the construction of a reliable safe courier's service. It would be a usage of military material for pure civil purposes without the creation of any budget-judicial base. The military would spend enormous financial means without approval of the House of Representatives that would not stand in a healthy ratio to the minium effect. At the same time the originating civil enterprises would be discouraged and private air traffic would lose its ground by military competition at the costs of the Reich. The utilization of the army goods in the field of aviation would become completely desorganized and immense values, which are necessary to erase our debts, would be squandered pointlessly. As well the Entente, which will notice this military organized air traffic, could see an offence against the conditions of the armistice and the obligations for the demobilisation because such a largely drawn up air traffic must give abroad the impression of a military excercise. If the National Assembly lays determining weight on such a Reichsluftkurierdienst then I am willing to organize the civil organization without costs for the Reich or with rather little subsidies, if the already existing civil air traffic is not sufficient because there are already four more companies, except the Luftreederei, licensed for air traffic without application for subsidies.

Zahl der zuletzt vor dem Waffenstillstand im Kriege verwendeten Flugzeuge in Summa: 16.000
Zahl der im Kriege überhaupt hergestellten Flugzeuge in Summa: 49.000
Zahl der bei Beendigung des Krieges vermutlich noch vorhandenen Flugzeuge

a) Riesenflugzeuge	7	
b) Gross-Flugzeuge	220	
c) C-Flugzeuge	4474	
d) Schul-Flugzeuge	1243	
e) Kampf-Flugzeuge (D)	1499	
g) Aufklärungs-Flugzeuge etc.	947 (Lichtbild-Flugzeuge)	
	in Summa: rd.	8.400

Zahl der bei Beendigung des Krieges vorhanden gewesenen Flugzeugführer Offiziere 2.267
Mannschaften 5.311
Summa: 7.578

Zahl der im Kriege ausgebildeten Flugzeugführer 7.578
+ 3.420 Verluste (tot u. vermisst)

Gesamtverluste an Flugzeugführern in Front und Heimat 7.159
davon tot und vermisst 3.420
verwunde 3.739

Erläuterungen hierzu:
1. An der Front
durch feindliche Einwirkung 920 tot, 1.224 verwundet
ohne -"- -"- 990 tot, 985 verletzt
vermisst 1.389
2. In der Heimat 1.375 tot, 1.284 verletzt

Quelle: Bundesarchiv Koblenz, Nachlass Euler

Above: Presentation for negotiations to the peace treaty.

For the regulation of the military the present unbelievable waste requires the civilization of the procurement questions as well as all questions of technical, scientific, and judicial nature, otherwise the military will establish a new war profiteer shop between war and peace without budget and without parliament."

Subsequently Euler demanded from the military authorities to allow only flights with purely military character to avoid conflicts with the regulation of the civil aviation. The war ministry followed this demand and kept a small number of airplanes for the flights between Döberitz und Weimar until the prohibition of every military air traffic.

In the endeavours to let develop a functioning civil air traffic Euler pointed all affected authorities and governments of the lands to the fact that the implemented legal regulations carried all-German character. The undersecretary of the state strictly acted against attempts of single states, e.g., Württemberg, Saxony, and Bavaria to buildup own air offices. Euler also explained precise ideas about the licensing processes for pilots, air vehicles and future airlines.

It was clear to Euler himself that he could not master alone the duties standing in front of him. In the first days of his activity as undersecretary of the state he tried hard to search for comrades-in-arms. Therefore, it was also not surprising that he turned to the aircraft industry and aviation research facilities first. Also the latter stood before almost insoluble problems. Production stood still but dismissals should absolutely be avoided. Moreover, the biggest insecurity ruled among the industrialists about the continuity of aviation in general.

As a result of consultations with Geheimer Regierungsrat Professor Dr. Hergesell (chief of the Aeronautical Observatory Lindenberg), Counsellor of Justice Dr. Niemeyer (earlier lawyer and notary, especially for aviation law), Major von Tschudi (earlier in the most different military leadership positions working in the field of aviation and later employee of Euler) as well as Director Rasch from the aircraft works in Staaken August Euler invited all aviation industrialists of Germany to talks about the principles of the German aviation administration.

This meeting which should also serve the explanation of the directives for the operating pinciples of the Reichsluftamt was fixed for the 20 December 1918. G. Dieterich, later member of the Reichsausschuss für Luft- und Kraftfahrwesen, wrote: "When in November 1918 as one of the most early legislative measures of the government of national representatives a temporary Reichsluftgesetz was issued, the Reichsluftamt was founded and an expert, known and seasoned in economic and industrial fields, was called on its top, then it was one of the first important activities in office of the new undersecretary of state Dr. August Euler to gather the representants of all interested expert circle's, interested in aviation and business,.."[18]

During this meeting it became clear that the whole aircraft industry of Germany was unified and ready to develop or to promote the future civil aviation with all available means and forces.

After this meeting Euler in his function as leader of the Reichsluftamt published two memoranda which appeared on 9 January and 15 February 1919.

The first memorandum served the renewed clarification of the activity and sphere of activity of the Reichsluftamt:

- Licensing of the pilots and airship captains, the air vehicles, the air traffic companies for air traffic;
- Participation in legal measures, which are issued

Facing Page: Enactment from 8 December 1918.

— 1407 —

Reichs-Gesetzblatt

Jahrgang 1918

Nr. 175

(Nr. 6573) Verordnung, betreffend die vorläufige Regelung des Luftfahrtrechts. Vom 7. Dezember 1918.

Auf Grund der Verordnung des Rates der Volksbeauftragten, betreffend die vorläufige Regelung der Luftfahrt, vom 26. November 1918 (Reichs-Gesetzbl. S. 1337) wird folgendes vorgeschrieben:

§ 1

Lenkbare Luftfahrzeuge (Luftschiffe und Flugzeuge) dürfen außerhalb der Flugplätze nur verkehren, wenn die Behörde sie zugelassen hat.

§ 2

Luftfahrzeuge müssen verkehrssicher und so gebaut, eingerichtet und ausgerüstet sein, daß Feuers- und Explosionsgefahr sowie Belästigung von Personen und Gefährdung von Personen und Sachen nach Möglichkeit ausgeschlossen ist.

§ 3

Genügt ein zugelassenes Luftfahrzeug den Anforderungen der Verkehrssicherheit nicht mehr, so kann die Behörde es vom Verkehr außerhalb der Flugplätze ausschließen.

§ 4

Wer außerhalb der Flugplätze ein Luftfahrzeug führen will (Luftschiff-, Flugzeugführer), bedarf der Erlaubnis der Behörde.

Die Erlaubnis ist zu erteilen, wenn der Bewerber seine Befähigung durch eine Prüfung dartut und keine Tatsachen vorliegen, welche die Annahme rechtfertigen, daß er nicht geeignet sei, Luftfahrzeuge zu führen.

Die erteilte Erlaubnis wird durch einen Führerschein nachgewiesen.

§ 5

Werden nachträglich Tatsachen festgestellt, welche die Annahme rechtfertigen, daß eine Person nicht geeignet sei, Luftfahrzeuge zu führen, so kann die Behörde ihr die Erlaubnis dauernd oder für bestimmte Zeit entziehen.

§ 6

Aufstieg-, Landungs- und Flugplätze dürfen nur mit Genehmigung der Behörde angelegt, schon vorhandene Plätze nur mit dieser Genehmigung in Betrieb gehalten werden. Die Behörde kann die Schließung bereits genehmigter Plätze anordnen, wenn es aus Gründen der Verkehrs- oder der Landessicherheit geboten erscheint.

§ 7

Zuverlässigkeits- und Wettbewerbsfahrten von Luftfahrzeugen sowie alle sonstigen Veranstaltungen mit Luftfahrzeugen bedürfen der Genehmigung der Landeszentralbehörde.

Erstreckt sich die Veranstaltung über den Bereich mehrerer Bundesstaaten, so sind zur Genehmigung die Zentralbehörden der Bundesstaaten gemeinsam zuständig, deren Gebiet bei Aufstieg und Landung berührt wird.

Vor der Erteilung der Genehmigung ist das Reichsluftamt zu hören; erhebt es Widerspruch, so ist die Genehmigung zu versagen.

§ 8

Die gewerbsmäßige Beförderung von Personen oder Sachen durch Luftfahrzeuge (Luftfahrtunternehmen) bedarf der Genehmigung der Behörde; die Genehmigung kann auch von der Leistung einer Sicherheit abhängig gemacht werden.

Erstrecken sich die Fahrten über den Bereich mehrerer Bundesstaaten, so sind zur Genehmigung die Zentralbehörden der Bundesstaaten gemeinsam zuständig, deren Gebiet bei Aufstieg und Landung berührt wird.

Vor Erteilung der Genehmigung ist das Reichsluftamt zu hören; erhebt es Widerspruch, so ist die Genehmigung zu versagen.

§ 9

Vorbehalten bleibt die Bestimmung darüber, inwieweit diese Vorschriften auf andere Luftfahrzeuge und luftfahrzeugähnliche Geräte und auf die militärische Luftfahrt Anwendung zu finden haben.

§ 10

Vorbehalten bleiben:

1. die Bestimmungen, die zur Ausführung der §§ 1 bis 9 erforderlich sind, insbesondere über die Prüfung, Zulassung und Kennzeichnung der Luftfahrzeuge und über die Ausbildung, Prüfung und Zulassung der Führer,

2. die sonstigen zur Erhaltung der öffentlichen Ordnung und Sicherheit erforderlichen Bestimmungen über den Verkehr mit Luftfahrzeugen außerhalb der Flugplätze,
3. Bestimmungen über den Verkehr innerhalb der Flugplätze,
4. Bestimmungen über räumliche Begrenzungen des Fliegens im Inland und über das Überfliegen der Grenzen durch in- und ausländische Luftfahrzeuge.

§ 11

Vorbehalten bleibt, die Zuständigkeit des Reichsluftamts einerseits und der von den Landeszentralbehörden zu bestimmenden Behörden anderseits für die Durchführung dieser Vorschriften zu ordnen.

§ 12

Solange die grundlegenden Bestimmungen nach § 10 Ziffer 1 bis 4 nicht erlassen sind, hat das Reichsluftamt die ausschließliche Befugnis, nach seinem Ermessen im Einzelfall Luftfahrt zuzulassen.

§ 13

Diese Vorschriften treten sofort in Kraft.

Berlin, den 7. Dezember 1918.

Der Staatssekretär des Innern

Dr. Preuß

Facing Page & Above: Enactment from 8 December 1918.

as legal foundation for the licensing for air traffic;
- Mediation of the business dealings between all that are interested in aviation like Imperial, state and military authorities, the working circles, the aircraft industry, the airlines etc.;
- Support of the German negotiators at the peace negotiations;
- Treatment of the question related to aviation with the federal states of the German Empire;
- Support of flight competitions and flight exhibitions.

To remove the obviously resulting confusion Euler clarified that, against all assertions of the earlier Luftamt of the Soldier's Council of the aviation troops, the Reichsluftamt is neither job agency, nor airplane sales agency or air travel office. Questions regarding the demobilisation of aviation staff were to be directed to the Demobililsation office. Moreover, he underlined thatthe Imperial Utilization office was responsible for the utilization of military goods.

He could make hardly any hope to thousands of soldiers and officers returning form the front that they would ever pilot an airplane again.

Probably August Euler already anticipated that only a few of the 16,000 airplanes available at the end of the war would escape destruction.[19]

However, in his memorandum Euler developed a vision for the German aviation. In the difficult economical and political situation in early 1919 Euler tried to show the aircraft industry and the pilots perspectives without concealing that aviation could not continued in the same amount like in the war times. He underlined that "available war aviation means ... were not competetive compared to other means of traffic and transportation".[20] As the

Facing Page, Top: Berlin, Wilhelmstrasse 72, back, on the right below Euler's flat.

Facing Page, Bottom: Assembly room in the Reichsluftamt.

Right: Entrance area of the Reichsluftamt.

most essential disadvantage he called the fact that especially at night the airplanes were not safe means of transportation.

He asked the aviation industry to adapt itself radically. Euler analysed: "In the peace years from 1910 to 1914 the industry was at least busy with the preparation for the war which was expected in the whole world. Even if the war had not broken out it would have been still an employment program for many years for the reason that one expected it, in any case, a considerably bigger employment possibilty existed, very different to the time after the war.

Consequently the amount of the aircraft industry and aviation was bigger before the war than it can be for the next future today. During the war the relevant state of aviation has multiplied, so that we stand in front of a complete over-development compared to the opportunities of a peaceful use.

Therefore, the industry must adapt itself, just as the pilots, and the biggest part has to take over a different activity."

August Euler foresaw clearly that the aviation industry could only achieve business success if the international aircraft industry developed. This needed not only purely technical progress but also the removal of all political and enconomic obstacles which could have hampered aviation.

In particular in the second memorandum "Die praktische Anwendung der Luftfahrt" (The Practical Use of Aviation) from 15 February 1919 August Euler drew new perspectives for a civil German aviation. He named already new fields of activities, for example business trip traffic and aerial rescue which were never pursued before. Future airplanes should transport post, papers, and other goods. The transport of persons, also for the purpose of arriving at a holiday destination, is to be taken into consideration.

Emphatically the undersecretary of state asked the airplane factories to develop airplane types which would do justice to the new intended purposes.

However, Euler saw the actual situation still too optimistic in this time. The Treaty of Versailles should smash all hopes concerning a steady development of the German aircraft construction a few months later. The construction restricitions of the peace negotiations brought the heaviest impediments to the German aircraft industry for the next years.

Wide space in both memoranda took the question how the aviation industry of Germany should organize itself. From her foundation on all German airplane factories had lived mostly from state orders because neither private principals nor civil societies (airlines) existed who could have ordered airplanes for their purposes. Thus it was explicable that the aviation industry was at first interested in a nationalization of aviation. However, Euler contradicted this strange request.[21] He had in mind a kind of "Air Traffic Trial Society of Germany". "All airlines, enterprises, airship and airplane factories, flight engine factories, airfield enterprisers, the state and the ctities unite in any still to establish common form of activity...".

Euler did also suggest "that the industry should agree that one factory should only produce giant

Nachrichten für Luftfahrer

Herausgegeben vom

Reichsverkehrsministerium (Reichsamt für Luft- und Kraftfahrwesen)

Jahrg. 1. | Berlin, 8. Oktober 1920. | Nr. 1.

Above: Copy No. 2 of the first ediction of the Nachrichten für Luftfahrer.

airplanes, another only great airplanes, a third only 3-seaters, 2-seaters or telegram airplanes or airships, etc.". Here he disregarded factors of a free market economy and the free spirit of entrepreneurs.

Efforts for the continuity and the development of the German aviation took in general a big space in his activity as chief of the Reichsluftamt.

His main task as chief of the office saw Unterstaatssekretär Euler surely not in the impediement of aviation, but in the support of a dynamic industrial branch. It was the most natural thing of the world for him to consult with experts, finally, there were still no employees avaiable to him until mid-1919.[22] For this reason Euler brought to life the "Reichsausschuss für die Luftfahrt" which met to its first meeting on 8 February 1919. To the participants belonged again: Geheimer Regierungsrat professor Hergesell, Counsellor of Justice Dr. Niemeyer, Major von Tschudi, professor Dr. Ing. Bendemann from the Deutsche Versuchsanstalt für Luftfahrt, Director G. Dieterich, Dr. Sperling from Verein Deutscher Motoren-Fahrzeug-Industrieller as well as Hauptmann Fisch and Oberleutnant Flörke, both new employees in the Reichsluftamt.

Above all the future duties of the Reichsausschuss and implementation regulations for the "Verordnung über die vorläufige Regelung des Luftfahrtrechtes" (Order about the temporary regulation of the aviation law) from 7 December 1918 as well as airline questions stood on the agenda.

In his (third) memornadum "The Internationality of the Aviation", published on 15 March 1919, August Euler developed visions of an internationally operating, land-covering central authority for aviation. However, here he was also far ahead of his time. The memorandum, published at first by the Reichsluftamt, had to be pulled back under the pressure of the Ministerium des Innern and be explained as a private opinion of Euler. He was attacked as "Internationalist" in the press. Germany had just lost a war and could not claim unduly to organize the order of the post-war aviation. Nevertheless, his thesis was revolutionary: "The aviation seems to be only a progress in the human culture, if it can be regulated internationally; her legislation should be an international. ... The aviation should be legaly controlled and administered by international offical institutions. In the single, today still by national borders separated countries authorities should be created which represent previous national and international interests. ... I (imagine) the establishment of an international aviation commission which is has her head in one of the cultural adavanced states of the world and in all single states aviation authorities erected and [I imagine] an aviation independent of national demarcations and national laws and working exclusively according to the instructions and orders of the international central authority."[23] In November 1944, 25 years later, this idea was continued by the US government. 55 states and authorities agreed on the conference in Chicago to bring a land-covering organisation to its life to lead the civil air traffic to world-wide equal standards: the Convention on International Civil Aviation (ICAO).

The problems in connection with the German traffic system were huge. After the end of the war the raw material shortage and the breakdown of the whole industry also affected the automobile industry, what lead to the fact that on 19 September 1919 a cabinet decision was made which caused the enlargement of the Reichsluftamt für Luft- und Kraftfahrwesen (RaLKW). The foundation was on 1 October 1919.

After this merging August Euler, who was promoted to secretary of state in May 1920, was

Der Unterstaatssekretär
des
Reichsluftamts

E/Kr.
J.Nr.105/19.

Berlin W8, den 9. Januar 1919
Wilhelmstraße 74

Zulassungs-Bescheinigung
zum Luftverkehr.
Nr. 1.

Der Deutschen Luftreederei G.m.b.H. Berlin wird auf Grund der Verfügung des Rats der Volksbeauftragten vom 7.Dezember 1918, Reichs-Gesetzblatt 175, die Erlaubnis erteilt, vom 10. Januar bis Ende Januar 1919 zu Propaganda-zwecken Luftverkehr mit Flugzeugen zu betreiben.

Die Flugzeuge sind gekennzeichnet:

L.V.G. C.V
L.V.G. C.VI
Sablatnig N
A.E.G. J.II
A.E.G. G.V.

Es sind nur Tagesflüge, welche von Berlin ausgehen und am gleichen Tage und ohne Zwischenlandung in Berlin wieder enden, erlaubt.

Diese Zulassung zum Luftverkehr ist auf jederzeitigen Widerruf erteilt und erlischt von selbst am 31.Januar 1919

An
Deutsche Luftreederei
G.m.b.H.,
Berlin.

Reichsluftamt

August Euler

Above: Licensing certificate No. 1. On this document were not listed a 4-engined Giant airplane Linke-Hoffmann and four two-engined airplanes of Gotha and Friedrichshafen.

aditionally in charge of the rebuilding of the whole German motor transport system. The independence of the Reichsluftamt was lifted as a result of the direct subordination under the Reichsverkehrsministerium. Euler could not resist against this in spite of several attempts.

With his typical pragmatic way of working August Euler began to solve these tasks. At the beginning of his work he had only four officals and less than a handful of secretarial staff was available to him, later the office developed step by step to an operable authority.

In particular one was busy to organize and to approve the civil air traffic under consideration of the restrictions which were imposed by the victorious powers.

A list of the Reichsluftamt from the end of 1919 displayed the following enterprises that received or had applied for a license (written in Italics) for air traffic:

1. *Flugzeugwerft Lübeck-Travemünde, Travemünde-Priwall*
2. *Luftfahrzeugbau Schütte-Lanz, Zeesen bei Königs-Wusterhausen*
3. Deutsche Luftreederei GmbH, Berlin
4. *Kondor-Flugzeugwerke, Berlin-Charlottenburg*
5. *Deutsche Flugzeugwerke, Leipzig*
6. *Albatroswerke, Berlin-Johannisthal*
7. *Gothaer Waggonfabrik, Gotha*
8. *Daimler-Motoren-Gesellschaft, Sindelfingen*
9. Sablatnik-Flugzeugbau GmbH, Berlin
10. *Flugzeugbau GmbH, Friedrichshafen*
11. *Halberstädter Flugzeugwerke AG, Halberstadt*
12. Hannoversche Waggonfabrik, Hannover-Linden
13. *Flugzeugbau GmbH Friedrichshafen, Warnemünde*
14. Rumpler-Werke AG, Berlin-Johannisthal
15. Junkers-Fokker-Werke, Dessau
16. *Luft-Fahrzeug-Gesellschaft mbH, Berlin-Charlottenburg*
17. *Bayerische Rumpler-Werke, Augsburg*
18. *Seekartell des Berufsverbandes für das Luftfahrtwesen, Kiel-Holtenau*
19. *Frankfurter Verkehrsverein, Frankfurt a.M.*
20. *Technische Werke Baden, Baden-Baden*
21. *Flieger-Gruppe e.V., Mannheim*

It is owed to Euler's personal engagement that a possibility was created in Germany to hand over the necessary information regarding aviation to all affected people – the "Nachrichten für Luftfahrer" (News for Aviators). The first issue of this offical information sheets which has kept the general structure until today, was published on 8 October 1920.

Reichsausschuss für Luft- und Kraftfahrwesen

As foundation meeting of the Reichsausschuss für Luft- und Kraftfahrwesen one can see the consultation of the representants of all in aviation interested circles of economy and expert associations which was called in by August Euler already on 20 December 1918. In the course of debate Euler directed the request to the present representatives to name experts with whom he could discuss the offical measures to be met by his office in advance.

G. Dietrich, member of the Reichsausschuss wrote about this:[24] "Untersecretary of state Euler let not arise any doubt that it was not his intention to see these representatives only as decorative addition to his new office, but that he saw them as real co-workers and accordingly intended to give them an immediate influence on the activities of his office. With this step the then youngest technical Imperial office entered a way that was not thought to be usual in the past.

Though advisory boards and expert's boards were already usual before the war and in some offices during the war, however, they were only involved in decisions from case to case, and they had rarely or never a real responsible influence on the development and the offical trend of affairs in these offices." Later Euler came under pressure by the press because of this establishment of the expert's board. However, at first the immediate integration of all circles interested in aviation was senseful and purposeful because the German aviation was only directed according to military goals (like in other countries) in the time from 1914 to 1918. Therefore everything related to the construction and use of air vehicles was determined purely from a military point of view.

The German military aviation was extinguished by the treaty with the victorious powers (see chapter 14 "The Treaty of Versailles, Demise and Restart of the German Aircraft industry"). Nevertheless, the possibility of the construction of an aviation for peaceful and civil traffic purposes as well as scientiific-technical tasks up to the sports flying was kept. The German civil aviation stood before its birth hour. In this sense the Imperial Committee should serve as an obstetrician.

The members of this committee were not representatives of certain circles of interest, but they were only appointed because of their personal suitability and skill in certain areas of aviation. Accordingly there were also specific scopes of work assigned to them for which they were in charge as permanent offical advisers of the Reichsluftamt. In detail there were: Prof. Dr. Bendemann (Technical and economic affairs, examination conditions for the licensing for airlines; competitions for engines and airplanes, photo-technical devices), Dir. Dieterich (Profitability calculations, Luftverkehrs-Versuchs-Gesellschaft/Airline-Trial-Association), Dir. Eckener (airship matters), Geheimer Regierungsrat Prof. Dr. Hergesell (General Scientific Affairs, Weather and News Service, Association Affairs), Dir. Joly (Airfield affairs, Reichsversuchsanstalt), Prof.

Junkers (Technical-scientific affairs), Dir. Kasinger (Industrial affairs, Aviation exhibitions), Dr. Council of Law Niemeyer (Aviation Law affairs, Reichs laws for air traffic, delegate for the peace negotiations), Dir. Rasch (secretary, delegate for the peace negotiations), Kapitänleutnant von Santen (Airplane and pilot's affairs), Privy Government Councilor Prof. Dr. Schütte (Airship and airship affairs), Dr. Sperling (Industrial affairs, aviation exhibitions, insurance and liability matters), Major a.D. von Tschudi (Association affairs, Aviator's care, Airfield affairs,Aviation sports affairs, aviation maps).

After the Reichsverkehrsministerium had enlarged the competence of Euler's Reichsamt for motor transport one also established a suitable Reichsausschuss for this area. Now according to the rules of operation the advicing of the now named Reichsamt für Luft- und Kraftfahrwesens had been transferred to this Reichsausschuss. It had, according to its purpose, to be heard in all questions of aviation and motor transport by the Reichsamt; as well it had to make suggestions and to make proposals for improvements in the field of aviation and motor transport. If necessary, Euler commissioned the committee also with the treatment of petitions and complaints.

All single questions which were assigned to the Reichsluftamt and its current successor, the Reichsamt für Luft- und Kraftfahrwesen which had to be worked on during their activity were at first assigned to the Committee for either preparation or evaluation or other statements. "In all questions his judgement has been heard or been recognized as authoritative, like in general the cooperation between the Reichsausschuss as decisive executing authority and the Reichsausschuss as authoritative advicory board must be called exceptionally harmonious. Also the opposition that one could expect and which resulted from the new nature of the whole institution and its use by older older offices unfamiliar with the new institution have been overcome or for the most part given up."[25] As a result of this division of labor the most important problems could be solved with defensible time exposure. Another advantage was that the decisions had not be made at the green table.

The Reichsausschuss für Luftfahrt had during its foundation at first the task to help to create the draft for the already before the war projected Air Traffic Law until the final presentation at the Nationalversammlung and the Reichsrat. Dieterich writes: "Which immense difficulties this one task met, the outsider can not judge: There were nearly no experiences existing for the airplane as means of transport in the public, for everybody accessible traffic. It is clear that the aerial legislative must often intervene to areas of the public and private law that base largely on century-old experiences in society and traffic which offer no conditions for the legal regulation of aviation."[26] More detailed information about the first German Air Traffic Law are explained below.

Almost all experts were equally inexperienced in the field of regulations for construction and use of airplanes and airships as means of transport. Though the war had brought big progresses in the area of technology, but understandably it had not contributed to the development of air vehicles as modern means of transportation. Thus the board of experts hat to look for new foundations which often differed radically from the technical and economic requirements conditioned by war standards. Also in this area the Reichsausschuss has performed an exceptionally valuable work. The first implementation regulations to the Air Traffic Law are mentioned here. These enclosed the uniform examination and acceptance regulations of air vehicles, their markings, the demands for the training of pilots, the equipment of airports, etc.

Deutsche Luftsport-Kommission

The resolutions of the Treaty of Versailles intended massive cuts for the airplane construction in Germany but did not prevent the development of the airsport. The exclusion of the Deutscher Luftfahrerverband from the Fédération Aéronautique International (FAI) was no reason for the German civil aviation to doubt its future fields of actvity. On the contrary, it forced to an improved organization. In August 1919, at the time of the exclusion of the Deutscher Luftfahrerverband from the FAI, the Reichsamt für Luft- und Kraftfahrwesen assigned the upper supervision of this young sport to the Luftsport-Kommission.

Herr v. Tschudi, who headed the Airsports-Commission, remebered: "The choice of the people for the commission mad hardly difficulties. It seemed reasonable to choose at first those who had performed the most essential work in the old commission and had acquired from it a long-term experience especially by the participation in international conferences. It was natural that experienced... pilots had to belong to the commission as well as scientific and industrial experts."[27]

August Euler transferred the following affairs to the Airsport Commission :

1. Installation of directives for breeding competitions (advertising of competitions);
2. Examination and approval of bidings;
3. Guidance of organizers;

Left: Meeting of the German Airsport Commission; from left to right: Dir. Kasinger, Kapt.-Ltn. Langfeld, Dir. Rasch, Oberstltn. Siegert, Prof. Berson, Dr. Hoff, Major v. Tschudi, Dr. Heimann, unknown (typist), Dr. Elias, Dir. V. Kehler, Sedlmayr, Ltn. Dörr.

4. Control of airsport;
5. Highest decision in airsport affairs;
6. Regulations for records, recognition of records and special achievements;
7. Suggestions for the use of available financial means;
8. Granting and extraction of sporty licenses;
9. Representation of the German airsport abroad;
10. Supervision of the Luftfahrerfürsorge.

To the duties of the commission also belonged the recognition of achieved records in the field of aviation and the biding of most different competitions (e.g. Rumpler Prize à 20,000 M). It belonged to the strategical duties of the airsport commission to hold contact to the international associations and organisations of airsport. One knew that the international isolation of the German aviator's association would not be long-lasting.

The First German Air Traffic Act

Finally, the exceedingly rapid development of aviation in all its areas at the beginning of the 20th century required clear rules to maintain and secure the order. Aerial-judically busy were offices and non-offical facilities as well, partly already in the 18th century but without concluding a noteworthy extent. This changed understandably by the end of the 19th century.

As examples, partly already in the 18th and 19th century are mentioned: The French local order from 23 April 1784 that made balloon take-offs depending from an approval, furthermore an order remitted in France in the year 1819, which forbade the rise of hot air balloons before the harvest and prescribed the entrainment of a parachute or a circular from 9 April 1892 of the Prussian Ministry of the Interior to the president of the government concerning the use of airships.

The jurisprudence began increasingly to deal with aviation – in Germany since circa 1908. However, the other side, the offical and administrative, that should have displayed a natural special interest in this field, was only little active until 1911. The reason for the change of this position can be explained by the already mentioned fact that the possibility of air traffic, at first only with airships, materialized more from this time on. However, on the other hand, there was already a steady increase of movements of airplanes, not only on airfields but also in cross-country flights and over populated areas.

To the first offical regulations of the air traffic with flight machines in the 20th century belonged the enacted Police acts from 29 July 1910, 1 October 1910 and 6 October 1910 about the rise of flight machine, which were issued by the Upper President of the province of Brandenburg respectively the Police president of Berlin together with an order of the Prussian minister for public works and the Prussian minister of the Interior "regarding state measures towards airship journeys and aviation" from 22 October 1910.[28 29]

According to state-contractual agreements in the area of avation are before 1911, apart from the land war order (Art. 29) of the Hague peace conferences in 1899 and 1907, aviators were not to be treated automatically as spies. Merely the ban of the dropping of projectiles and explosives from airships or "on similar new ways" was created.

Concerning the events of the year 1911 can be ascertained finally that the air traffic law was already discussed on the "Meeting of the Representatives of the Flight Science" on 3, 4, and 5 November 1911 in Göttingen, where August Euler participated as well.

The report of the meeting says in addition: "In the evening at 6½ o'clock the lectures of the of Dr. jur. Alex Meyer and referendar v. Rottenburg (both flight trainees of August Euler, who was present as guest speaker as well, remark of the redaction) took place in the Auditorium Maximum of the university. The

Right: Euler flight machine in Göttingen

first discussed the airship flights and the public law, the second private-juridicial and patent juridicial questions of the airship traffic. In the discussion Prof. Dr. von Bar, Göttingen, took the word for a discussion about international questions of the air law."

The progressing technical development of aviation, especially the forming of the regular air traffic, let arise from 1911 on not only in Germany, but also in the most other states a national aviation legislation. Moreover, also the border-crossing and therefore international air traffic was also widely regulated by respective interstate treaties.

On 6 December 1912 August Euler received an invitation which was signed by Reichspräsident Dr. Lewald to take part in a first discussion of legal regulations of air traffic. Euler was counted among the leading experts at this time because of his extensive experiences as pilot and industrialist. In preparation of this discussion which took place on 6 January 1913 in the building of the Reichstag, already "Main features for a regulation of the traffic with air vehicles" and "Main features for an order about the traffic with air verhicles" were compiled. These draughts coincided with little divergences with proposals that were brought into the legislative process after the end of the First World War.[30]

1913 can be also called the year in which urged by everybody recognizeable inexorable progressing development of air traffic – the legislation began to deal the first time more thorougly with air laws.

A time had been reached where the human mind had succeeded, on one hand to make airships, bodies lighter than air, to obey the rudder, on the other hand to arise in the air with the help of such bodies and to move on there. The long desired opening of the air space by airplanes was basically achieved. Consequently one had to make oneself familiar with the thought that air vehicles will develop to an important means of traffic in not so far times. At the same moment also the legislator had to deal with aviation.

This is also shown by a look at the railway and steamboat legislation as well as many laws and orders concerning the traffic with bicycles and automobiles. These laws and orders were mostly not welcomed by the prospective customers but after more exact considerations the critics had to come to the conviction that nothing works without an order and that the legislator did not remit the laws as chicanery against single persons, but had to remit them in the interest and for the protection of the collectivity. The legislation, which dealt, as in the present case, with new means of traffic, might only not appear as enemy of progress, but might merely work "ordering, clearing and supporting".

By the opening of the air space a new theatre was created, beside the solid earth and the sea, where juridically important actions of all kinds could occur. Consequently it was the first and most important task of the jurisprudence to determine, how the air over the different parts of the earth's surface has to be seen according to constitutional law and under international law.

Unity was achieved fast here: the airspace over the open sea and stateless areas is free in every respect. Hence, the use of the airspace over these parts of the earth's surface is free for commercial, scientific and private as well as warlike purposes of all nations and could not prohibited for anybody.

In contrast to the unity of the opinions in this question several different views have already formed about the other questions: as what should the airspace be considered that is situated over the state area which is sourrounded by state borders in state and international law. It prevailed the view that this part of the airspace was property – also if property in a limited sense – of the state situated below.

In 1912 August Euler was invited as guest to the discussions of the air traffic law, but since December 1918 he was in charge and had to do the same work. already on 30 April 1919 the Reichsluftamt presented the draft for the Reichsgesetz for Luftverkehr, on 2 May 1919 followed the drafts below:

- Decree about markings, state and control of the airfields;
- Decree about the licensing for traffic;
- Decree about the traffic with air vehicles with mechanic engine within and outside of airfields;
- Decree about markings on the earth;
- Decree about the examination and licensing of crews of air vehicles with mechanic engine;
- Decree about the check, licensing and markings of air vehicles for the traffic outside of airfields;
- Pattern and piece examination regulations.

In the reasoning of the draft for this version of the Reichsgesetz für den Luftverkehr undersecretary of state August Euler pointed towards the changed political, legal and technical conditions in comparison to January 1914, so that the old draft had to be entirely reworked. He justified the urgent need of the law and the later following implementing regulations as follows: "The experience gained in the meantime has caused the inviction of the Reichsluftamt and all incurred experts that an only "temporary regulation" of the aviation law is not to be recommened in the interest of the development of the German aviation. An only provisional legal condition at the very beginning would be an obstacle for the wished development of civil aviation and its industry and the fact that all foundations are given for a comprehensive legal regulation of aviation, that is meeting the needs of aviation and the interests of the collectivity for the foreseeable future and finally, that the legal regulation is not allowing any delay."[31] For the first time an all-German set of rules had been worked out, which should replace the provincial single regulations that had been applied until then. The first German air traffic law[32] was brought into force on 1 August 1922.

Euler's Leave

On 8 July 1920 August Euler submitted for personal reasons a holiday request to the acting Reichsverkehrsminister. He explained the applied duration of three months with family problems (death of the father in May 1920, demise of his mother in June 1920, illness of his wife Louise Euler) and the fact that the fate of the Eulerwerke in Frankfurt-Niederrad was uncertain. At this time one could not conclude that Euler would have the intention already in Summer 1920 to lay down the offical business. He assured his willingness to return to Berlin immediately if the requirements demanded this. To be informed permanently Euler let himself report the events and working main forces in both departments of aviation and transport to Frankfurt.[33]

Already a short time after his holiday's beginning critical articles in the press increased, at first against the Reichsamt für Luft- und Kraftfahrwesen, then directed against August Euler. Occassion offered the stagnant development of the passenger traffic by means of automobiles, no matter whether it concerned vehicles of trucking companies, e.g. taxis, or private passenger cars. All suffered equally from the forced-on distribution of fuel. Discontent ruled in the whole republic.

The decision of the government was generally taken up negatively because it was incomprehensible to unite the interests of motor transportation with the aviation's interests in one common office.[34] This allocation was taken as sign of low esteem for the development of motor transport in the public. In professional circles of the automobile industry one observed the decline of the German aviation industry very careful and and was afraid to suffer the same fate under August Euler's management. The demand for an own office for motor transport was sent as a reminder and at the same time the public attacks against Euler became more sharp.

This organizational change was also a big worry for Euler but for other reasons. With the insinuation of the Reichsamt für Luft- und Kraftfahrwesen under the Verkehrsministerium in May 1920 he saw a weakening of his position. Above all Euler was focused on his independence and own responsibility in all questions of aviation that was given to him in his first decree on 8 December. His initial efforts that the Reichsluftamt would develop into an own ministry (of aviation) failed. The differences between the Minister of Transport Bauer and Euler became more and more visible. With reference to his good relations to his present offical superiors, the state secretaries of the Interior Dr. Preuß and Dr. David as well as minister of transport Dr. Johannes Bell[35] he insisted to minister of transport Bauer[36] on independence in his office. He demanded: "This position, at which I look as well acquired right for the purpose of the article 129 of the Reichsverfassung, is not abolished, rather I have remained politically responsible still as a specialised ministerial undersecretary of state, i.e., I am immediately responible regardless of my expertly classification in the Reichsverkehrsministerium according to article 53, 54, and 57 of the Reichsverfassung and also to the House of Representatives, the Reichspräsident and the Reichsregierung."[37]

Euler had even as the leader of the Reichsamt für Luft- und Kraftfahrwesen no easy stand. His authority was damaged in particular by the officals assigned to him and their protection of interests (official's committees). Euler, who filled his activity as an offical superior with extreme devotion and willingness, could and would not accept that the officials insisted on a 7-hours working day. Moreover he did not feel as portable that he could not work on personal matters, even of officials, independently. These compulsions in the organisation of service and leadership of this according to his own wishes independent office was not acceptable for August Euler on a continuing base. Still before his vacation he complained in a writing from 29 May 1920 to minister Bauer: "The biggest part of the middle civil servants, embittered by petty, often only on misunderstandings based points of complaints, acts without restraint, and even still encouraged by the behavior of parts of the higher officals in the sharpest opposition to the leader of the Reichsamt. The whole or at least large parts of the working days are used exclusively to collect material against him, to explore his whole private life, without giving him knowledge about this before, directing disoriented accusations, partly of the most unobjective kind, immediately to his senior office."[38]

Already on 22 July 1920, only a few days after the holidays beginning the "BZ am Mittag" published first suppositions about a forthcoming change at the head of the imperial office of Aviation and Motor transportation. Openly one discussed in the press the names of suitable successors, although state secretary August Euler was merely on vacation. The *Berliner Zeitung* appreciated already on 27 July 1920 Euler's achievements and his positive work in an "obituary": "August Euler goes! With him a personality disappears from the political life as we do not find them to frequently in Germany. He combined determination and vigor in his person together with great practical and theoretical knowledge in the field of aviation as well as motor transportation... The name Euler is tied forever with the history of aviation. His career begun in 1908 as the first airman of Germany and led him soon to honor and recognition... Through his coarseness and his drastic expressions he belonged in airman's circles at that time to the most popular personalities.

During the war Euler stepped more in the background. In contrast to Fokker, Grade, and other well-known pilots he did not know how to procure the necessary capital to play a similar role as the afore mentioned. To become an employee may not have fitted to the independent nature of this man, after he had been his own director, mechanic, and chief pilot in his own person.

There is little to say about his activity as leader of the R.L.K. The main work was not construction and advancement but the liquidation of the army aviation, the fight against the Entente commission, and lack of fuel on one hand and against the stormy urge of the aeronautical youth on the other hand. This, as well as the unhappy composition of his variform office made it impossible for him, to bring his orgainzational abilities completely to bear..." [39]

In his last writing from Frankfurt a.M., passé on 8 October 1920, so shortly before expiration of his allowed 3-month vacation, Euler clarified towards the Reichsverkehrsminister Bauer: "I hand over the enclosed writing (Account on the grievances in the Reichsamt für Luft- und Kraftfahrwesen, the author) with the polite request to grant me leave until the decision about decision and execution of the said writing and matters by the Reichs government or the cabinett ... , because I do not think that I am obliged to lead the office entrusted to my management under other conditions and rights than the conditions agreed with the government."[40]

Apparently the minister did not follow the request of his secretary of state because Euler did not return in his office. In November 1920 August Euler submitted a request about the temporary transfer in the state of retirement to the minister of transport Gröner which was granted to him on 30 November 1920.

However, August Euler withdrew at the age of 53 years into the private life and received a pension from the treasury of the state up to the end of his life. Later the retired Euler summed up: "To be an undersecretary of state was my most thankless charge."[41]

The Reichsluftamt became the Reichsamt für Luft- und Kraftfahrwesen. According to a decision of the Reichspräsident Euler got the title secretary of state.

It is the Germany of the parliamentary majorities. Governments come and go. Euler remains, survives them.[42]

Chapter 29 (Excerpt from the Memoirs of August Euler)[43]

Based on the favor of parties new ministers appear over and over again, rule some months and either disappear forever or try to regain the lost minister's chairs by all kinds of tricks or manoeuvres.

Euler outlasts them all.

Thus it goes ... over years. He is the only one, who does not participate in the parties game. He don't want to be exponent of a party or a political group, but fair custodian of German aviation. And aviation belongs all Germans together.

...

One day minister of transport General Gröner appears in Euler's bureau.

"Herr General, what leads you to me?"

"Well, Herr secretary of state, this is not said with a few words - - ", the general replies in very light tone and slightly abashed.

"Do we not want to sit down, Herr General? Please – "

Gröner takes a seat in the presented armchair. Euler sits opposite to him, observes him sharply. At first it is spoken about uninteresting things, nevertheless, a secret tension vibrates in the background which waits only for discharge.

Finally, the general beginns: "You are already more than three years in your office, Herr secretary of state?"

"Since December eighteen."

"And you are not belonging to a party?"

This should be known too well, Herr General!"

Now Gröner becomes livier. "See, and this does not go in the long run!"

"What does not go in the long run?" Euler's voice sounds sharp.

"Just the fact that a leader stands at the head of an independent Reichsamt who is not belonging to a party according to the constitution. The Reichstag calls this as incompatible with the constitution."

"When I assumed my office, there was never a discussion that I should do this as an exponent of a party. And if one had expected this of me, I would never have accepted the office. I had seen myself as representant of the German aviation since my assumption of the office and it is unpolitical and belongs to no party, she may be called as she wants!"

Euler has got up and goes with big steps in the room up and down.

"I also said: up to now it went well, but in the long run it does not go. You must join a party and allow her to represent you!"

Euler stops again in front of the general and briefly gives a lough.

"A party? Which party? Maybe your own party?"

"One does not want to influence you in it. You can choose."

"Let us make it short, Herr General! I have chosen long ago! The Deutschnationalen [German Nationalists] don't stand far right enough and the Communists not far left enough. Thanks!"

Now Gröner also gets up. Both men stand close to each other.

"Herr secretary of state, you are probably not enough offical to be able to understand the situation properly?"

Euler twitches the shoulders. His face remains dead. No muscle moves in it.

"So you don't want?", the general continues annoyed.

"As I see, you have understood my words absolutely properly, Herr General!"

Gröner takes a deep breath. Drums with the fingers nervously on the tabletop.

"Are you aware of the fact that one can force you to take your resignation?"

Euler remains calm, very calm.

"I remain what I am and what I always was, Herr General! Herr Reichspräsident can put me quietly to disposition. Therefore, I do not need to be ashamed!"

General Gröner has stepped to the window. He looks some moments in silence outward. Then he suddely turns around and comes up to Euler again. He has become considerably quieter and politer.

"Let's just say, Herr secretyry of state, should we not talk about all today evening in the Deutsche Gesellschaft [a restaurant] with a glass of beer?"

Euler shakes the head. "I am too much of an offical for that, Herr General. I have agreed on a position as an apolitical and independent professional minister with my assumption of the office. I persist on this!"

"And, nevertheless, we will talk once again about that!", said Gröner resolutely and with strong voice, as if this is his last trump. Then he said goodbye. Euler accompanied him to the door of the antechamber.

Some weeks later Euler got to know the general would intend to integrate the Reichsamt für Luft- und Kraftfahrwesen into his ministry of transportation and would use his party's influence in the Reichstag. Gröner had not still turned to Euler himself with this matter. However, it is not a far way from Gröner's office room to Euler's. working room. And a rumour spreads fast.

Finally, Gröner stretches out the first offical feeler. He demands from Euler, that he is communicating about his office and his budget. Euler declines definitely. He writes back that he himself represents his budget in front of the Reichstag. People who want to play their game with Euler on this way know the first German pilot badly.

Two weeks later he asks the Reichspräsident to put him to disposition. His request was approved. With relief Euler draws a deep breath. He is free again and his own master.

With unbroken energy and fighting spirit Euler returns to Frankfurt. He becomes a private individual, goes on travelling, enjoys – sport. With 54 years of age he discovered his love and talent for the tennis sport. He plays in summer on places at the Forsthausstrasse and in winter in the old Euler flying hangar on the flight area.

Euler plays the new sport not only to entertain himself. He invites himself approved players for competition, grows in her achievements and becomes an equal opponent to them. He studies the tennis sport like a science in literature and practice. The victory-used racing cyclist and car racing driver, the combatative pilot and record airman also becomes a victorious tennis player.

Besides he starts to the Black Forest-Championship in cross-country skiing – and wins! In Baden-Baden he wins a tournament in ballroom dancing. "First became a well-preserved bonvivant!", newspapers wrote.

In spite of his advanced age the first German airman has remained young. Once, when he was made the proposal to give a political speech in the Berlin Sportpalast, where he had participated in so many bicycle races, he denied with the remark: "The people would yell out: "August, faster!""

The town at the Main, where he found his adoptive home, could not hold him. So much as Frankfurt had become dear to him as town of his work and successes, so much did it drive him from the tangle of streets and houses of the city in the width and loneliness of the nature.

Endnotes

1. The way of departure of Euler stands in crass contradiction to his whole achievement as office leader in the time from 10 December 1918 to 30 November 1920, nevertheless, it reflects the nature of this man. His habit not to divide power or to keep his independency and the resulting authoritarian, partly dictorial way of work with his subordinates formed a big obstacle to remain longer on the political stage of a partly chaotically operating republic. In Euler's 2-year long term in office he himself and his comrades-in-arms finally did what was objectively possible under the then domestic and foreign political circumstances.[42] Schreiben des Kommandierenden Generals der Luftstreitkräfte an den Chef des Generalstabes des Feldheeres vom 10.9.1917 [Letter of the Commanding General of the Air Force to the Chief of General Staff of the Field Army on 10 September 1917].
2. Reichsgesetzblatt, vol. 1918, No. 163, issued on 27 November 1918.
3. Reichsgesetzblatt, vol. 1918, decree No. 6569 about the establishment of the Reichsluftamt on 4 Dezember 1918.
4. BA Koblenz, estate Euler, signature N1103-282
5. Ibid: At the end of the war Siegert numbered the available material values in form of aviation stations, buildings, airplanes, engines, photo devices, spares and raw material with 1,012,000,000 Mark. The available living flying personnel represented costs of training including crashs and consumption of fuel with a value of 322,000,000 Mark.
6. Ibid: Main points were especially tasks like the prevention of "wild flights", which served the exportation of property and personalities.
7. Ibid: In November 1918 a department "Air Mail" was provisionally established by the Inspection of the Aviation troops.
8. Reichsgesetzblatt, vol. 1918, No. 175, issued on 9 December 1918.
9. BA Koblenz, estate Euler, signature N1103-283.
10. Die Entstehung des Reichsamtes für Luft- und Kraftfahrwesen, special print from "Motor", January/February 1920.
11. Ibid.
12. BA Koblenz, estate Euler, signature N1103-283.

13. Journal *Motor*, January/February 1920, Article: Das Reichsamt für Luft- und Kraftfahrwesen.
14. Whether and when August Euler was moved into the status of an civil servant ist not clearly proven until today. However, everything points to this fact because he later received a pesnion from the treasury.
15. Licensing certificate No. 1, Archive Deutsche Lufthansa AG, Köln.
16. BA Koblenz, estate Euler, signature N1103-298, Schreiben Reichsluftamt vom 24.2.1919 an diverse Dienststellen [Writing of the Reichsluftamt to different service offices on 24 February 1919].
17. Ibid.
18. Die Entstehung des Reichsamtes für Luft- und Kraftfahrwesen, special print from *Motor*, January/February 1920.
19. BA Koblenz, estate Euler, signature N1103: a total of 49,000 German airplanes was produced during the years of war.
20. Untersecretary of state August Euler, memorandum from 9 January 1919.
21. See also Euler's memorandum "Die Verstaatlichung der Luftfahrt?" [The Nationalisation of Aviation] from 10 May 1919.
22. Only in the course of the year 1919 several officals were assigned to the Imperial Air Office from the Ministry of the Interior.
23. BA Koblenz, estate Euler, signature N1103-294, August Euler, 3rd memorandum "Die Internationalität der Luftfahrt" [The Internationality of Aviation].
24. Journal *Motor*, issue January/February 1920, "Das Reichsamt für Luft- und Kraftfahrwesen".
25. Ibid, p 9.
26. Dieterich, G., "Der Reichsausschuß für Luft- und Kraftfahrwesen", in "Das Reichsamt für Luft- und Kraftfahrwesen", W. Büxenstein Druckereigesellschaft, Berlin, 1919.
27. Ibid, p 12.
28. Amtsblatt der Kgl. Regierung zu Potsdam und der Stadt Berlin, 1910.
29. Deutsche Zeitschrift für Luftfahrt, vol. 1910, issue 20, p 18 and issue 22, p 16.
30. BA Koblenz, estate Euler, signature N1103-009
31. Unterstaatssekretär des Reichsluftamts, Begründung des Entwurfs eines Reichsgesetzes für den Luftverkehr, Berlin, 30.04.1919, BA Koblenz, estate Euler, signature N1103-285.
32. See RGBl. I p 681.
33. Representative of Euler was the later leader of the General Air Office in the Imperial Aviation Ministry, privy councillor (later head of government department) Willy Fisch.
34. BZ am Mittag, 1 June 1920, article "Wiederaufbau des Autoverkehrs" [Reconstruction of Motor traffic]: The imperial traffic ministry subdivided itself at this time into a) railroading, b) shipping and c) Aviation and motor transportation.
35. Johannes Bell,first Reichsverkehrsminister of the Republic of Weimar from 13 February 1919 to 30 April 920.
36. Gustav Bauer, from 21 June 1919 to 26 March 1920 Reichskanzler, from 1 May 1920 to 24 June 1920 Reichsverkehrsminister.
37. BA Koblenz, Signature N1103-330, Euler's letter to Reichsverkehrsminister Bauer on 19 May 1920.
38. Letter from Euler to Reichsverkehrsminister Bauer on 29 May 1920, BA Koblenz, estate Euler, signature N1103-330.
39. BZ am Mittag, 27 July 1920, article "Wechsel im Luftfahrtamt".
40. Letter from Euler to Reichsverkehrsminister Bauer on 8 October 1920, BA Koblenz, estate Euler, signature N1103-330.
41. Kronenwerth Egon, "Der tolle Euler" [The stunning Euler], Umschau Verlag, Frankfurt, 1992
42. With effect from [1]st March [1921] the office was led by head of government Traugott Bredow.
43. Unpublished manuscript , Euler-Archiv, Feldberg.

16. The Merits of August Euler for the Development of Aviation in Germany

What distinguishs August Euler from the other pioneers of German aviation? In what does his big merit lie, why were his great achievements forgotten?

Euler was indisputeable not the endowed constructor of flight machines in spite of the huge number of submitted and granted patents as well as utility models. Also he was not the passionate pilot because already in 1912, three years after his maiden flight at the International Airship Exhibition, Euler left the flying to others and devoted himself with full power to the management of his enterprise beside other important tasks.

Euler owned the necessary foresight for the development of the motor flight like no second pilot of the first hours.

It is to be owed to his personal engagement that the forces were bundled up for the support of aviation heavier than air in Germany and continue to work until today in many cases.

The number of German airmen was still very small in 1910. It was a brightly mixed society which dedicated itself to the reckless aviation. Beside young engineers, well-known sportsmen tried to prove their skills in the "most modern" sport. Officers competed with forward striving students, amateur handicraftsmen and adventurers stepped on the airman's stage. It is slightly conceivable that it was not easy to bring these totally different men under a hat. It is to be owned to Oskar Ursinus in this case that on 22 April 1910 in Frankfurt German aviators and flight engineers assembled to found the "Vereinigung der Flieger". The meeting took unanimously the view that an association was necessary to fight the exploitation of airmen and to protect the economic interests of all German airmen.[1]

Therefore August Euler counted to the founding members of the "Deutscher Fliegerbund", a union of pilots for pilots. Today the AOPA-Germany, Verband der Allgemeinen Luftfahrt e.V. exists at this place and represents since 1964 the interests of nearly 20,000 private and professional pilots, just 100 enterprises, airfields, and various aviation associations.

August Euler is at first member of the Deutscher Luftschiffer-Verband since 1911. When this association also opens itself to the flying after the principle "heavier than air" and organized itself as Deutscher Luftfahrer-Verband in 1912, he is taking over the leading position in the board of the independent airplane department. Euler had a decisive portion in the whole organisation of the aviation in Germany with this function. He was raised to the state of a honorary member by the successor organisation Deutscher Aeroclub (DAeC).

Therefore there was no hesitation for August Euler in 1911 when he was offered the responsibility for the leadership of the convention "Flugzeug-Industrie" within the Verband Deutscher Motorfahrzeug-Industrieller e.V. (VDMI). He was already an active member of this association since 1901 in the field of automobile sports. As 1st chairperson he represented with devotion the interests of the aircraft industry in relation to the military administrations of Prussia and Bavaria. Although the Euler-Werke, measured in the total volume of accepted airplanes, took not a prominent position compared to the other production facilities in Germany, August Euler took care of a closed appearance of the German aircraft industry up to their decline to the end of the war. Energetically he turned against the reproaches of some representatives of the Reichstag short before the war's end, the aircraft industry would have got rich by the war production in irresponsible manner at the expenses of the German people.[2] Today his mind lives on in the Bundesverband der Deutschen Luft- und Raumfahrtindustrie e.V. (BDLI).

August Euler was untiring in the struggle for a speedy growth of the German aircraft industry and he used all all means available to him to shift the main attention of the German military but also of the sciences away from the airship in the direction of the engined airplane.

As a co-initiator and member of the committee of the National-Flugspende August Euler had direct influence on the application of donation money for the purpose of a rapid development of the aeronautical engineering since 1912. By the farsighted decisions in the committee of the National-Flugspende Germany succeeded in compensating the aeronautical and aerotechnical deficits in the shortest term.

In the time of the preparation of the Allgemeinen Luftfahrt-Ausstellung (ALA) August Euler persuaded scientists in Göttingen by his talks and discussions in November 1911 of the need to bundle the scientific knowledge. Euler's suggestions led to the fact that on the opening day of the ALA, on 3 April 1912, the most famous representatives of science founded the Wissenschaftliche Gesellschaft für Flugtechnik e.V. (WGF, later Wissenschaftliche Gesellschaft der Luftfahrt – WGL). The traditions of this association are preserved up to the present day in the Deutsche Gesellschaft für Luft- und Raumfahrt – Lilienthal - Oberth e.V. (DGLR) and this makes sure that all private individuals and institutions interested in aviation are united.

Also since 1912 August Euler was involved like no second German pilot and enterpriser as a member of the Technischer Ausschuss der Deutschen Versuchsanstalt für die Luftfahrt (DVL) – now passed over in the Deutsches Forschungszentrum für Luft- und Raumfahrt (DLR).

When a leader was searched at the end of the war in 1918 who seemed suited on the political level the solve the upcoming problems of German aviation, the choice necessarly fell on August Euler. This, in all areas of aviation experienced man, put the points for a heavy but roughly ordered new beginning of aviation under civil conditions. For this job Euler left his family and airplane factory for years.

Of course August Euler, the "German pilot No. 1", was an active member of the "Alte Adler" since its foundation until his old age.

It puts the question to itself, why has the personality of August Euler has fallen into oblivion so fast?

One explanation could be founded in the personality of August Euler: purposefully, obstinately, independently, just a leader, who was never forced to to subordinate or to integrate himself because of his financial autonomy.

Euler stood in the spotlight of politics between 1918 and 1920 at a time when the German aviation suffered most in all areas. Even then his visions about a unified international airspace, demonstrated in his 3rd memorandum, were formulated way too early. He had to fail on the political level because his political views came shortly after Germany's defeat and therefore simply too early.

August Euler resigned to the retirement as failed for the wide public. Later he rejected all attempts to use his person for the rebuilding of aviation, especially for the military avation.

This should not be seen as reproach but other pilots of the first hours and highly decorated pilots of the First World War let use themselves to make a "new German mind" grow.

Not August Euler. He did not allow, especially in the 1930's, the NS regime to use him! Every political engagement, for whatever direction, was alien to him.

This may have been also the reason for the fact that numerous publications about the early days of aviation in Germany did not honor Euler, but rather the "Heros of the Air". Apparently the person August Euler was not suited to be provided with a gloriole.

However, the author of this book came after many years of research to the conclusion that beside August Euler no other personality in Germany existed who put the development of German aviation so unselfishly and partly altruistic in the centre of his life.

Endnotes

1. To the founding members counted furthermore: Hans Grade, Baron Ellery v. Gorissen*, Erich Lochner*, Karl Jatho, Erich Thiele*, v. Rottenburg* (* Euler' s pilot trainees)
2. BA Koblenz, signature N1103-338, 1 April 1918, A. Euler, Der Fall Daimler, Denkschrift für die deutsche Luftfahrt [The Case Daimler, Memorandum for the German Aviation].

17. Epilog by Prof. Hanns Peter Euler (August Euler's Grandson)

The resignation as secretary of state for aviation and motor transport has not been easy for August Euler as a personality always high engaged in all situations of life. On one hand he was prescribed for the foundation and advancement of the German (and international) aviation with body and soul, on the other hand he did not tolerate restrictive conditions which hindered him in his independence and in his before by government decree assured scopes of action.[1]

In addition, he considered himself as a personality independent of (restricting) party political programs and was guided exclusively by factual issues and he was of course steered by own evaluations and convictions. He gathered around himself employees and experts in the Reichsamt who were also approved experts and belonged to no party – so far as known to him. Strictly he stayed away from government-political consultations and cabinet meetings, what he – understandable – brought in a distance to cabinet Bauer and later General Gröner or was supposed to him. The reproached lacking devotion to the ruling parties prompted the cabinet Bauer and later General Gröner to put secretary of state Euler before the alternative to let himself present from one of the ruling parties or to join such a party what August Euler definitely rejected.[2]

August Euler's final decision to resign fell, when with the subordination of his independent Reichsamtes für Luftfahrt- und Kraftfahrwesen under the "political" Verkehrsministerium Gröner's"[3] his office was stripped of its independence that he had negotiated and got by government decree.

Furthermore, there came attempts in the press to blame the Reichsamt and him as a person for the lack of raw material and the stagnant development in the area of motor transport and civil aviation and other conditions which were mostly caused by the very restrictive obligations of the Treaty of Versailles.

From now on August Euler presented himself after his resignation during suitable opportunities as "independent gentleman", what should lend expression to his party independence and individual independence. On one hand he devoted himself on account of the Treaty of Versailles to the destiny and whereabouts of the property of his airplane factory including his airfields in Frankfurt/Niederrad, connected with all the economic and political difficulties of the 1920s, on the other hand he followed his sportive (tennis tournaments, dancing contests), artistic (music, poetry), and social inclinations and he was in both, all industrial and also society-political matters, a requestd person as many contacts and still existing documents of exchanges with important personalities at home and abroad prove.

The question of the resumption of his airplane manufacture stood not at disposal because of the conditions of the Treaty of Versailles. In 1923 A. Euler reacted very angrily with a letter to a wrting of the Amtsgericht Höchst a. M. (H.R.A. 251 from 10 January 1923) with the demand to apply for the deletion of the Euler-Werke in the commercial

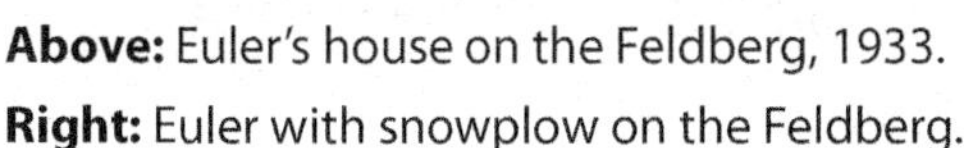

Above: Euler's house on the Feldberg, 1933.

Right: Euler with snowplow on the Feldberg.

Above: August Euler as independent gentleman.

register because the company had according to the information of the chamber of commerce its work "already since years finished".[4] Euler wrote back:

"...The company Euler-Werke still exists, the activity as airplane factory had to be put to a halt on account of the peace treaty of 1918.

A conversion was impossible in 1918, 1919, 1920 as a result of seizures and occupation by French troops. Later the conversion failed because of the dilatoriness of the responsible authorities to make good the considerable damage. For the equipment of the whole factory, the machines, the whole material, means of transportation, trucks, etc., were paid after five years of delay, believe it or not, 2 million paper Mark a few weeks ago. This is not even enough for the engine of a new truck. Every compensation for extracted use, closing down, flight, and building ban of airplanes was refused.

In addition the head of the district authority in Höchst has crowned the whole thing and has demanded a forced rent for allotmentier purposes for my whole real estate on the airfield.

I do not delete my company, the authorities carry the guilt that I cannot rebuild or continue my blossoming peace-factory-company.

In foreseeable future if the factory is got going again, this depends for the most part on the authorities.

Your's faithfully
August Euler"

No matter to what extent this writing to the district authority Höchst concerning the resumption of the airplane manufacture was to be taken seriously, there is at the end of the 1920s the idea – after activities of the city council of the City of Frankfurt, together with Ernst Udet, a narrow and long-standing friend of August Euler, to found a common new airplane factory with bringing in the Euler-Werke. The idea had matured in any case so far that a draught contract was worked out already in 1927.[5] However, this plan was never implemented and there is no information known about the historical background until now.[6] Obviously the negations failed because of lacking pledges of the city council of the City of Frankfurt.[7]

August Euler celebtrated his 60th birthday as independent gentleman in his home in Frankfurt, Forthausstraße 104, as one says looking back in the *Frankfurter Allgemeinen Zeitung*: "The Südwestdeutsche Luftverkehrs-AG, the Lufthansa and the Frankfurter Verein für Luftfahrt, sent him three pilots over the house, who dropped bouquets, while inside Parseval, Eckener, Junkers, Rumpler, and Fokker congratulated. Euler withdraw into the Schwarzwald to the Euler-House on the Feldberg"[8]

Already in the turbulent Twenties August Euler also got to know the Feldberg in the Schwarzwald (Black Forest), where he became a frequent guest in the winter in the Feldberg Hof and gathered much prominence around himself.[9] As a passionate skier he made big ski tours and particiapted in ski races in the birth place of German skiing.[10]

During these years also the thought matured to establish his age retirement home in his new adoptive country. He acquired an area of about 28,000m^2 at approx. 1,300m sea height from the municipality of Menzenschwand in the region Seebuck (Feldberg massif). There he established in 1932, also in his 64th year, his age retirement home which he also entitled as "Adlerhorst" (eyrie).

The generously invested house, which he himself had sketched, was put on all around his pieces of furniture and the inventory of his residence in Forsthausstrasse 104 in Frankfurt with all installations (wooden casings, libraries, etc.) and originated in a record time of only four months (1.6. to 4.9.1932) and was ready for occupation since 3.10.1932. August Euler has – as typical for him – personally controlled and documented the construction progress by photographing the establishment of his retirement home each day.[11]

The object was planned so from the very beginning that next to the private home a big winter sports hotel (200 beds) with name Aviatik (building design in 1936)[12] should originate and also according to his passion a tennis court was established which exists until today as the highest situated tennis sand place in Germany.

August Euler had the vision to let arise the most important winter sports place in Germany (compared to Garmisch-Partenkirchen) in the Feldberg area and has exerted himself for this among other things with the responsible authorities by production of an economic assessment about the creation of a "Feldberg municipality" already in the year 1934.[13] Then the municipality Feldberg was founded with effect from 1 April 1939. Also this hotel project was shortly before its realization in 1938 after all leveling works were concluded. The general material stop before the outbreak of the Second World War prevented this already by all responsible authorities – against all regional and local resistances – granted project.

At the end of the 1930s other developments excited August Euler's attention. The German aviation history was still unwritten and first publications came out under the influence of National Socialism. He himself had resisted all requests to support the national socialist propaganda, what other flight pioneers – for other understandable, often economic reasons – not always did. Thus the determining pioneer's achievements of the German engine flying were attributed to other pioneers (e.g. Hans Grade in Italiaander's book, 1938, or because of defective research in *Buch der deutschen Fluggeschichte* by Peter Supf (1936) or Fokker (1932) and found their way in important German universal encyclopedias as for example Brockhaus. This development in the writing of the German aviation history excited August Euler's nuisance and prompted him to public statements and accounts from an opposing point of view, as for example in the writing "Luftfahrt der Erinnerungen nach 30 Jahren", 1939, in which he puts out gapeless all wrong assertions but without wanting to defame for example Hans Grade.[14]

On 20 November 1938 he celebrated his 70th birthday at the Feldberg in the circle of famous aviation pioneers and aircraft industrialists (like Messerschmidt, Heinkel) and under presence of many of his former road companions from the early pioneer's time, as for example Feries von Hiddessen, the first offical postal airman of history. The media reported in detailed contributions about August Euler just as live broadcasting from the "eyrie" took place.

Above: August Euler, 1943.

August Euler himself was still engaged in many questions of aviation and also employed a secretary at his old age for his comprehensive correspondence. Making music, to tennis and skiing were for him, so far as the conditions allowed, a permanent employment, and he received many visits and entertained his guests.

In 1933 his personal physician and friend Dr. Otto Mock, ski doctor and author on the Feldberg wrote a self-experienced story with August Euler, called "The Ill Eagle", in which he describes in a very fitting way character and personality "August Euler", when the latter suffered a severe cancer of intestine with great and long-lasting pains and could overcome this successfully.[15]

After outbreak of World War Two it became quieter around August Euler, although he received visits in his "eyrie" again and again, more often also from soldiers and aviation units which stayed for a

Above: August Euler in the circle of his guests on the occasion of his 70th birtday (1938).

rest in the Feldberg area as for example among others Egon Kronenwerth, later the author of the book *Der tolle Euler* (The awesome Euler).[16]

After the end of the Second World War his possession was taken once more by the French occupation forces. This time, however, he succeeded, especially because of his excellent French linguistic proficiency to prevent that the "eyrie" was confiscated as an accommodation for French occupation forces. Just in time he had smashed the heaters of the central heating in his house, so that the intended accommodation was not habitable.

The years after the war were also hard years of renunciation for August Euler and at old age he was daily supplied by the neighborhood (especially family Keller and family Kern) and in addition supported by his oldest son.

In 1952 August Euler was awarded with the Great Cross of Merite of the Order of Merite of the Federal Republic Germany by Bundespräsident Theodor Heuss who already wrote about August Euler in his book about the life and deeds of Robert Bosch (1946). August Euler was an honorary member in many technical and aerotechnical associations (e.g. Deutscher Aero-Club, Schnauferl Club, Vereinigung der Alten Adler, etc.). August Euler still attended the first meeting of the WGL after World War Two in 1951 in Braunschweig.

He passed away at the age of 89 years on 1 July 1957 in his "eyrie" on the Feldberg. The City of Frankfurt bestowed him with his honorary grave on the Frankfurt main cemetary a last honor.

August Euler, who coformed a thrilling time full of technical innovations, met many famous personalities on his life's way, and lived through socal upheavals including two World Wars, was in habit to say 'good bye' to his guests on the Feldberg with a self-written song (with several strophes) for the lute: [17]

"You can visit me in Menzenschwand
near the fir wood's slope ,
There I live at the forest's rim
well between old beechwood!
A tennis court, a pilot's house,
a flagstaff, a streamer!

And apart from that, I could care less
about these world's fidgeting.
And if you come to my slope,
There is coffee, tea and cake.
Yes, there you can, you can,
You can visit me."

Remark (Hannes Täger): The original German text used repeatedly the common German phrase "Ihr könnt mich mal". This phrase is often used in the German language in connection with the insult "Ihr könnt mich mal am Arsch lecken" ["You can lick my ass!"]. Every German will immediately notice the double meaning of Euler's words. It was probably Euler's way to cope with all the years of frustration in his former business life and especially the later political job.

Above: August Euler's grave of honor, 2007.

Endnotes

1. Compare Kronenwerth pp. 80.
2. Compare. August Euler's letter from 13.07.1935 to the Reichspostministerium [Imperial post ministry] concerning the accusation and suspicion that he belonged to the Sozial Democratic Party (Euler-Archiv).
3. Ibid.
4. August Euler's answering letter from 24 January 1923 to the district authority, Euler-Archiv.
5. Draft agreement 1927, Euler-Archive, Feldberg.
6. Dr. G. Hallerbach wrote about this in his unpublished manuscript "Luftfahrt in Frankfurt a.M.": "A revival of the aircraft construction in Frankfurt after the conclusion of peace with the Treaty of Versailles brought the year 1927. In 1926 the town had submitted its airfield at the Rebstock to an extensive rebuilding and removal and had maintained negotiations with the Kasseler Flugzeugwerk at the same time... However, the matter failed shortly before its finalization. In the meantime, a new project had appeared. Undersecretary of state a.D. August Euler and Ernst Udet intended to create a company with a foundation capital of 200,000 Mark with participation of the town and the goal to build a modern airplane shipyard. although this project was very serious, it came never to a final result, because the city as partner intended to settle the newly founded factory on the airfield Rebstock ... Apparently Euler and Udet disagreed with the choice of the factory site."
7. August Euler's letter to the City Council of the city of Frankfurt from 13.04.1927, Euler-Archive, Feldberg.
8. Frankfurter Allgemeine, 25 February 1967. Der tolle Euler – "Ich glaube, ich habe früher gehopst" – Das abenteuerliche Leben des ersten deutschen Flugzeugbauers, by Dieter Vogt.
8. Compare A. Vetter, Feldberg im Schwarzwald, Selbstverlag der Gemeinde Feldberg (Schwarzwald), 1982, p 472.
10. Vetter, A.,1982, p352.
11. Euler-Archiv, Feldberg.
12. Ibid.
13. Vetter, A., 1982, p 378.
14. Euler-Archiv, Feldberg.
15.See also Kronenwerth, Der tolle Euler, Umschau Verlag, ISBN 3-524-.88042-8.
16. Compare the entries in the guest book of the house Euler.
17. Kronenwerth, pp 157.

Appendix 1: Excerpt from the Nationale of

Worknr	Description	Military Marking	Engine				Wing Area, m^2	Controls
			Brand	Power	# Cyl	RPM		
1	Original "Voisin", biplane		Gnóme				40.0	Side control with 3 axes
2	"Euler" flight machine, biplane, exhibition object at the ILA		Adler				40.0	
3	"Euler" flight machine, biplane (demon-stration machine)		Antoin-ette				40.0	
4	Chanute glider, Original "Voisin"						28.0	
5 – 7	Chanute glider, "Euler"							
8	Cancelled							
9	"Euler" flight machine, biplane		Gnóme	50	7	1200	40.0	2 tail controls
10	"Euler" flight machine, biplane							Without
11	"Euler" flight machine, biplane		Gnóme	50	7	1200		
12	"Euler" flight machine, biplane		Gnóme	50	7	1200		Without
13	"Euler" flight machine, biplane, biplace							
14	"Euler" flight machine, biplane		Argus	50	4	1200	40.0	
15	"Euler" flight machine, biplane		Gnóme	50	7	1200	40.0	Comb. Height-, Side- and Banking controls

the Euler-Werke

Airframe	Weight, kg	Propeller			Orderer	Built Month/Yr	Remarks
		Brand	Diam	Pitch, m			
	515	aluminium from Voisin			August Euler	041909	Did not fly
	480				August Euler	06/1909	Did not fly
	480				August Euler	07/1909	Flown at the ILA in Frankfurt
					August Euler		Destroyed at the ILA in Frankfurt t
					Frankfurter Verein für Luftschiffahrt	09/1909	
"Euler" with skids	440	Chauviere	2.60				Crashed from 180 m height
	440				v. Gorrissen		Only fuselage produced
	440	Chauviere	2.60		v. Gorrissen		
	440	Chauvière	2.60		August Euler		
					Frankfurter Flugsport-Klub		
	530	Chauvière	2.50		Thiele		
"Euler" with skids	440	Chauvière (Gnóme)	2.50	1.4	Lochner	07/1910	

Worknr	Description	Military Marking	Engine				Wing Area, m^2	Controls
			Brand	Power	# Cyl	RPM		
16	"Euler" flight machine, biplane, biplace		Gnóme	50	7	1200	40.0	ditto
17	"Euler" flight machine, biplane, earlier No. 12		Gnóme	50	7	1200	40.0	ditto
18	"Euler" flight machine, biplane, 1-seater, light apparatus		Gnóme	50	7	1200	20.0	ditto
19	"Euler" Flight machine, Biplane, training machine		Argus	50	4	1200	40.0	ditto
20	"Euler" Flight machine, Biplane, 2-seater, light apparatus		Gnóme	50	7	1200	20.0	ditto
21	"Euler" flight machine, biplane		Gnóme	50	7	1200	25.0	ditto
22	"Euler" flight machine, biplane, biplace		Gnóme	50	7	1200	35.0	ditto
23	"Euler" flight machine, biplane, type "Hessen" [Hesse]		Opel	65	4	1220	28.0	ditto
24	"Euler" flight machine, biplane, "Großherzog" [Grand Duke], Wnr. 1, biplace		Gnóme	70	7	1200	19.0	ditto
25	"Euler" flight machine, biplane, type "Großherzog" [Grand Duke] Wnr. 2, biplace		dto.	70	7	1200	22.0	ditto

Airframe	Weight, kg	Propeller			Orderer	Built Month/Yr	Remarks
		Brand	Diam	Pitch, m			
ditto	440	Chauvière (Gnóme)	2.60	1.32	Dr. Gans-Fabrice	10/1910	
ditto	440	Chauvière (Gnóme)	2.60		August Euler	11/1910	smashed by Prince Heinrich v. Preußen
"Euler" without skids	380	Chauvière (Gnóme)	2.50	1.45	August Euler	06/1911	sold to Reichhardt on 7th Juni 1911
ditto	530	Chauvière (Argus)	2.30		August Euler	01/1911	sold to Frankfurter Flugsport-Klub
ditto	300	Chauvière (Gnóme)	2.80	1.15	Witter-städter		
"Euler" without skids	280	Chauvière (Gnóme)	2.60	1.32	Werner Dücker	01/1911	
ditto	290	Chauvière (Gnóme)	2.60	1.32	Flugsport Club	03/1911	sides without walls
ditto	390	Chauvière (Opel)	2.60	1.25	Carl Jörns	05/1911	
ditto	280	Chauvière (Gnóme)	2.50	1.60	August Euler	06/1911	sold to Reichardt, destroyed on 2nd Juni 1911
ditto	290	Chauvière (Gnóme)	2.60	1.60	August Euler	05/1911	smashed by Reichardt (Mingolsheim)

Worknr	Description	Military Marking	Engine				Wing Area, m²	Controls
			Brand	Power	# Cyl	RPM		
26	Euler biplane, type "Flugsport", biplace		ditto	50	7	1200	30.0	ditto
27	Euler biplane Wnr. 2, "Großherzog" [Grand Duke] Wnr. 1, biplace		ditto					
28	Euler biplane, training machine for Bavarian Army		Opel	68	4	1220	35.0	Comb. Height-, Side- and banking controls
29	Euler biplane, biplace, replacement for No. 22		Gnóme	50	7	1200	35.0	ditto
30	Euler biplane (former Wnr. 18 or 10?)		Gnóme	50	7	1200	20.0	ditto.
31	Euler monoplane Wnr. 1		Gnóme	70	7	1200		patent Euler
32	Euler biplane, military type "Flugsport" [Flightsport]		Gnóme	50	7	1200	30.0	ditto
33	Euler biplane, type "Gelber Hund" [Yellow Dog] Wnr. 1, height control backwards		Gnóme	70	7	1200	24.0	ditto
34	Euler triplane No. 1		Gnóme					
35	Euler biplane, military type "Flugsport" [Flightsport]		Gnóme	50	7	1200	30.0	Comb. height-, side- a. banking controls
36	Euler flight machine biplane, teaching machine (former No. 19)		Argus	50	4	1200	40.0	ditto

Airframe	Weight, kg	Propeller			Orderer	Built Month/Yr	Remarks
		Brand	Diam	Pitch, m			
ditto	290	Chauvière (Gnóme)	2.60	1.40	Bavarian Army	07/1911	
	290					06/1911	Crash Reichardt near Magdeburg
ditto	390	Chauvière (Opel)	2.60	1.40	dto.	07/1911	
ditto	290	Chauvière (Gnóme)	2.60	1.40	Frankfurter Flugsport-club	06/1911	
ditto	380	Chauvière (Gnóme)	2.50	1.45	Reichardt	07/1911	Bought back because used as training machine
"Euler" 4 wheels	335	Chauvière (Gnóme)	2.60	1.65	August Euler	08/1911	
"Euler" without skids	290	Chauvière (Gnóme)	2.60	1.40	Pressain Army	09/1911	destroyed 19.10.1911 in Döberitz (Ltn. Mudra)
ditto	262	Chauvière (Gnóme)	2.60	1.60	August Euler	08/1911	
	320						
"Euler" without skids	290	Chauvière (Gnóme)	2.60	1.40	Bavarian Army	10/1911	
ditto	530	Chauvière (Argus)	2.30		Frankf. Flugsport-club	02/1912	

Worknr	Description	Military Marking	Engine				Wing Area, m^2	Controls
			Brand	Power	# Cyl	RPM		
37	Euler-flight machine biplane, militry type "Flugsport" replacement No. 32		Gnóme	50	7	1200	30.0	ditto
38	Euler flight machine biplane, teaching machine (repair, former No. 28)		Opel	68	4	1220		ditto
39	Euler flight machine biplane, height control backwards, type "Gelber Hund" groß		Mer-cedes	65	4	1250		ditto
40	Euler flight machine biplane, Vorführ-demon-stration machine		Opel	68	4	1220		ditto
41	Euler flight machine, height control backwards, type "Gelber Hund" groß"		Opel		4	1220		ditto
42 – 44	Euler-flight machine biplane, height control backwards, type "Gelber Hund" groß]"	B.12/12 – B.14/12	Gnóme	70	7	1200		ditto
45	Euler-flight machine biplane, height control backwards, type "Gelber Hund" klein		Gnóme	70	7	1200		ditto

Airframe	Weight, kg	Propeller			Orderer	Built Month/Yr	Remarks
		Brand	Diam	Pitch, m			
ditto	380	Chauvière (Gnóme)	2.60	1.40	Prussian Army	10/1911	
ditto	450	Chauvière (Opel)	2.60	1.40	Bavarian Army	11/1911	
ditto	460	Chauvière (Dunlop)	2.60	1.40	ditto	01/1912	
ditto	450	Chauvière (Opel)	2.60	1.40	ditto	01/1912	(Repair for the Bavarian Army, fromer #28 & #38)
ditto	450	Chauvière (Opel)			August Euler		
ditto	320	Chauvière (Gnóme)			Prussian Army admin-istration	04/1912 – 08/1912	
ditto	320	Chauvière (Gnóme)			U. Placzy-kowski, Dort-mund	04/1912	

Worknr	Description	Military Marking	Engine				Wing Area, m^2	Controls
			Brand	Power	# Cyl	RPM		
46	Euler flight machine biplane, military type "Flugsport", 2 seats, height control affixed ahead		Gnóme	50	7	1200	30.0	ditto
47	Euler training machine biplane		Opel	65	4	1200		ditto
48	Euler flight machine biplane, instruction machine, height control in front of the main area		Opel	65	4	1200		ditto
49	Euler flight machine biplane, military type "Gelber Hund" groß, height control affixed behind		Deutsch-Daimler	70	4	1200		ditto
50	Euler flight machine biplane, military type "Gelber Hund" groß, height control affixed behind		Gnóme	70	7	1200		ditto
51	Euler flight machine biplane, military type "Gelber Hund" groß, height control affixed behind		ohne					ditto
52	Euler flight machine biplane, military type "Gelber Hund" groß, height control affixed behind		Gnóme	70	7	1200		ditto

Airframe	Weight, kg	Propeller			Orderer	Built Month/Yr	Remarks
		Brand	Diam	Pitch, m			
ditto	340	Chauvière (Gnóme)	2.60	1.40	Werner Dücker, Düssel-dorf	04/1912	Destroyed 14.07.1913 by Herrn v. Rottenburg
ditto	440	Chauvière (Opel)	2.60	1.40	Bavarian Army admin.	05/1912	
ditto		Chauvière (Opel)	2.60	1.60	ditto	05/1912	
ditto	460	Chauvière (Daimler)	2.60	1.40	ditto	05/1912	
ditto	320	Chauvière (Gnóme)	2.70	1.40	Prussian Army admin.	05/1912	
ditto	230	Chauvière (Gnóme)			ditto	05/1912	
ditto	320	Chauvière (Gnóme)	2.70	1.40	Prussian Army admin.	05/1912	

Worknr	Description	Military Marking	Engine				Wing Area, m^2	Controls
			Brand	Power	# Cyl	RPM		
53	Euler flight machine biplane, teaching machine,		Gnóme	50	7	1200	40.0	Side control with 3 axes
54	Euler flight machine monoplane		Gnóme	50	7	1200		modified controls
55	Euler flight machine biplane, teaching machine, wings type "Gelber Hund" klein, height control ahead, tail type record machine		Gnóme	50	7	1200		ditto
56 – 63	Euler flight machine, type "Großer gelber Hund", height control affixed behind	B.39/12 - B.46/12	Gnóme	70	7	1200	30.0	patent Euler
64	Euler flight machine, type "Großer gelber Hund", height control affixed behind, engine ahead	B.80/12	Deutsch Daimler	70	4	1200	37.0	ditto
65	Euler flight machine triplane No. 2, engine ahead, height control affixed behind, engine ahead	B.79/12	Argus	100	4	1300	42.0	height and side control directly by lever, dual controls
66	Euler flight machine biplane, school machine (big wings), height control affixed behind		Gnóme	50	7	1200	46.0	

Airframe	Weight, kg	Propeller			Orderer	Built Month/Yr	Remarks
		Brand	Diam	Pitch, m			
ditto	320	Chauvière (Gnóme)	2.60	1.40	August Euler		On 30.5.1913 destroyed by Ltn. Eichhorn. Wings type "Großherzog", tail type "Prinz Heinrich"
steel tube skid	294,75 ohne Benzin	Chauvière (Gnóme)	2.60	1.40	August Euler	09/1912	
ditto	320	Chauvière (Gnóme)	2.60	1.40	August Euler		
wheels	320	Chauvière (Gnóme)	2.70	1.40	Pruss. Army admin.	08/1912	
ditto	400	Garuda (Daimler)	2.60	1.55	August Euler	10/1912	
ditto	580	Garuda (Argus)	2.60	1.65	August Euler	01/1913	
ditto	340	Chauvière	2.60	1.40	August Euler	01/1913	

Worknr	Description	Military Marking	Engine				Wing Area, m^2	Controls
			Brand	Power	# Cyl	RPM		
67	Euler flight machine, type "Großer Gelber Hund", (Racing machine), height control affixed behind	B74/12	Gnóme	80	7	1250	30.0	patent Euler
68 – 75 & 77	Euler flight machine, type "Großer Gelber Hund", height affixed behind	ohne	ohne Motor				30.0	ditto
76	This machine was not manufactured							
78	Euler flight machine, type with staggered (forewards and sidewards) wings: 1,75 m, engine ahead		Argus	100	4	1300	with tail	normal controls
79	Euler flight machine, type: monoplane No. 4	A41/12	Argus	100	4	1300	23.00	normals controls
80	Euler flight machine biplane, school machine, height controls affixed behind (gondola from Prince Heinrich machine No. 18)		Gnóme	50	7	1200	50.0 without tail	lever and foot controls
81	Euler flight machine biplane, type "Kleiner Gelber Hund" (former Wnr. 30), height controls and engine aft, new: gondola, chassis, side controls, 2 [attached wings]		Gnóme	50	7	1200	34.0 without tail	
82	Euler flight machine, biplane, military type 1913, height control and engine aft	B23/13	Gnóme	80	7	1200	34.5 without tail	hand wheel a. foot control

Airframe	Weight, kg	Propeller			Orderer	Built Month/Yr	Remarks
		Brand	Diam	Pitch, m			
Normales with 2 wheels	320	Chauvière (Gnóme)	2.50	1.90	August Euler	12/1912	Fuel & oil resevoir for 7 hours
ditto	290				Pruss. Army admin.	11/1912 – 01/1913	
normal chassis with 2 wheels	470				August Euler	02/1913	
ditto	550	Garuda (Argus)	2.60	1.65	August Euler		
ditto	330	Chauvière (Gnóme)	2.60	1.40	August Euler		all parts new, except gondola
ditto	340	Chauvière (Gnóme)	2.60	1.40	August Euler		destroyed on 10.7.1913
2 wheels, wood wrapped	360	Chauvière (Gnóme)	2.50	1.90	Pruss. Army admin.	05/1913	Participation in Prince-Heinrich-Flight 1913, 10.5.1913 destroyed

Worknr	Description	Military Marking	Engine				Wing Area, m^2	Controls
			Brand	Power	# Cyl	RPM		
83	Euler flight machine biplane, type "Kleiner Gelber Hund" Wnr.1, former postal flight machine, new parts: gondola, side control, skid		Gnóme	50	7	1200	30.0 without tail	lever- & foot control
84, 87 – 99	Euler flight machine biplane military type 1913	B34/13, B35/13 – B44/12	Gnóme	80	7	1200	37	lever- a. foot control
85	Euler flight machine biplane, new school machine		Gnóme	70	7	1200	30	lever control
86	Euler water flight machine triplane, with glide boat		Gnóme	100	9	1200	50	ditto
100	Euler flight machine Yellow Dog, teaching machine		Gnóme	80	7	1200	30	ditto
101	Euler Raceing monoplane No. 5		Adler	80	7	1200	26	lever- a. foot control
102 – 104	Euler monoplane, type No. 4	A32/13 – A34/13 (A41/12)	Argus, Mercedes	100, 75/85	4, 6	1300, 1400	25	lever- a. foot control
105 – 116	Euler biplane, type "1914", series 1	B160/13 – B171/13	Mercedes	100	6	1400	45.5	lever- a. foot control
117	Euler biplane, type "1914"		Argus	100	4	1300	45.5	ditto
118	Euler fuselage biplane "14", series 2	B40/14 – B51/14	Daimler-Mercedes	100	6	1400	46.0	ditto
130 – 145	Euler fuselage biplane "14", series 3 & 4	B142/15 – B157/14	Daimler-Mercedes	100	6	1400	46.0	ditto
146, 148 – 164	Euler biplane "14", series 5	B403/14 – B420/14	Daimler-Mercedes	100	6	1400	46.0	ditto
147	Euler biplane, engine aft		Gnóme	100	9	1200	46.0	ditto
165–184	Euler fuselage biplane, series 6	B331/15 – B.350/15	Benz	110	6	1400	48.0	ditto

Airframe	Weight, kg	Propeller			Orderer	Built Month/Yr	Remarks
		Brand	Diam	Pitch, m			
normal with 2 wheels		Chauvière (Gnóme)	2.60	1.40	August Euler		destroyed on 23.10.1913 by Ltn. Heppe
normal with 2 wheels, woods wrapped	380	Chauvière (Gnóme)	2.50	1.90	Pruss. Army admin.	08/1913	B.34/13 was a donation airplane (National Flight Donation)
normal with 2 wheels	380	Chauvière (Gnóme)	2.70	1.40	August Euler		
Hinged chassis with 2 wheels	800	Chauvière (Gnóme)	2.60	2.10	August Euler		dismantled July 1914
normal with 2 wheels wood wrapped	380	Chauvière (Gnóme)	2.60	1.40	August Euler		
steel tube struts	500	Garuda (Argus)	2.60	1.65	August Euler		dismantled 1st July 1914
normal with 2 wheels wood wrapped	550	Integrale (Argus, Mercedes)	2.60	1.50	Pruss. Army admin.		
steel tube struts, with nose wheel	710	Integrale (Mercedes)	2.70	1.42	Pruss. Army admin.	11/1913 – 05/1914	engine with exhaustpot
without nose wheel	700	Integrale (Mercedes)	2.70	1.43	August Euler	05/1914	
without nose wheel	740	Integrale (Mercedes)	2.70	1.43	Pruss. Army admin.	05/1914	new shape of the damping area
without nose wheel	740	Integrale (Mercedes)	2.70	1.43	Pruss. Army admin.	10/1914 – 11/1914	
ditto	740	Integrale (Mercedes)	2.70	1.43	Pruss. Army admin.	11/1914 – 03/1915	
ditto	500	Integrale (Gnóme)	2.70	1.43	August Euler		
ditto	775	Integrale (Benz)	2.70	1.54	Pruss. Army admin.	03/1915 – 08/1915	Gotha (2), Köln (18)

Worknr	Description	Military Marking	Engine				Wing Area, m^2	Controls
			Brand	Power	# Cyl	RPM		
185, 186	Euler fuselage biplane	B481/15, B482/15	Benz	110	6	14	48.0	ditto
187	model machine for series 7		Mercedes	120	6	1400	48.0	ditto
188	Euler biplane engine ahead MG II		Mercedes	160	6	1400	48.0	ditto
189, 189a, 189b	Euler biplane engine aft MG I		Mercedes	160	6	1450	48.0	ditto
190–201	Euler fuselage biplane, series 7	B1361/15 – B1372/15	Mercedes	120	6	1400	48.0	ditto
202	" with M.G. III engine ahead model machine		Mercedes	160	6	1450	–	ditto
203	" " engine aft M.G. IV		Mercedes	120	6	1400	–	ditto
204–231	Euler fuselage biplane, series 8 & 9	C3605/15 – C3632/15	Mercedes	160	6	1400	35.7	ditto
232–234, 236–299	numbers cancelled							
Ohne (232)	Euler triplane		Mercedes	220	8	900/ 1400		lever- & foot control
235	Euler fuselage biplane	C9319/16	Mercedes	160	6	1400		ditto
300–303 (233, 234)	D I Euler biplane type Yellow Dog	D4000/16, D4001/16	Oberursel	80/100	7/9	1200		ditto
304–324	Euler fuselage, series 10 (D I)	D2330/16– D2350/16	Oberursel	100	9	1200		ditto
325a, b –351	Euler fuselage biplane, series 10 (D II)	D2351/16– D2379/16	Oberursel U 0/U I	80/100	7	1200	13.7	ditto
352–401	Euler fuselage biplane, series 10 (D II)	D250/17– D 299/17	Oberursel U 0/U I	80/100	7	1200	13.7	ditto

Airframe	Weight, kg	Propeller			Orderer	Built Month/Yr	Remarks
		Brand	Diam	Pitch, m			
ditto	775	Integrale (Benz)	2.70	1.54	Pruss. Army admin.	08/1915	Zwickau (1), Köln (1)
ditto	775	Integrale (Mercedes)	2.70	1.54	Pruss. Army admin.		
ditto	600	Integrale (Mercedes)	2.70	1.85			11.11.15 destroyed
with/without nose wheel	600	Integrale (Mercedes)	2.70	1.85	Pruss. Army admin.	11/1915 – 12/1915	sent to Döberitz
without nose wheel	775	Integrale (Mercedes)	2.70	1.54	Pruss. Army admin.	06/1915 – 01/1916	Hannover, Gotha
without nose wheel	915,5	Integrale (Mercedes)	2.70	1.54		01/1916	Gotha
metal suspension		Integrale (Mercedes)	2.70	1.54		02/1916	Gotha
metal suspension	879,5	Reschke (Mercedes)	2.80	1.70	Pruss. Army admin.	01/1916 – 12/1916	Böblingen (11), Karlsruhe (2)
2 wheels, without nose wheels	1000	Prop. Zek X R (Mercedes)	2.80	1.70	Pruss. Army admin.	12/1916	Frankfurt a/M
ditto		Reschke (Mercedes)	2.80	1.70	Pruss. Army admin.	05/1916 – 12/1916	Hannover
ditto		Reschke (G"N)	2.60	1.70/2.00	Pruss. Army admin.	11/1916 – 12/1916	Adlershof/ Frankfurt a.M.
ditto	400	Reschke (Mercedes)	2.60	2.00	Pruss. Army admin.	12/16 – 3/17	Versuchspark Ost (10), Großenhain (5), Paderborn ((5)
ditto	340	Reschke (Mercedes)	2.60	2.00	Pruss. Army admin.	02/17 – 05/17	Warschau, Hannover (je 4), Großenhain, Erfurt (je 1), Köln (2), Schleißheim (11), Thorn (3),
ditto	340	Reschke (Mercedes)	2.60	1.95	Pruss. Army admin.	06/1917 – 09/1917	Baden-Oos (21), Adlershof (24), Hannover (12),

Worknr	Description	Military Marking	Engine				Wing Area, m²	Controls
			Brand	Power	# Cyl	RPM		
402–431	Euler fuselage biplane, series 10 (D II)	D1200/1–D1229/17	Oberursel U I	100	9	1200	13.7	ditto
432	Euler triplane D.R. 4		Oberursel	160	18	1200	-	ditto
433	Euler triplane D.R. 5		Mercedes (D IIIa)	160	6	1200	18.00	ditto
434	Euler triplane D.R. 6		Göbel	160	9	1300	23.00	ditto
435	Euler quadraplane D 4		Gnom	100	9	1200	18.00	ditto
436	Euler triplane D.R. 7		Göbel	110	9	1300	13.50	ditto
437	Euler biplane D 6		Siemens Sh 3	160	9	900	14.50	ditto
438	Euler biplane D 5		Mercedes	160	6	1200	15.00	ditto
439	Euler triplane D.R. 9			110	9	900	13.50	ditto
440	Euler biplane D 7		Mercedes	160	6	1200		ditto
441	Euler biplane D 9			200	9	1200		ditto
442	Euler biplane D 10		Mercedes	160	6	1200		ditto
443–503	Euler biplane B III		Mercedes	100	6	1200	32.15	ditto

Airframe	Weight, kg	Propeller			Orderer	Built Month/Yr	Remarks
		Brand	Diam	Pitch, m			
ditto	340	Reschke (Mercedes)	2.62	2.15	Pruss. Army admin.	6/17 - 2/18	
ditto	650	Reschke (Mercedes)			Euler-Werke	04/1917	dismantled July 18
ditto	680	Reschke (Mercedes)	2.78	2.00	ditto	04/1917	"
ditto	534	Reschke (Mercedes)	2.70	2.65	ditto	03/1918	smashed in Berlin
ditto	400	Reschke (Mercedes)	2.62	2.15	ditto	04/1918	dismantled 30.7.18
ditto	389	Reschke (Mercedes)	2.62	2.10	ditto	05/1918	
ditto	496	Reschke (Mercedes)	2.83	3.50	ditto	04/1918	
ditto	687	Reschke (Mercedes)	2.78	2.00	ditto	05/1918	dismantled July 18
ditto	390	Reschke (Mercedes)			ditto		
ditto		Reschke (Mercedes)	2.78	2.00	ditto	08/1918	dismantled Sept. 18
ditto	680	Reschke (Mercedes)			ditto		
ditto		Reschke (Mercedes)	2.78	2.00	ditto	07/1918	
ditto	700	Reschke (Mercedes)	2.70	1.45	Pruss. Army admin.	07/1918 – 11/1918	partly only airframes

Appendix 2: Euler's Reichspatents & Utility Patents

August Euler's innovative portion in the development of German aircraft construction is – inspite of the rather high number of patent and utility patent applications – to be estimated (with the exception of the first years) in the long term as not important because because more and more new players appeared and sped up the advancement of airplane technology. A big number of his patent and utility patent registrations found elsewhere only little use. Nevertheless, one can make clear one thing with the example of his efforts and achievements: roughly daily the public was surprised with news. In the beginning in this fact rather practical people – like Euler – were involved instead of scientists.

Euler recognized on account of his activity as aircraft constructor and pilot very fast and directly the weak spots of the industrial branch that was still in its development. Euler registered more than 120 Reichspatents and utility patents between 1910 and 1918. The following mentioned examples should serve to get a deeper impression in the construction of the first German airplanes.

The probably most important patent of Euler was already described in chapter 12. Many of the other inventions are due to the new needs and knowledge of aviation. On the other hand the demands of the orderers, especially of the Prussian Army administration, resulted in innovations in the whole aircraft industry, thus also in the Euler-Werke. With some well-chosen examples this should be explained exemplarily.

Multiplanes with Foldable Wing Ends According to DRP 268368 (DRP 272770)

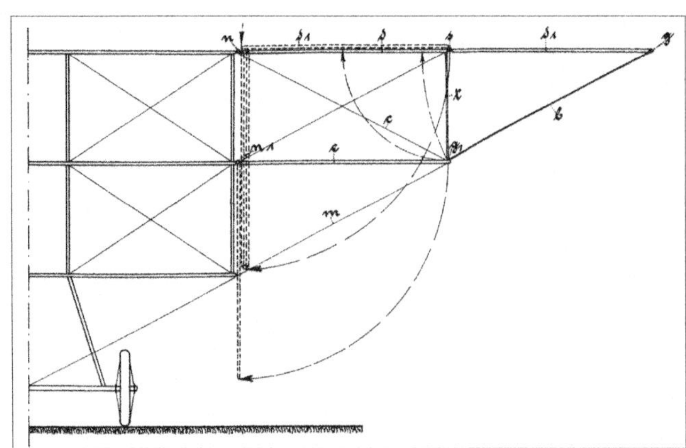

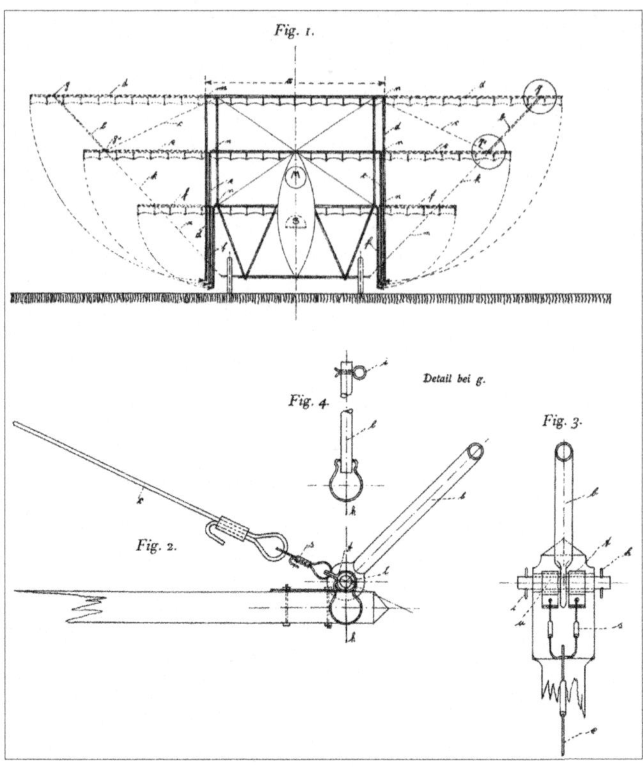

Left: Additional patent 272 770 to patent 268 368.

Germany stands before the First World War! In 1913 the Inspektion des Militär-Luft- und Kraftfahrwesens issued new acceptance conditions for the acquisition of army airplanes.

Beside the demand tht the airplanes had to be "manufactured basically in all parts from German material" clear logistical demands were formulated, e.g.:

"19. Quick assembling and disassembling (as a norm assembly with five men in two hours, disassembly in one hour) was demanded; an easy opportunity to load it on railway waggons and land vehicles, profile freedom for railway and street transport."

To be able to meet this demand in a competetive way the folding mechanism was obvious.

For the first time Euler realised his patent with the water flight machine, Werknummer 86.

Turnbuckle, especially for flight machines according to DRP 288 619 (Utility patent 579 178).

August Euler recognized that the bracing of the wings was a time-consuming work. Even under

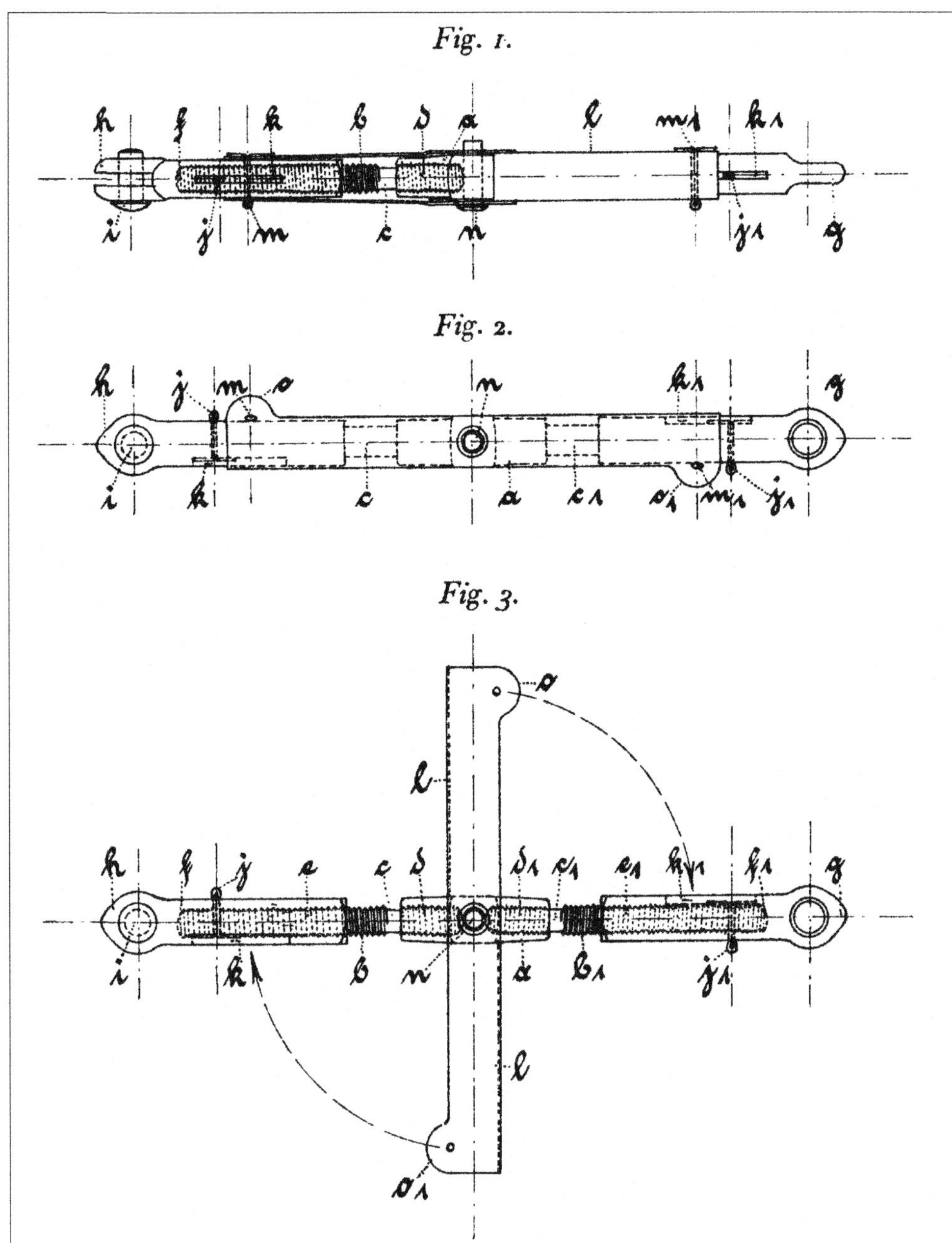

Right: Euler's patent for a turnbuckle.

rather favorable conditions in the factory this work required a lot of care. The performance of the airplane depended highly on the way of bracing as well from the tractive forces within a pair of wings. If the airplane was adjusted in the factory at first it had nevertheless to be dismantled in general for the purpose of the delivery to the troops. The assembly of the airplane in the respective destinations occurred largely by the pilots themselves what not always led to the desired success, in particular because every pilot had his own theory about the mutual influencing of the bracing of the lower and upper wings. To step aside of this general practice August Euler developed a bracing device which made sure that the works settings could be restored quickly during the assembly in the field.

Utility Patent			
Content **Registered-number** **File number**	**(a) signed in** **(e) grated** **(zg) withdrawn** **(z) rejected** **(l) defunct**	**Description of the Claims** **("t.m.t." = " … thereby marked that…)**	**Fig.** **(Remark: The drawings originate from a survey of the Euler-Werke, source: Bundesarchiv Koblenz, Signature N1103)**
Start- and landing chassis for biplane E. 13796/77 450 651 Signed in as patent (E. 15635 XI/77 h2) but it was rejected because details were already published first in the journal *Flugsport*.	27.01.1910 (a) 26.01.1911 (e)	Connection of the chassis axis b with the chassis rack axis a by rubber rings; on the rack axis swivelling arranged skid, linked with the rack by rubber elastic c; small wheel f, which is preventing the impact of the front part on the soil; spanning and stiffening g; wooden rack in all fields horizontally, vertically and diagonally braced.	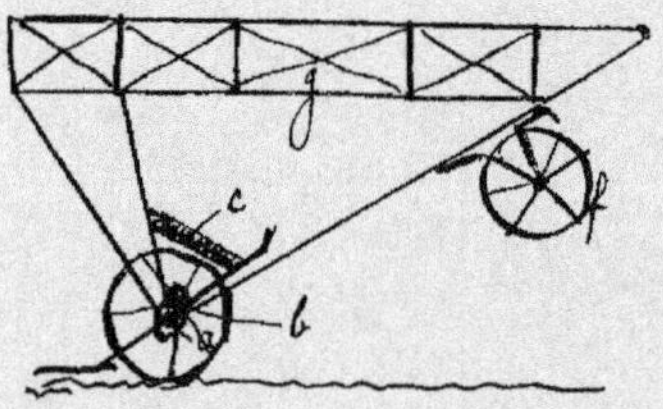
Combined height and rudder control for air vehicles E. 13802/77 418 598	02.04.1910 (a) 20.04.1910 (e) 02.04.1913 (l)	Control column b moves by rod p the lever u, which lies in the middle of the elevator pipe v; wire bracing to the end t of the control column; control column adjustable forwards in pipe e, but it takes e along in a rotation and operates the rudder by cable sheave h. Both controls are also operated by hand wheel a.	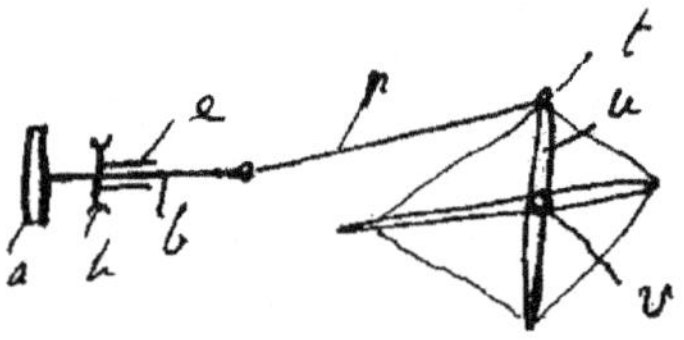
Elastic wheel for air vehicles (has been announced as a pentent before) E. 14147/77 431 928 Patent application occured (E. 15339 II/63 d) but was unfortunately rejected.	20.04.1910 (a) 20.08.1910 (e) 07.11.1916 (f)	Hub a and rim b are connected by one, two or several rubber latten c.	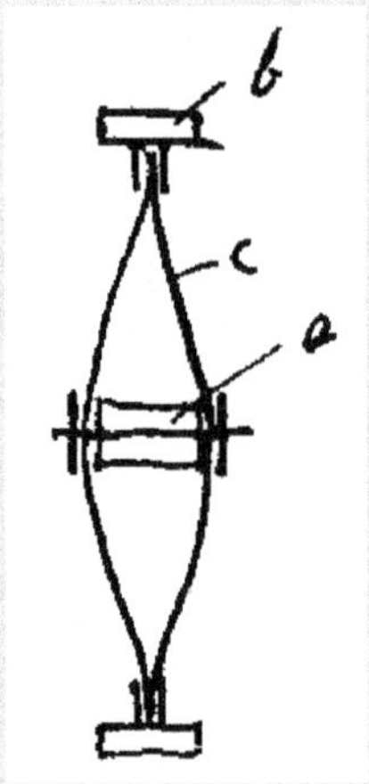

Utility Patent			
Content **Registered-number** **File number**	**(a) signed in** **(e) grated** **(zg) withdrawn** **(z) rejected** **(l) defunct**	**Description of the Claims** **("t.m.t." = " ... thereby marked that...)**	**Fig.** **(Remark: The drawings originate from a survey of the Euler-Werke, source: Bundesarchiv Koblenz, Signature N1103)**
Double connection piece for flight machine wings E. 14540/77 436 260	23.07.1910 (a) 25.07.1910 (e) 25.07.1913 (f)	The aluminium made connecting piece a grasps the rod b between the upper and lower wing and the horizontal rod c, which is holding on the wing's warping; by monoplanes the piece is only grasping rod c below the curved wood.	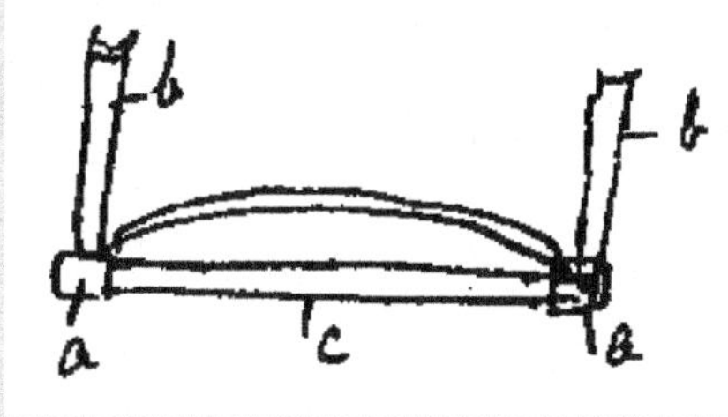
Shifting lever for engines, carburettors, ignition apparatuses, wing adjustments etc. of flight machines E. 14569/77	26.07.1910 (a) 26.09.1910 (e) 10.06.1913 (f)	With notches a outfitted aluminium corner d where the lever c is kept in the desired position by a rubber band b.	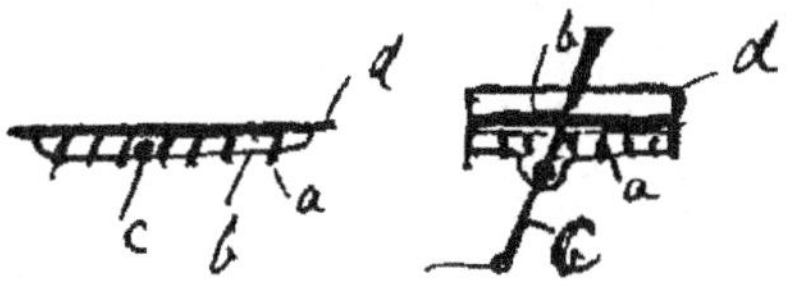
Measuring corner for the measuring of the angle of incidence of wings of biplane flight machines E. 14570/42 432 931	26.07.1910 (a) 27.08.1910 (e) 10.06.1913 (f)	Thigh b is laid to the front edges and the corner is pushed upwards to a at the lower edge. By unscrewing of the screw c until it is meeting the surface the entering angle is determined.	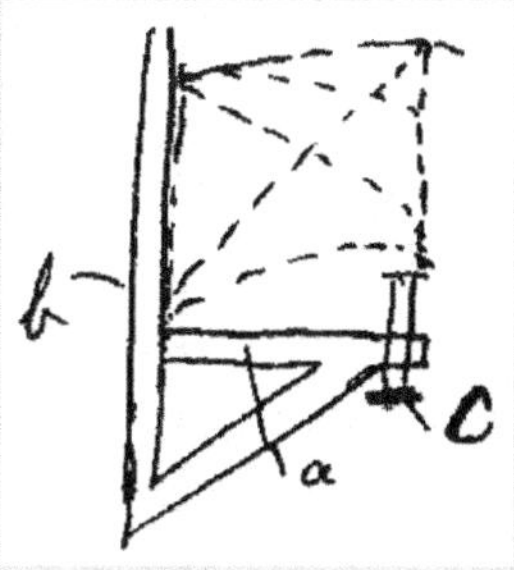
Auxilliary wing for flight machines for the regulation of the horizontal cruise in flight direction during .... displacements of weight in flight E. 14856/77 443 507	14.10.1910 (a) 08.11.1910 (e) 1913 (f)	Auxiliary wing a on the rear upper tail surface, swivelling by means of lever b and two wire ropes c over little self hampering role e which is operated by a hand wheel d.	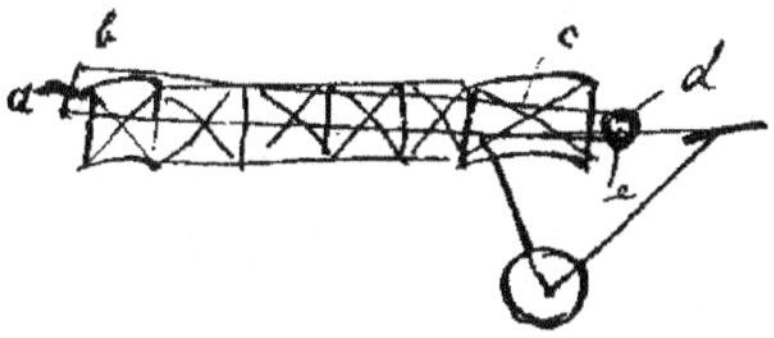

Utility Patent			
Content **Registered-number** **File number**	**(a) signed in** **(e) grated** **(zg) withdrawn** **(z) rejected** **(l) defunct**	**Description of the Claims** **("t.m.t." = " ... thereby marked that...)**	**Fig.** **(Remark: The drawings originate from a survey of the Euler-Werke, source: Bundesarchiv Koblenz, Signature N1103)**
Bracing of aeroplane wings, chassis and rod connections E. 15014/77 447 415	23.11.1910 (a) 09.12.1910 (e) 15.11.1913 (l)	On the on top of each other and in the middle between two supported struts c lieing parts of two equal airplane parts d, e are arranged in against each other directed little pedestals a, their points are connected with the next positioned points c and with each other by tension wires.	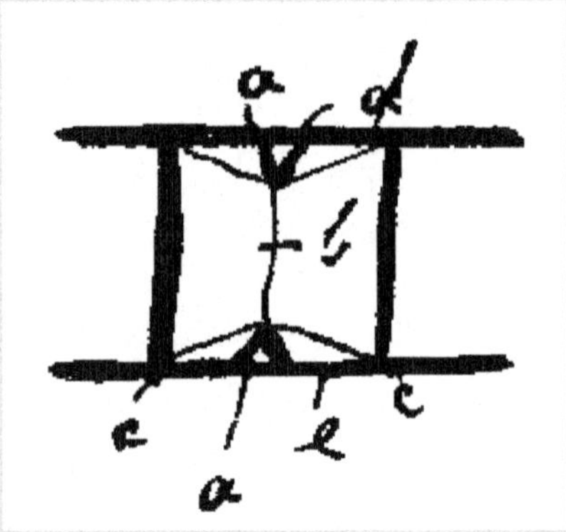
Unilaterally braced wings for flight machines E. 14881/77 443 003	21.10.1910 (a) 27.10.1913 (l)	Between the ribs bands b are spanned from the front frame A to the rear frame B and to wit even, crosswise or angular and over the frame A below the frame B. From the back sideof frame A stripe c spanned to the bottom side of surface Fläche a.	
Connecting piece for divided aeroplane woods E. 15191/77 451 882	04.01.1911 (a) 05.01.1914 (f)	Pipe a, in which itself the sloped ends b, c of the woods are lieing over each other that they are filling the pipe. Held together by spanning or screws e.	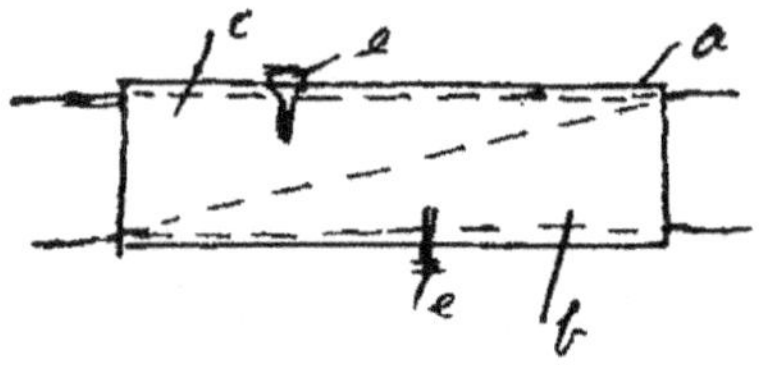
Starting-up axis for flight machines E. 15245/77 452 778	14.01.1911 (a) 22.12.1913 (l)	14.01.1911 (a) 22.12.1913 (l)	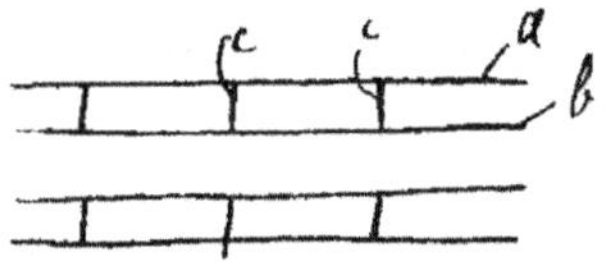
Starting-up chassis for flight machines E. 15289/77 453 815	23.01.1911 (a) 25.01.1917 (f)	Over the steel pipe axis a the perforated, exactly on it fitting canister b is shifted and over it the exactly fitting wheel axis c. This is held on the left and right by the wearing part d and splint e.	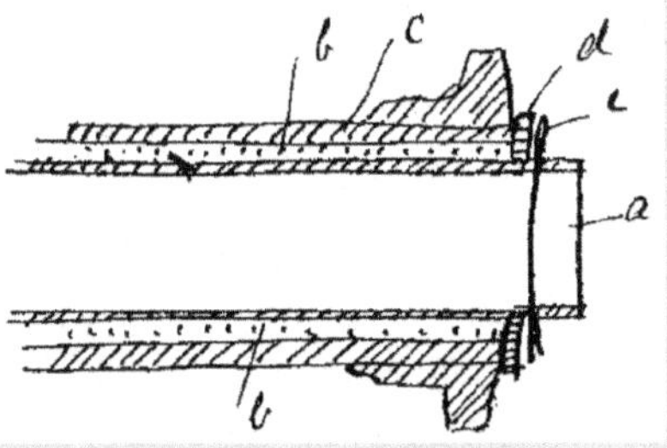

Utility Patent			
Content **Registered-number** **File number**	**(a) signed in** **(e) grated** **(zg) withdrawn** **(z) rejected** **(l) defunct**	**Description of the Claims** **("t.m.t." = " ... thereby marked that...)**	**Fig.** **(Remark: The drawings originate from a survey of the Euler-Werke, source: Bundesarchiv Koblenz, Signature N1103)**
Combined side, heights and banking controls for flight machines E. 15262/77 456 228	16.01.1911 (a) 16.01.1914 (f)	On the cross c-d which can swing around the props e, a big lever a is sitting, from there wires g go to the height control, wires i to the banking control and lever b with coil f, from there wires h guide to the rudder; a and b are swingable around c. a and b operate both and solo the elevator control, furthermore a operates the banking control, b the rudder.	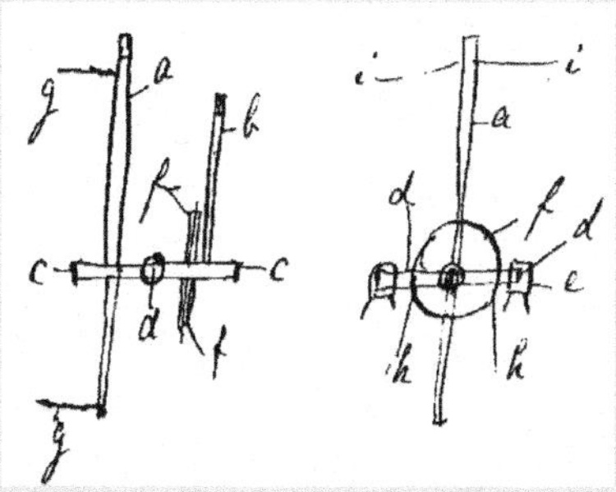
Combines head and tail height control E. 15290/77 461 098	23.01.1911 (a) 1914 (f)	The axis d, on which the lever a, b swing, both operate the elevator control n, is sidewards extended and has the lever k on its end that is with each other crossing (?) an adjustable tail surface n operates - in the opposite direction as the elevator control m, while it takes part in the movements of the levers a, b. The effect of the elevator control is thereby stengthened.	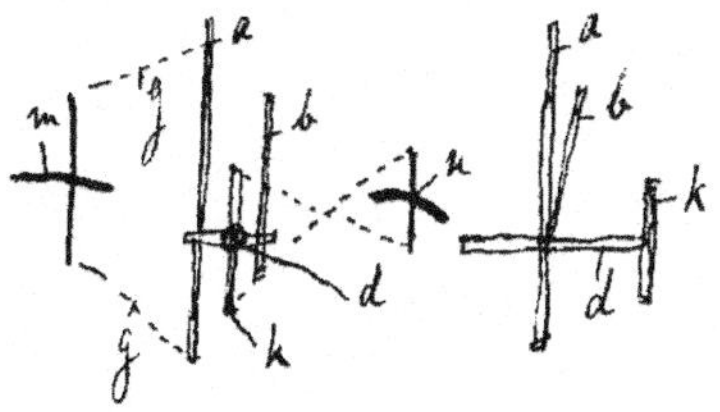
Rudder for aeroplane E. 15291/77 453 816	23.01.1911 (a) 18.2.1911 (e) 28.01.1914 (f)	rudder with this shape b with pipe a which sits moveable in eyelets of the tail surface and is support rod for the tail surfaces as well, is solid connected; several rudder with the points connected by wires, also connected aft.	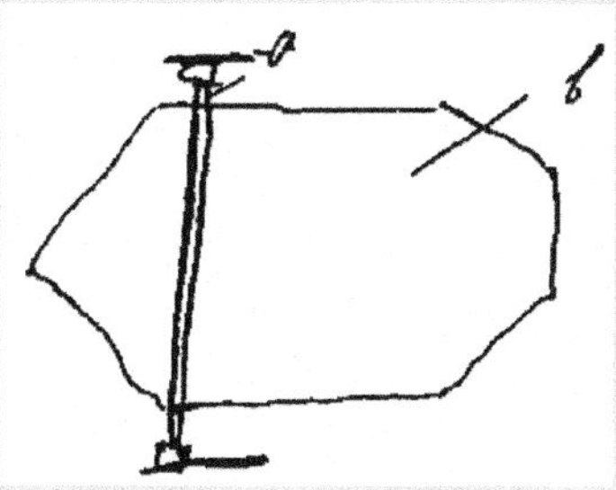
Fixture of height controls for flight machines with protective skid E. 15292/77 453 817	23.01.1911 (a) 18.02.1911 (e) 25.01.1914 (l)	Elevator control pipe c is held by metal piece b with washer b and splints. Elevator control lever d is outfitted with protective skid f.	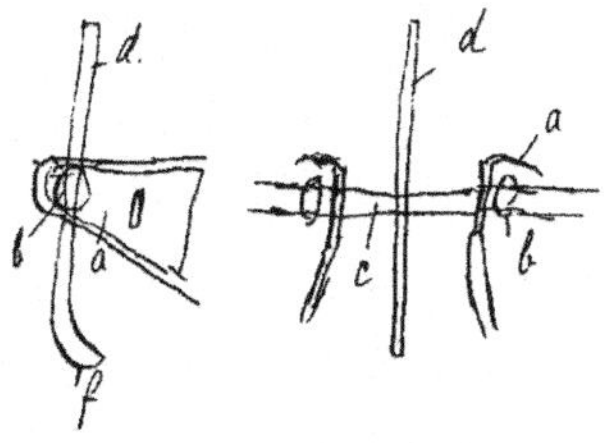

Utility Patent			
Content **Registered-number** **File number**	**(a) signed in** **(e) grated** **(zg) withdrawn** **(z) rejected** **(l) defunct**	**Description of the Claims** **("t.m.t." = " ... thereby marked that...)**	**Fig.** **(Remark: The drawings originate from a survey of the Euler-Werke, source: Bundesarchiv Koblenz, Signature N1103)**
Tail skid for aeroplane E. 15293/77 hGm 453 818	23.01.1911 (a) 18.02.1911 (e) 25.01.1914 (l)	Skid a is firm and sits solid below the tail surface, it springs only so much as the wood bends. Tension wires c absorb the forces.	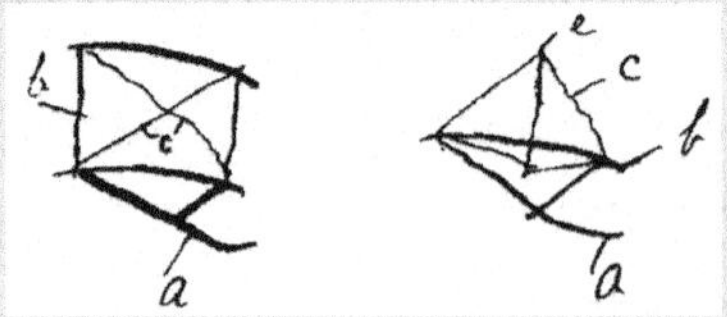
Double-sided control buckle for aeroplane parts, especially for height control, rudder and banking control E. 15294/77 hGm 466 391	23.11.1911 (a) 29.04.1911 (e) 29.03.1917 (l)	Steel tube a (that can be shfted over a steel tube b) is slit on one or several sides above and below and the slit ends are bend and combined to the eyelet c. The tension wires go through these control wires. The eyelet can move around the tube, the wire inside the eyelet.	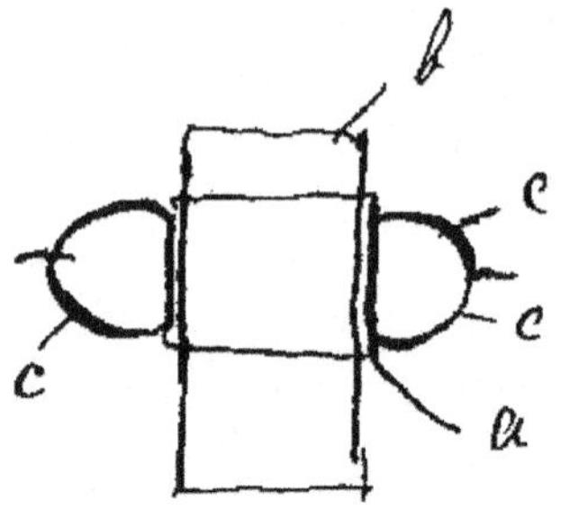
All-around flexible tail skid for flight machines E. 16512/77 hGm 487 186	24.10.1911 (a) 14.11.1911 (e) 30.12.1911 (l)	Skid k sits horizontally swingable on l, which sits on axis b, which swings vertically in bearing a (fastened with splint s). Upper end of the skid is connected bouncing with the tail strut by rubber rings p, o in a manner that it is swinging springy on and with the T-shaped axis b-l on the vertical and horizontal level.	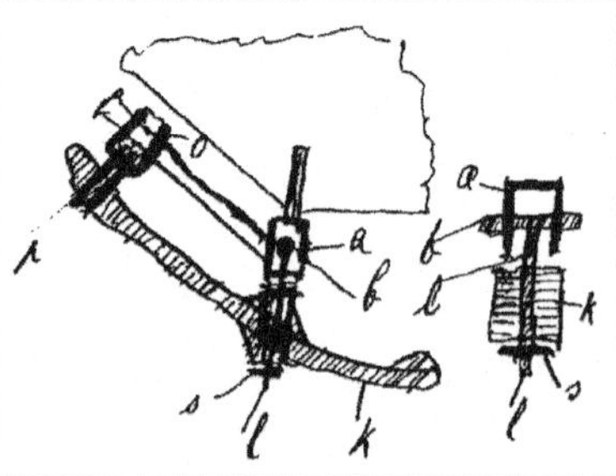
Starting-up and landing chassis for a biplane war flight machine with height control surface aft E. 16512/77 hGm 487 187	24.10.1911 (a) 14.11.1911 (e) 30.10.1917 (l)	In itself closed chassis is independent of the wings. Mounted before the wings and with 2 slantwise upwards running frontal struts a, which prevent somersault. Beside struts a in the middle 2 struts b, in the rear 1. strut c connected with tail by spiky upward running lattice of the tail skid k, with the tail only connected by pipe e which is connecting the axis of the rudder and strut f (compare. 487186).	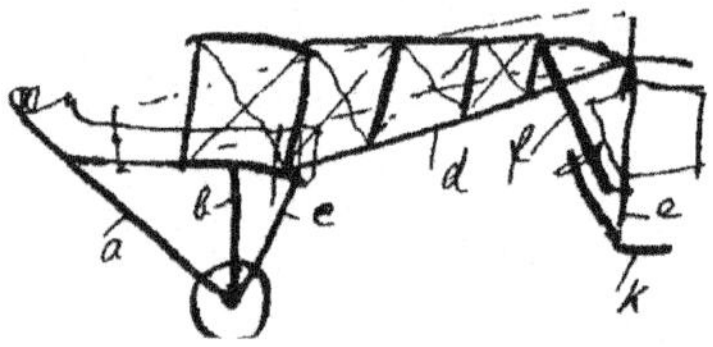

Utility Patent			
Content **Registered-number** **File number**	**(a) signed in** **(e) grated** **(zg) withdrawn** **(z) rejected** **(l) defunct**	**Description of the Claims** **("t.m.t." = " ... thereby marked that...)**	**Fig.** **(Remark: The drawings originate from a survey of the Euler-Werke, source: Bundesarchiv Koblenz, Signature N1103)**
Connecting framework between main wings and tail surface in flight machines E. 16863/77 hGm 496 001	15.01.1912 (a) 30.01.1912 (e) 22.01.1918 (l)	Tail surface e is embedded around more than the half of the propeller's diameter s over the imagined extension of the propeller axis A-B.	
Device for the folding down of the outer ends of the wings of biplanes and mulitiplanes E. 16963/77 hGm 499 003	22.01.1912 (a) 24.02.1912 (e) 11.02.1918 (l)	The foldable ends d, e of the wings are connected on solid parts a with hinges. d, e are connected with each other by rods b; e upwards with a by tension wire c; c and b grasp e in gl. e is spanned downward by tension wire k. If gl, b and c solved, then one can fold down the whole.	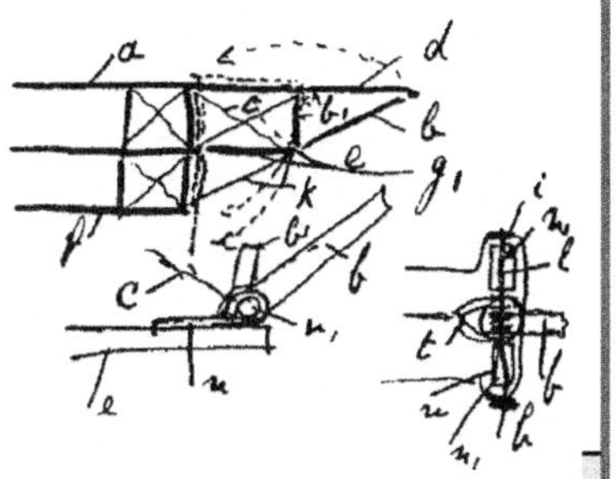
Starting-up chassis for flight machines which can be easily sparated from the wings E. 17141/77 hGm 504 365	15.03.1912 (a) 01.04.1912 (e) 15.03.1915 (f)	Chassis a and wing frame bb independent. Chassis a can be shifted in it in front (Fig. 2 on top) Rear part connected from a with longeron n from f by screws or bolts s; leading part connected with rods i, g, f with leading longeron from b. f, g resolvable with a screw l. In the height of the lower wing b is the wing piece k installed in the chassis and lashed up.	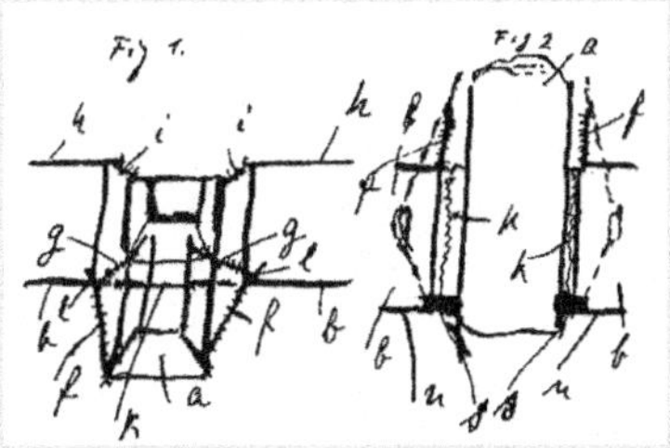
Flight machine with two engines and with two air screws E. 17187/77 hGm 505 735 Patent application occured (E. 17943 XI/77 h5) but wass rejected.	27.03.1912 (a) 22.04.1912 (e) 01.04.1918 (l)	Engines and propeller screws a, b, c, d lie on an imgagined axis A-B and a, b touch in front, c, d behind the wings.	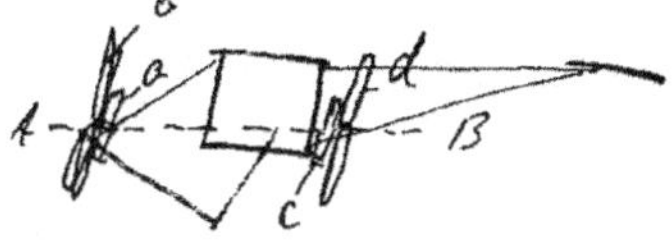

Utility Patent			
Content **Registered-number** **File number**	**(a) signed in** **(e) grated** **(zg) withdrawn** **(z) rejected** **(l) defunct**	**Description of the Claims** **("t.m.t." = " ... thereby marked that...)**	**Fig.** **(Remark: The drawings originate from a survey of the Euler-Werke, source: Bundesarchiv Koblenz, Signature N1103)**
Aiming device for flight machines with fixed built-in machine-gun E. 17206/77 hGm 505 966	30.03.1912 (a) 16.04.1912 (e) 03.04.1915 (l)	Aim device of flight machine with fixed build in machine-gun f (a, b seats, d, e control) two rear sights g, gl, two bead sights k, kl, of which the latter are adjustable (with lever i) from the seats by the hand wheels K which are outfitted with a scala. The machine-gun operator on seat b (notch sight gl, bead sight kl are computed for him) is able to notice, if the pilot on seat a, (notch sight g, bead sight k are computed for him) has aligned the machine with the target and to fire.	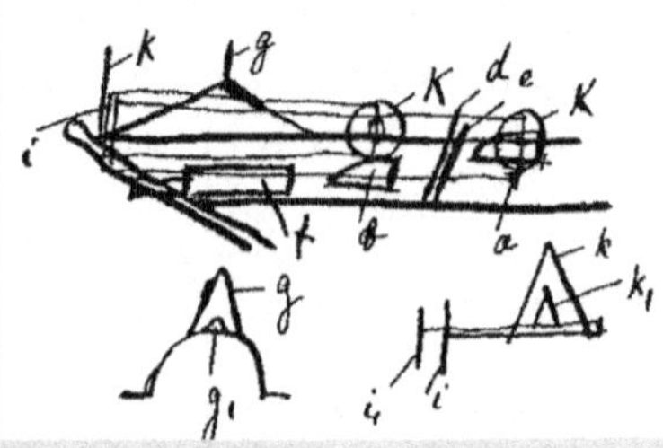
Banking control for airplanes by one-sided lenthening or shortening of the wings E. 17558/77 hGm 516 365	26.06.1912 (a) 12.07.1912 (e) 29.06.1918 (l)	Banking control by enlargement of the wing on one side and decrease in size of the wing on the other side in fact by shifting the upper wings b. b which are conneted with the lower wing a by rods c which are sitting in the joints. The rods e can be shfted by the lever f and the pushing rod c, by which means also b becomes shifted.	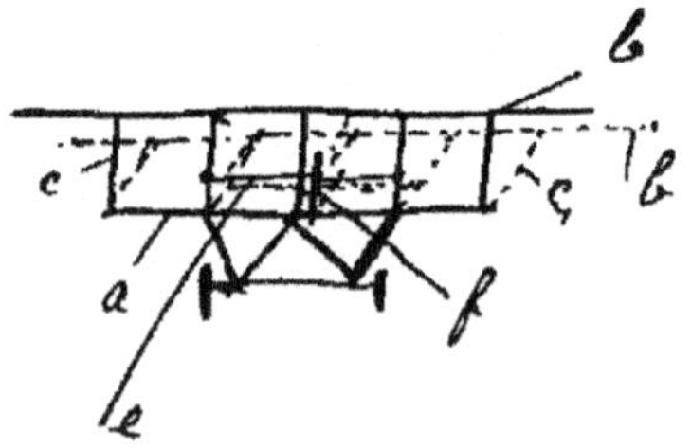
Combined height, rudder and banking control for flight machines E. 17569/77 hGm 516 734	30.03.1912 (a) 17.07.1912 (e) 12.06.1918 (f)	Lever a operates heights and banking controls, han wheel f the rudder. f is vertically and on the upper end of a fixed. a is at the sides swingable on axis c, which is firmly linked with the lever e which operate the height control, so that the latter are only making the forward and backward moves but not the sideward moves.	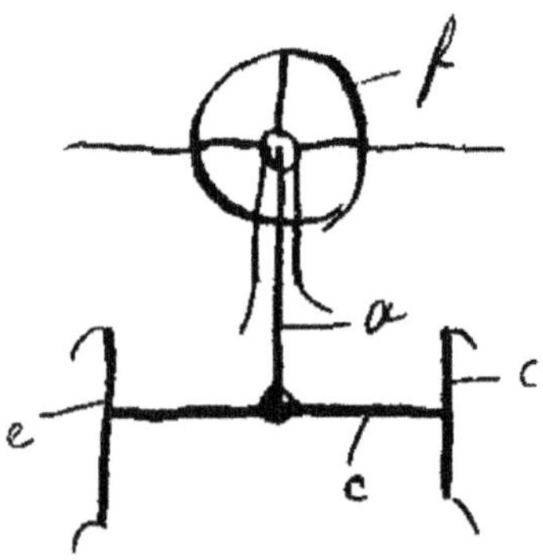

Utility Patent			
Content **Registered-number** **File number**	**(a) signed in** **(e) grated** **(zg) withdrawn** **(z) rejected** **(l) defunct**	**Description of the Claims** **("t.m.t." = " ... thereby marked that...)**	**Fig.** **(Remark: The drawings originate from a survey of the Euler-Werke, source: Bundesarchiv Koblenz, Signature N1103)**
Combined height, rudder and banking control for flight machines E. 17688/77 hGm 521 076	26.07.1912 (a) 30.08.1912 (e) 27.07.1915 (l)	Control lever d with auxilliary lever b, bl is connected by rods a, c in such a way that all forward and backward moves and sideward moves of the control lever d are also made by the levers b, bl. (Hand wheel on d, is operated by the lever g and wire cables and operats the three-armed lever e, f, which is for his part operating the rudder.).	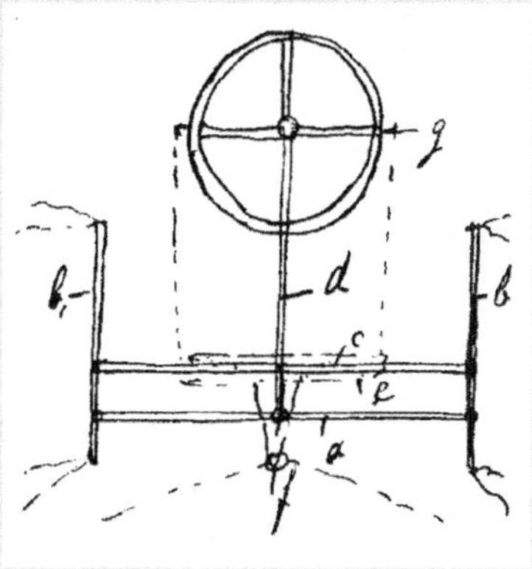
Safety and protective wheels for flight machines E. 17960/77 hGm 534 878	28.09.1912 (a) 17.12.1912 (e) 01.10.1915 (l)	Around the pilot's and the passenger's seat b, bl lie the tyres d, which carry pneumatics c on the inner side. These tyres are connectedspringly by elastic bands e with the vehicle body.	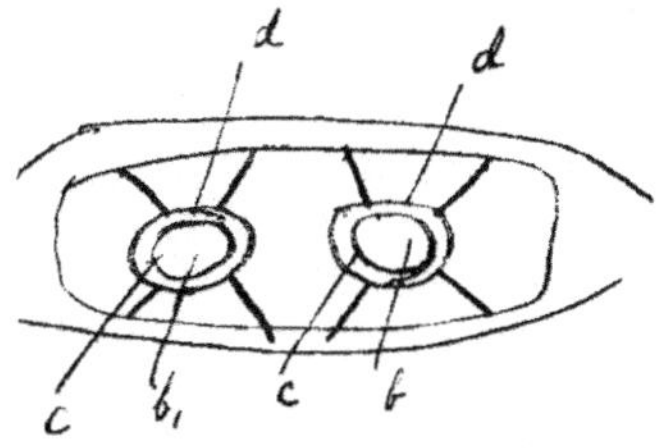
Radiator with shifted cooling ribs, especially for flight machines E. 18822/77 hGm 550 343	20.03.1913 (a) 03.04.1913 (e) 24.03.1919 (l)	Radiator is adjusted to the vehicle body K. The colling ribs b are shifted and all with the flat side parallel to the direction and move of the vehicle.	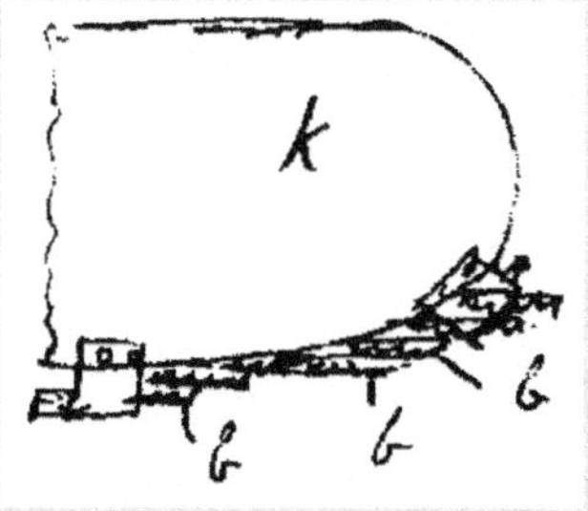
Auxilliary flaps with compulsory guidance for the baking control of flight machines E. 18828/77 hGm 549 198 Patent application occured (E. 19033 XI/77 h 5) but was rejected.		Banking controls with the ailerons a, al are characterised so, that auxillary flaps which are connected with the controls or lever by wires d, dl, e, el through the roles i, k on both its upper side and also its lower side and therefore necessarly guided in a way that if by means of operating the control leverthe flap is pulled down, the other one is pulled upward and therefore the effect strengthened.	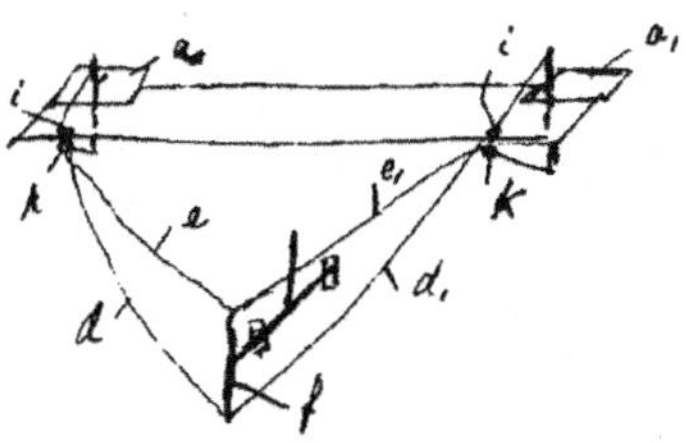

Utility Patent			
Content **Registered-number** **File number**	**(a) signed in** **(e) grated** **(zg) withdrawn** **(z) rejected** **(l) defunct**	**Description of the Claims** **("t.m.t." = " ... thereby marked that...)**	**Fig.** **(Remark: The drawings originate from a survey of the Euler-Werke, source: Bundesarchiv Koblenz, Signature N1103)**
Role for wire or rope guidance E. 18846/47 bGm 551 339	25.03.1913 (a) 11.04.1913 (e) 29.03.1916 (l)	Role for wire guidance t.m.t. with channeling provided wheel rim b is put over a length of pipe a,around which they can run, to prevent a sliding of the wires a piece of metal d is stuck through one end of the pipe and bent over the roles. This piece of metal is held on with special split pins c.	c d b b a
Surface framework for flight machines which is held together by bracing E. 18887/77 hGm 551 688	04.04.1913 (a) 17.04.1913 (e) 07.04.1916 (l)	Wing scaffolding of a shape that the single unequally thick struts b, c can put through each other and the ends can put throught the edge struts a and the cohesion is caused by diagonally running tension wires. tension wires run through the system. Go through crossroad points of two struts b, c under formation of a knee.	e c a c e a b b c
Device for the connection of a tube end with any other piece E. 18909/47 hGm 551 806 Patent apllication occured (E. 19081 XII/47 a) but was rejected.	07.04.1913 (a) 10.04.1916 (l)	t.m.t. the tube end a is slit on two sides and bent, so that it forms flanges b, which are put on the connecting piece, so that a short cuff-like pipe piece e, which is outfitted in the same way with flanges d, is pushed over a, so that the flanges d are cover the flanges b. Flanges b, d are fastened with bolt e on f.	d a e d b e b f

Utility Patent			
Content **Registered-number** **File number**	**(a) signed in** **(e) grated** **(zg) withdrawn** **(z) rejected** **(l) defunct**	**Description of the Claims** **("t.m.t." = " ... thereby marked that...)**	**Fig.** **(Remark: The drawings originate from a survey of the Euler-Werke, source: Bundesarchiv Koblenz, Signature N1103)**
Fixture of tension wire for flight machines E. 18918/77 hGm 551 712	09.04.1913 (a) 12.04.1916 (l)	Bracing wire connection for wings, which are braced upward and downward in such a way that through the eyelets d a bracing wire e is running through the holes of a thin but concerning its surface relatively big metal sheet b which is seating on the edge strut a of the surface and is fastened with thin screws g or nails but incorporating the bracing wire with its plane.	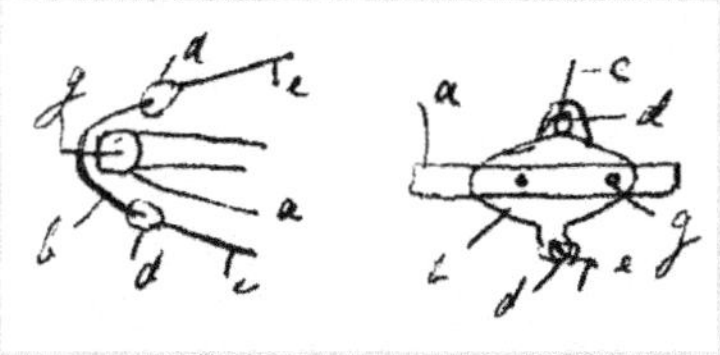
Lever device for the adjustment of wing parts of flight machines E. 18960/77 hGm 553 900 Patent application occured (E. 19110 XII/77 h7) but was rejected.	16.04.1913 (a) 18.04.1919 (l)	Lever device in such a manner that the bracing masts b, bl are sitting in hinges c, cl on the edge cross-beams h of the solid surface a.	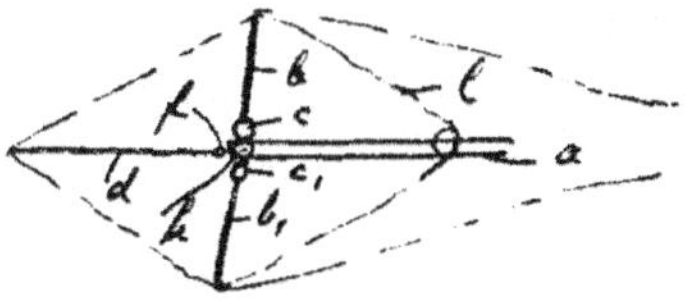
Bracing device for flight machines E. 18975/77 hGm 552 848 Patent application occured (E. 19111 XI/77 h8) but was rejected.	18.04.1913 (a) 19.04.1913 (l)	On the flat upper one of the bracing mast is an on both sides bent upward metal a, which forms a pile I by the benting on each side and it's over each other folded edges are outfitted with bolts in the bracing mast.	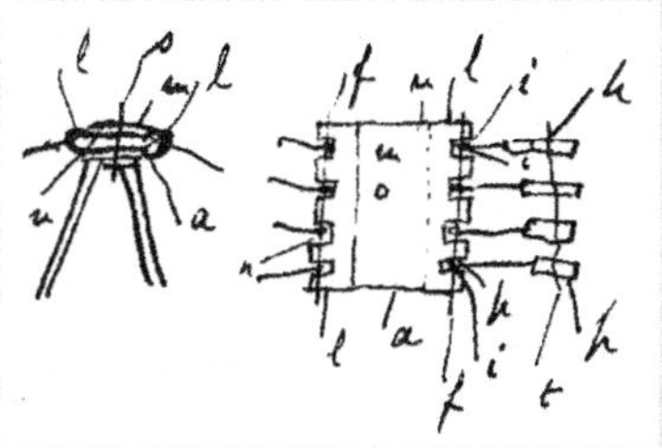

Utility Patent			
Content **Registered-number** **File number**	**(a) signed in** **(e) grated** **(zg) withdrawn** **(z) rejected** **(l) defunct**	**Description of the Claims** **("t.m.t." = " ... thereby marked that...)**	**Fig.** **(Remark: The drawings originate from a survey of the Euler-Werke, source: Bundesarchiv Koblenz, Signature N1103)**
Swimming and driving body for air vehicles E. 19006/77 hGm 558 147 Patent application occured (E. 19140 XI/77 h7) but was rejected.	23.04.1913 (a)	Swimmer whose swimming bodies a are constructed role-shaped and are fastened turnable, sod that it can roll on the water.	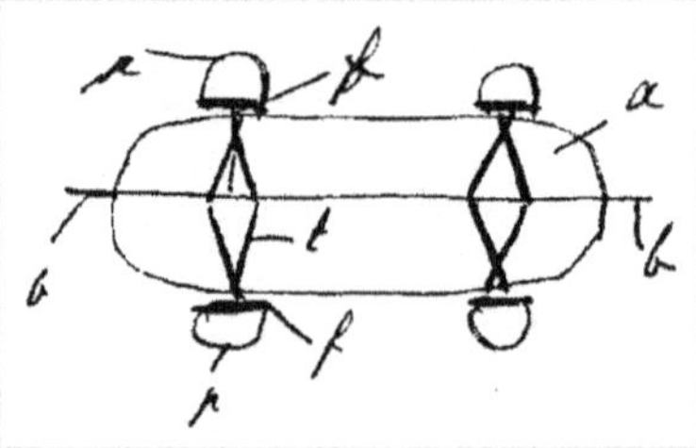
Foldable tail surfaces for flight machines E. 19016/77 hGm 553 757 Patent application occured (E. 19646 XI/77 h) but was rejected.	22.04.1913 (a) 26.04.1916 (e)	In such a way that it is consisting of two independent surfaces a, b which lay next to each other, where the internal edges are at least partially in contact with to the rear end of the airframe c and by means of a row of upwards foldable hinges fastened	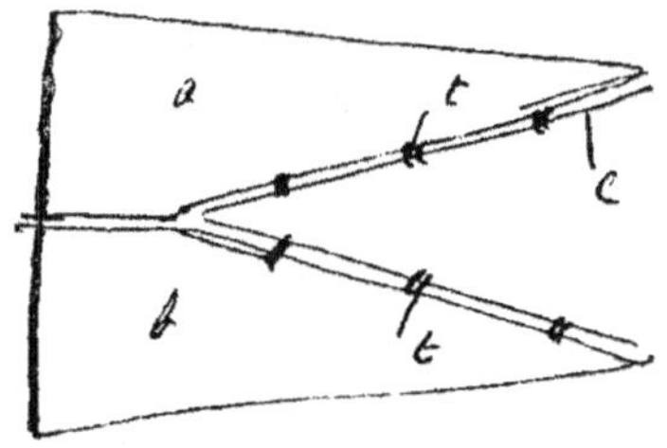
Foldable bracing bridge for wings of flight machines E. 19024/77 hGm Patent application occured (E. 19158 XI/77 h) but was rejected.	23.04.1913 (a)	t.m.t. struts are hinge-like and slightly solveable stiffened at the wing cross-beam and support longeron to the chassis bridge by wires s, t, which lead to the front and rear edge of the wing surface.	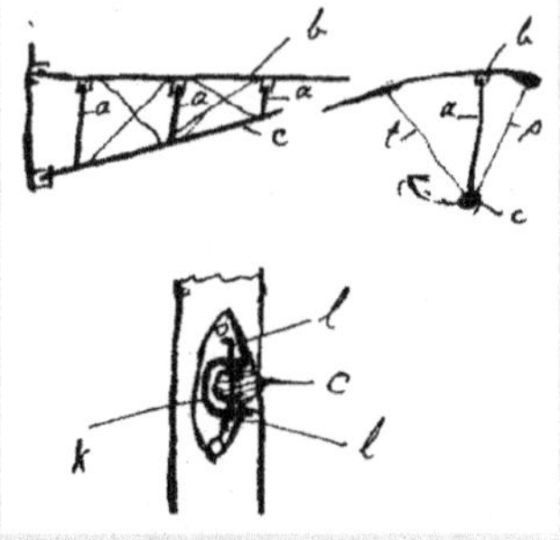
Fixture of the wing bracing of flight machines E. 19048/77h Gm 555 115	02.05.1913 (a) 01.05.1919 (l)	Fixation of the wing covering of flight machines or the ribs of the wing framework a through stitching in a way that the ribs a are enveloped with fabric b and the covering is stitched on it.	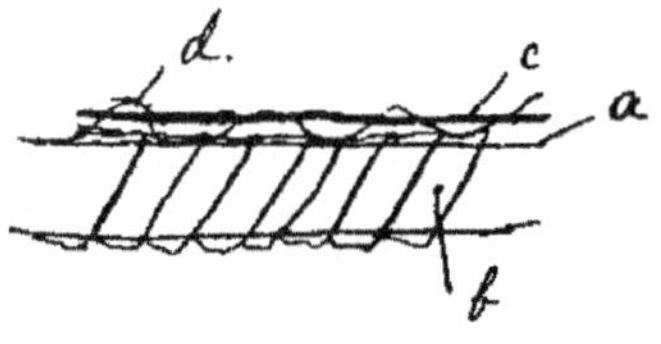

Utility Patent			
Content **Registered-number** **File number**	**(a) signed in** **(e) grated** **(zg) withdrawn** **(z) rejected** **(l) defunct**	**Description of the Claims** **("t.m.t." = " ... thereby marked that...)**	**Fig.** **(Remark: The drawings originate from a survey of the Euler-Werke, source: Bundesarchiv Koblenz, Signature N1103)**
Bracing of flight machines E. 19044/77 hGm 555 116 Patent application occured (E. 19164 XI/77 h) but was rejected.	28.04.1913 (a) 28.04.1919 (l)	Bracing wires d, e are fastened to a ring, a plate or other spanning organs a, b, which is sitting on one hand on the upper or lower bracing mast f, t.m.t. the lower bracing organ b with nut c, that can be screwed on and screwed off on the lower bracing mast f with its threads.	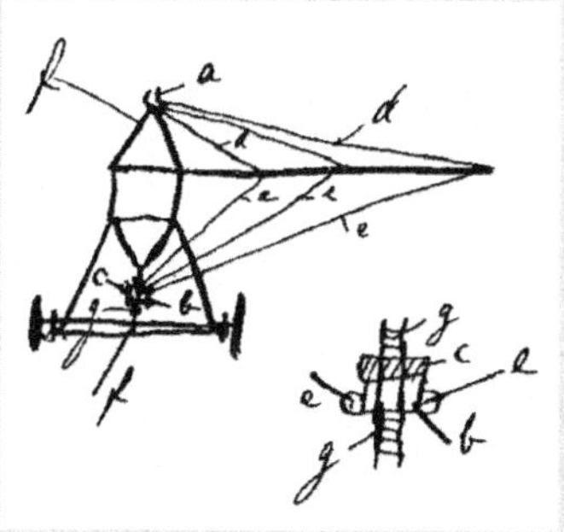
Foot control for flight machines E. 19085/77 hGm 555 712		Foot control with right and left pedal a which turns every axis b in such a way that each one has a lver c which is connected by a wire with te control, that means that a is not fastened on b, but hinge-like in front at d on b sitting auxilliarly lever m when hooks in front of role n roll on plate d.	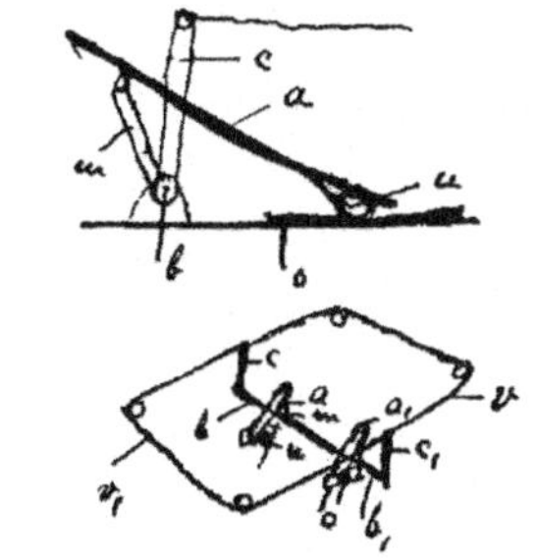
Adjustable tail surface for flight machines E. 19253/77 hGm 559 858 Patent application occured (E. 19296 XI/77 h5) but was rejected.	02.06.1913 (a) 14.06.1916 (l)	t.m.t. the bracing rings d - which are used to fasten the bracing wires c to the bracing masts b - can be pulled up and down from the pilot's seat by a wire rope hoist g which is going over roles h on the bracing mast.	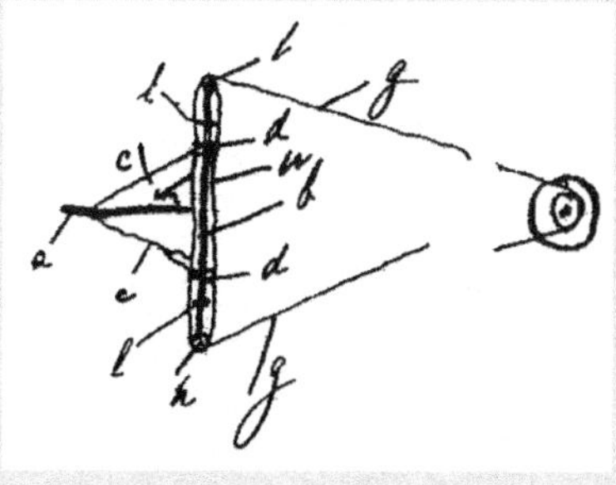
Fixable lever for flight machines E. 19304/46 bGm 561 434	25.06.1913 (a) 26.06.1919 (l)	Fixeable lever, consisting of a main and an auxilliary lever a, b which can be fixated by nose d which is griping into a gearing e and fixating the main lever a, if the upper ends of a and b are pressed apart.	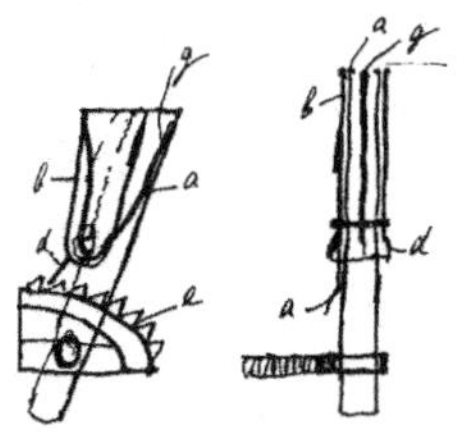

Utility Patent			
Content **Registered-number** **File number**	**(a) signed in** **(e) grated** **(zg) withdrawn** **(z) rejected** **(l) defunct**	**Description of the Claims** **("t.m.t." = " ... thereby marked that...)**	**Fig.** **(Remark: The drawings originate from a survey of the Euler-Werke, source: Bundesarchiv Koblenz, Signature N1103)**
Sealing for glas pipes, especially for gasoline level measurement device on lfight machines E. 19589/77 hGm 568 442 Patent application occured (E. 19504 XII/47 f) but was rejected.	20.08.1913 (a) 15.09.1913 (e) 23.08.1916 (l)	Sealings, which sit on each of its ends in a metal shoe d, f on a joint ring l, l1 each, t.m.t. the shoes, of which one is moveable, are connected with each other Two-part ... glass pipe rohr of parallel wires i are connected in kind of the bicycle spokes, where wires d. can firmly span bolt nuts k.	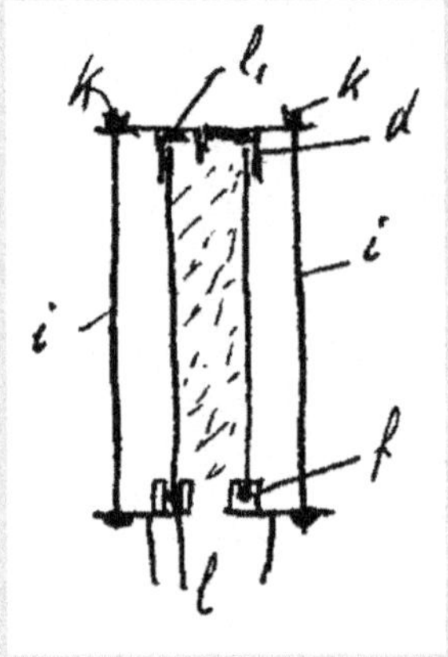
Petrol regulation for flight machines E. 19652/77 hGm 572 588 Patent application occured (E. 19542 XI/77 h5) but wss rejected.	02.09.1913 (a) 11.10.1913 (e) 03.09.1916 (l)	Petrol regulation, where by the rotation of a small wheel c which sits on an axis b a fuel cock a is operated in the pipe. Between tank and carburettor is pushed in, t.m.t. the pipe guides directly from the tank to the carburettor and the small wheel c which is operating the cock is perforce connected with an equally big small wheel e next to the pilot's seat by a wire cable g, which can be rotated by a lever l.	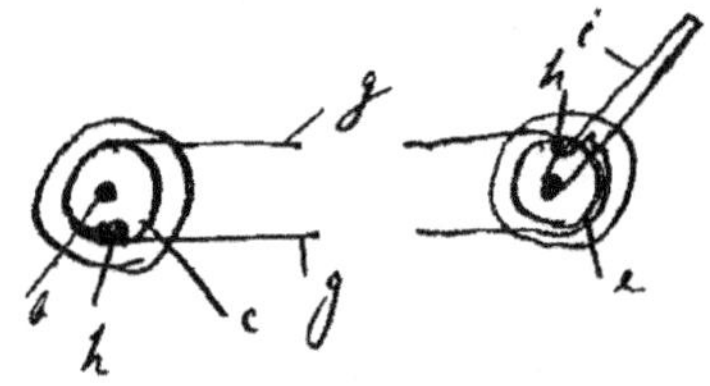
Shoe for struts of flight machines E. 19710/77 hGm 571 664	13.09.1913 (a) 04.10.1913 (e) 15.09.1916 (l)	Shoe for the struts which are claimed under pressure, t.m.t. on a lower embossed plate a a second plate b is fastened with bolts d or the like, plate b is embossed so that it is displaying a hole which corresponds to the cross section and its bend up rims from a tube part c for the incorporation of the end of the strut m.	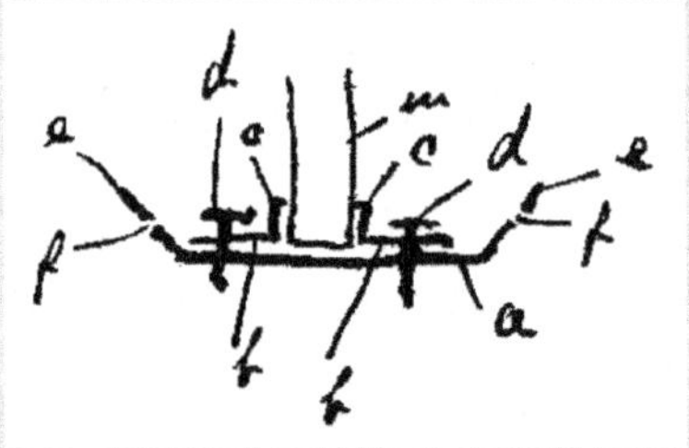

Utility Patent			
Content **Registered-number** **File number**	**(a) signed in** **(e) grated** **(zg) withdrawn** **(z) rejected** **(l) defunct**	**Description of the Claims** **("t.m.t." = " ... thereby marked that...)**	**Fig.** **(Remark: The drawings originate from a survey of the Euler-Werke, source: Bundesarchiv Koblenz, Signature N1103)**
Turnbuckle for flight machines E. 19805/77 hGm 579 178	30.09.1913 (a) 25.11.1913 (e) 06.10.1919 (l)	Turnbuckle, t.m.t. the parts to be braced, wires, wire ropes etc are fastened in a known manner at two suared bracing sheats f, f1 with threads that sit on two screws without head b, b1 and are fixed and on safety on it after the establishment of the right tension during the first assembling by splints.	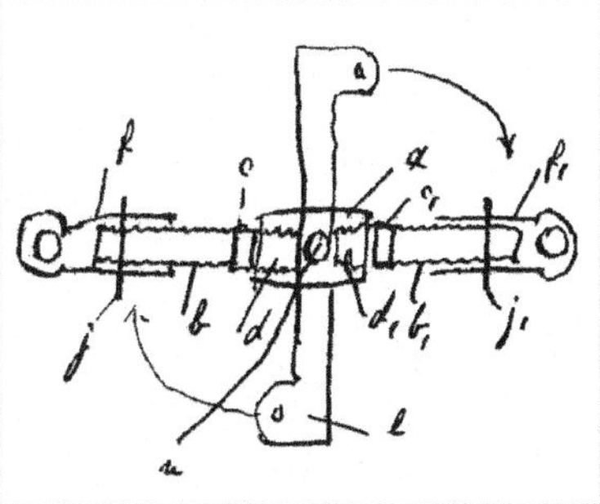
Shoe for fastening of tube struts and diagonal bracing E. 19830/77 hGm 574 772	06.10.1913 (a) 27.10.1913 (e) 10.10.1919 (l)	Shore t.m.t. if at the same point of the main cross-beam several struts from different directions und diagonal braces should be fastened at once, then the upper plates b, b1 are outfitted with two shoes with fishplates c, c1 which eject each other and display each one a hole.	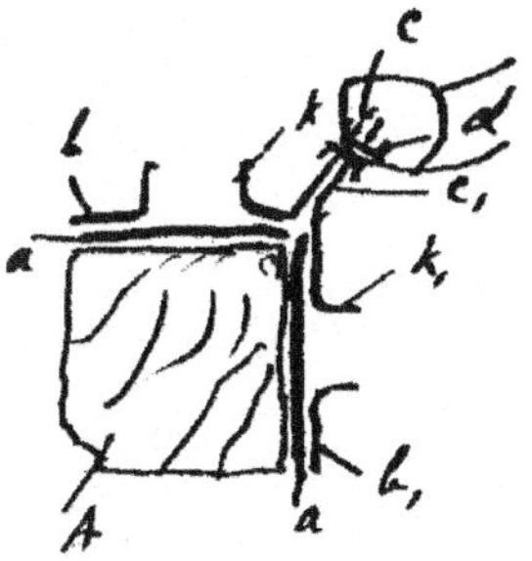
Silencer for flight machines E. 19829/46 cGm 577 868 Patent application occured (E. 19662 I/46 c6) but was rejected.	03.10.1913 (a) 15.11.1913 (e) 10.10.1916 (l)	Silencer t.m.t. the exhaust valves b enter into a tube c which is running along an upper end of the cylinder, from which the gases are guided through a derivation pipe e below the body of the machine where they escape through the backward bent open end g.	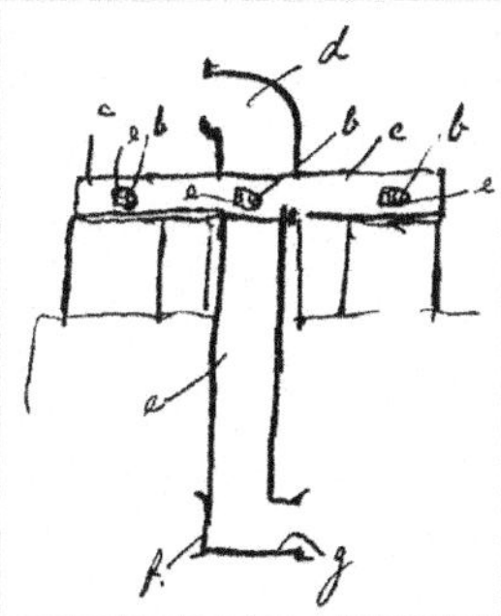
Hinge for wings of flight machines E. 19865/77 hGm 575 489	15.10.1913 (a) 30.10.1913 (e) 16.10.1919 (l)	Hinge arrangement tm.t. the edge cross-beam of one surface is outfitted over his length with a channeling d, that over this cross-beam a tube is pushed, so that e hollow cavity is created between the channeling and the pipe wall e, that the tube c has openings alongside of the channeling d, in which eyelets f fit, that lay with their eyes i in the hollow cavity between d and c ...	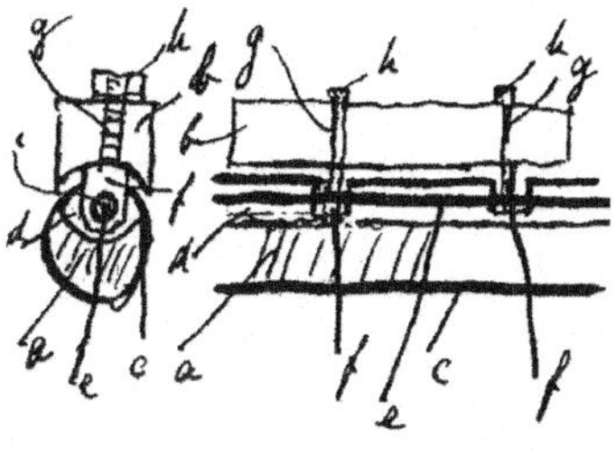

Utility Patent			
Content **Registered-number** **File number**	**(a) signed in** **(e) grated** **(zg) withdrawn** **(z) rejected** **(l) defunct**	**Description of the Claims** **("t.m.t." = " ... thereby marked that...)**	**Fig.** **(Remark: The drawings originate from a survey of the Euler-Werke, source: Bundesarchiv Koblenz, Signature N1103)**
Chassis for flight machines E. 19871/77 hGm 579 495 Patent application occured (E. 19694 XI/77 h4) but was rejected.	15.10.1913 (a) 27.11.1913 (e) 18.10.1919 (l)	Chassis t.m.t. the main struts and perhaps a number of bracing wires are united on the right and left in 2 tins a, a1, which are connected by a fixed axis and each outfitted with a slot b and on the lower side in front and behind with a recess c each, that a number of concentric rubber rings h can be laid from below in these recesses and be bent upwards ...	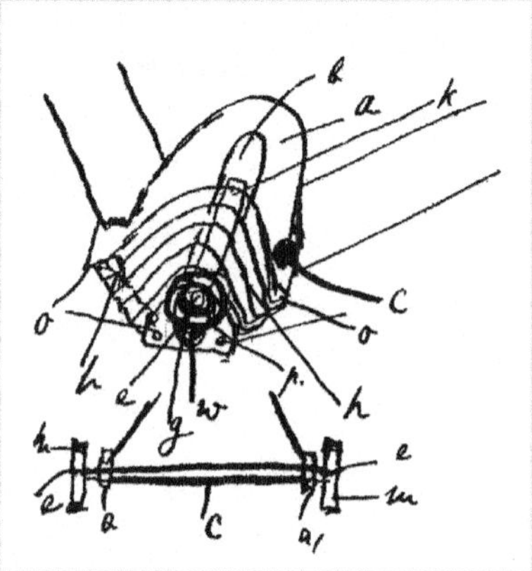
Bracing for flight machines E. 19882/77 hGm 576 095 Patent application occured (E. 19699 XI/77 h8) but was rejected.	15.10.1913 (a) 04.11.1913 (e) 20.10.1916 (l)	Bracing for flight machines t.m.t. strong spoke wires each with broadened heads c on its end are used and are fastened through these heads in a known manner at the braced parts by eyelets and rings.	
Shoe for the fixture of struts of flight machines E. 20187/77 hGm 586 076	13.12.1913 (a) 15.12.1919 (l)	Shoe, consisting of a lower a and upper plate b of which the upper one has a hole with a curved up, a pipe extension creating edges k and on the sides fishplates e with holes f, t.m.t.. also the lower plate e is outfitted with a number of fishplates e which feature holes f as well and are laid on the suitable fishplates of the upper plate ...	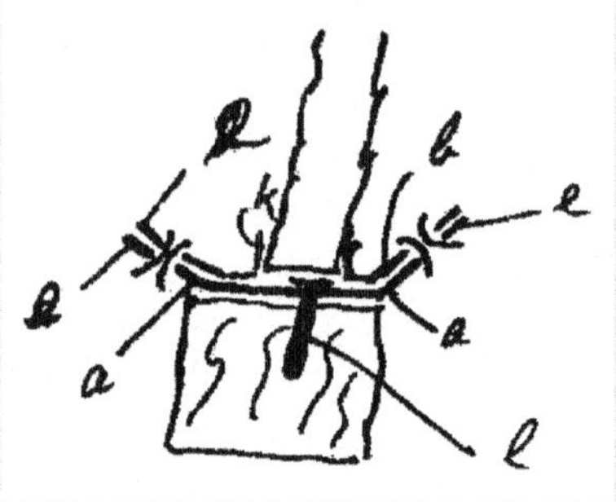

Utility Patent			
Content **Registered-number** **File number**	**(a) signed in** **(e) grated** **(zg) withdrawn** **(z) rejected** **(l) defunct**	**Description of the Claims** **("t.m.t." = " ... thereby marked that...)**	**Fig.** **(Remark: The drawings originate from a survey of the Euler-Werke, source: Bundesarchiv Koblenz, Signature N1103)**
Fuel line for engines of flight machines E. 20541 596 574 Patent application occured (E. 20164 I/46 c1) but was rejected.	28.02.1914 (a) 30.01.1917 (e)	Petrol line for airplane engines, which own a pressurized petrol tank a and a gravitational tank b, which are connected with each other, t.m.t. a pipe c is guiding from the pressurized fuel tank to a three-way cock e, that a pipe g is also guding from the bottom of the tank b to e and from there a pipe to the engine and that e according to its position the 3 pipes which enter it or only 2 connects or all 3 closes.	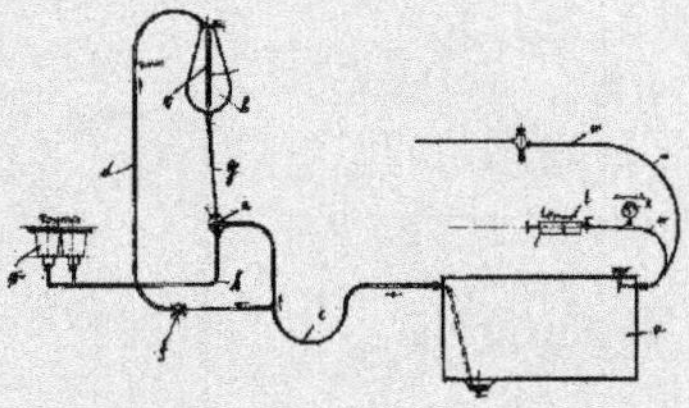
Wing bracing E. 20654/77 hGm 597 295 Patent application occured (E. 20247 XI/77 h8) but was rejected.	18.03.1914 (a) 28.03.1914 (e) 18.03.1920 (l)	Wing bracing t.m.t. the ends of the axis of the impellers serve as fixture points for the under bracing.	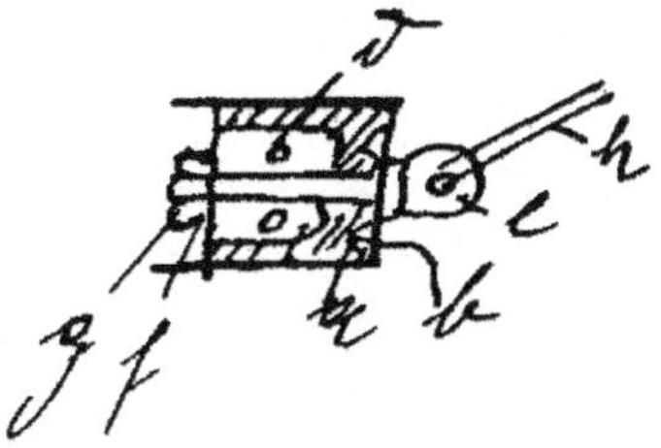
Aircraft fuselage 20713/77 hGm 598 972	27.03.1914 (a) 09.04.1914 (e) 27.03.1920 (l)	Airframe marked by the arrangement of a steel frame a, which surrounds the vehicle body d and is fastened at the engine block k radiator bearing c ... or pyramide f chassis e and one or several wing struts g, so that all parts form a firmly closed whole.	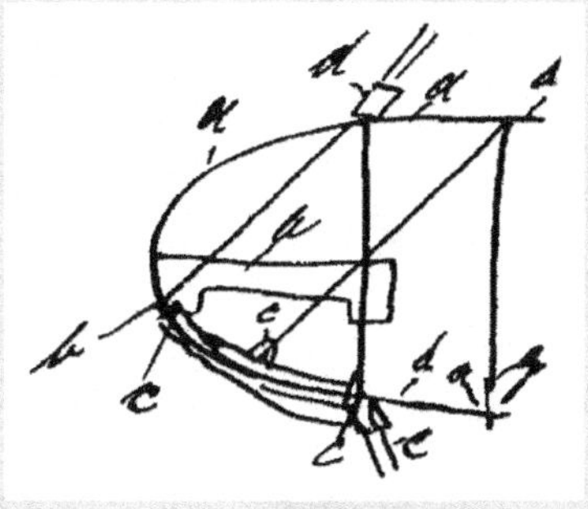
Fuel cleaner E. 20818/46 cGm 602 875 Patent application occured (E. 20362 I/46 c2) but was rejected.	15.04.1914 (a) 05.05.1914 (e) 20.04.1920 (l)	Fuel cleaner which is switched into to the pipe which is guiding from the petrol tank to the carburettor, t.m.t. the pipe a which is coming from the tank is giuding to a hollow cylinder b, in the latter are arranged above the entrance window a shovel c, above it a sieve e and above this the pipe a which is guiding to the carburettor.	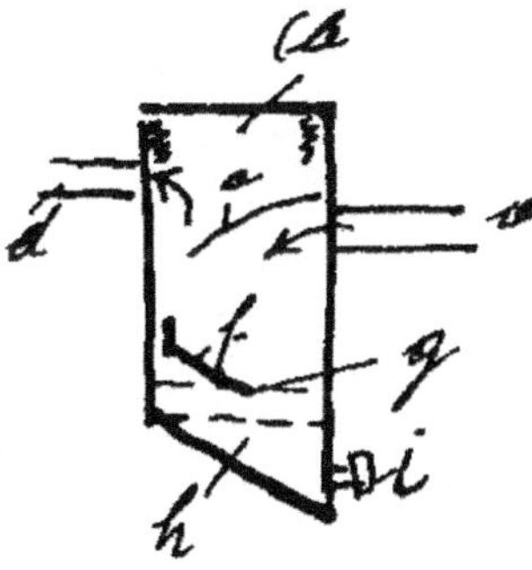

Utility Patent			
Content **Registered-number** **File number**	**(a) signed in** **(e) grated** **(zg) withdrawn** **(z) rejected** **(l) defunct**	**Description of the Claims** **("t.m.t." = " ... thereby marked that...)**	**Fig.** **(Remark: The drawings originate from a survey of the Euler-Werke, source: Bundesarchiv Koblenz, Signature N1103)**
Device for the fixture of the silencer on the wings of flight machines E. 21929/77h 633 958	13.07.1915 (a)	Thereby marked that the exhaust pipe is provided with 2 pins St parallel to its axis, which guide to 2 sheats H, which are fastened with enveloping sheets B to the edges of the wing.	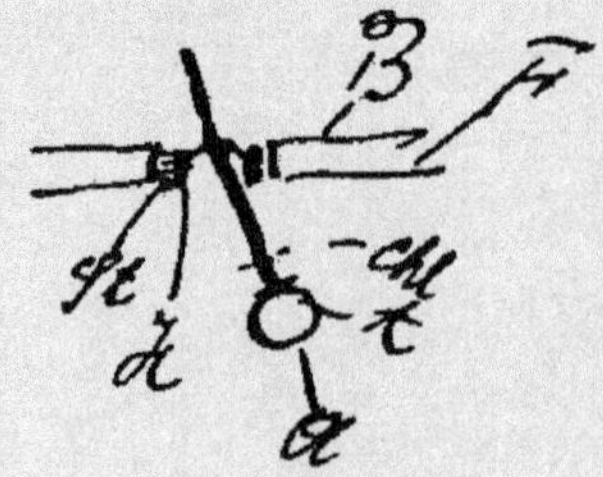
Bombing device for airplanes E. 22042/77h Gm 664 407 Patent application occured (E. 21243 XI/77 h1) but was rejected	07.09.1915 (a) 11.12.1915 (e)	t.m.t. the bombs are hanged on two camshafts which lay one above the other, of which the lower is firmly outfitted with flexible cams and the upper one outfitted with hinged standing cams. The upper shaft is operated by a driver disc, driver and push rod are operated with a little lever.	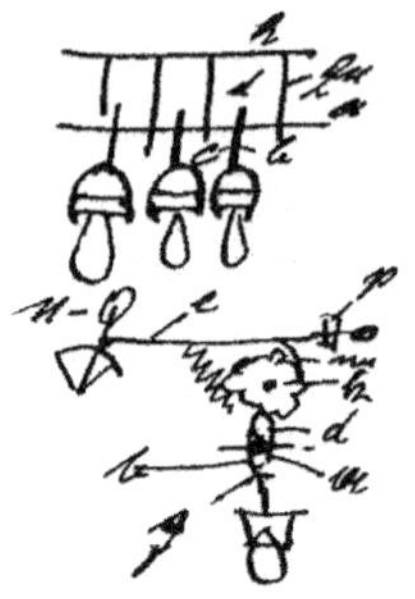
Arrangement of machine-guns for airplanes E. 22070/70 hGm 664 408	27.09.1915 (a) 29.09.1921 (l)	t.m.t. a rail or the like of it is attached for the machine-gun carrier as a steel tube with teething b, on its lower end is a rail c located. the machine-gun carrier is construed as a vehicle, which is moving on 2 hinged metal sheet bodies d, d1 which include against each other arranged rollers e, e1.	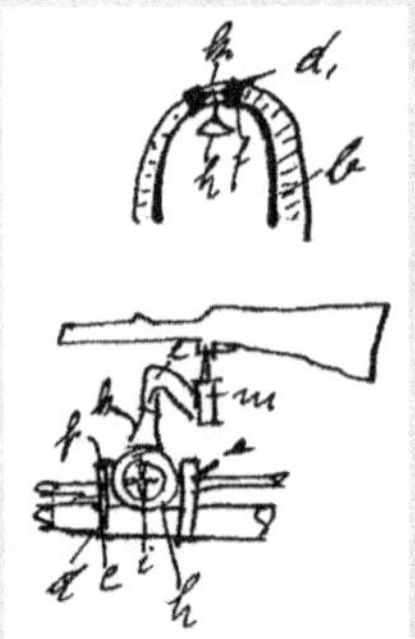
Arrangement of machine-guns for airplanes E. 22091/77 hGm 664 410	04.10.1915 (a) 08.10.1921 (l)	Thereby marked that the machine-gun carrier is fastened - additional to a tappet on the edge of the airframe - to an on all sides swingable arm of variable length in the center of the airframe in flight direction.	See patent application 299699

Utility Patent			
Content **Registered-number** **File number**	**(a) signed in** **(e) grated** **(zg) withdrawn** **(z) rejected** **(l) defunct**	**Description of the Claims** **("t.m.t." = " ... thereby marked that...)**	**Fig.** **(Remark: The drawings originate from a survey of the Euler-Werke, source: Bundesarchiv Koblenz, Signature N1103)**
Arrangement of petrol tank for airplanes E. 22126/77 hGm 640 375 Patent application occured (E. 21333 XI/77 h8) but was rejected.	01.11.1915 (a) 05.11.1921 (l)	t.m.t. the 2 different big tanks a, b in front and behind the pressure center are balanced out namely by different distances ofthe latter. Tanks are connected by a tube d, d1, in which a length of tube f with a sieve rests...	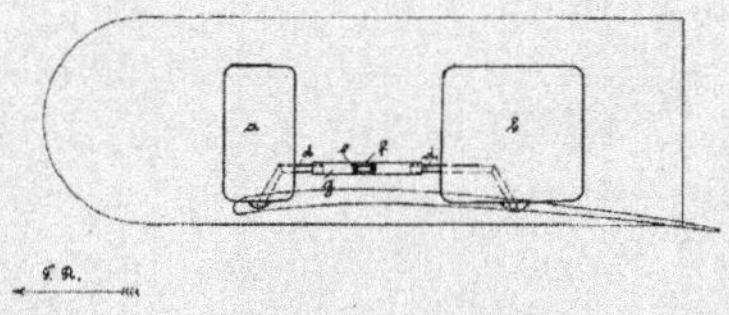
Cushioning for airplanes E. 22116/77 hGm 675 339	21.10.1915 (a) 27.10.1921 (l)	t.m.t. any number of spiral springs a, a1, a2 etc can be arranged on one hand on a chassis shoe b swingable two-part lever c, c1 and on the other hand on shoe b itself in a way that axis e which was put through the moveable end of the lever c can move up and down in a slot f inside the shoe b.	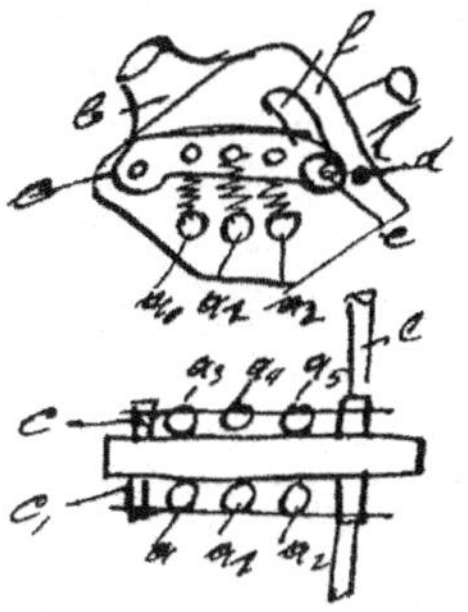
Rope guidance role for airplanes E. 22332/77 hGm 644 480	06.03.1916 (a) 08.03.1919 (l)	t.m.t. a central main sheet on both sides stores two little auf beiden Seiten zwei kleine loose axes, on the latter are the control rope wheels loosely slided and then from both sides two casing halves so shoven on the loose axis, that they - connected on the outside with the center sheet - form a closed whole. ...	
Control lever for airplanes E. 22357/77 hGm 664 417	19.03.1916 (a) 19.03.1922 (l)	t.m.t. the pivot point of the lever b is arranged above the wheel axis c and the wire cable d or d1 for the rudder or banking control over a moveable segment e which is moveable around the pivot point a and goes through the center of the main control axis.	

Utility Patent			
Content **Registered-number** **File number**	**(a) signed in** **(e) grated** **(zg) withdrawn** **(z) rejected** **(l) defunct**	**Description of the Claims** **("t.m.t." = " ... thereby marked that...)**	**Fig.** **(Remark: The drawings originate from a survey of the Euler-Werke, source: Bundesarchiv Koblenz, Signature N1103)**
Electrically fired machine-gun E. 22382/77 hGm 670 662 Patent application occured (E. 21590 XI/72 h) but was rejected.	27.03.1916 (a) 28.03.1919 (l)	t.m.t. the ignition of the cartridge is instead on the mechanical way for example occurring by an electromagnetic ignition apparatus and that the spark plug which is formed as a cap makes the electric current supplied to it in its explosive chamber of the cartridge arranged electrodes as spark jump over and ignites the powder...	None
Arrangement of machine-guns for airplanes E. 22441/77 hGm 664 418	25.04.1916 (a) 27.04.1919 (l)	t.m.t. a fixed firing second, third etc. machine-gun in an airplane is operated regards the aiming according to patent 258 918. The target point is changeable over the visor line of the pilot.	Refer to Patents
Hand control lever for airplanes E. 22588/77 hGm 664 420	12.07.1916 (a) 14.07.1919 (l)	t.m.t. the pivot point of the on all sides moveable control lever below the axis of rotation for the height control is arranged on these at the below welded on support. The same, below fork-like shaped ever, allows the banking control.....	None
Adjustment of the angle of inclination of airplanes' wings E. 22792/77 hGm 666 139 Patent application occured (E. 21933 XI/77 h8) but was rejected.	18.10.1916 (a) 20.10.1922 (l)	t.m.t. the wing spar can be adjusted or fixed mechanically on adjustable screws within the different necessary banking angles in flight by threads and nuts. Controlling equipment about scale.	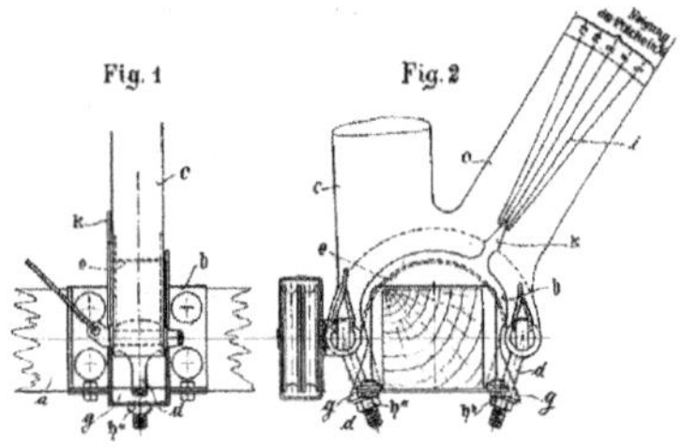 Fig. 1 Fig. 2

Utility Patent			
Content **Registered-number** **File number**	**(a) signed in** **(e) grated** **(zg) withdrawn** **(z) rejected** **(l) defunct**	**Description of the Claims** **("t.m.t." = " ... thereby marked that...)**	**Fig.** **(Remark: The drawings originate from a survey of the Euler-Werke, source: Bundesarchiv Koblenz, Signature N1103)**
Buffer-lake axis bearing for aircraft chassis E. 22796/77 hGm 664 427 Patent application occured (E. 21934 XI/77 h4) but was rejected.	19.10.1916 (a) 21.10.1922 (l)	t.m.t. pressure and pull or buffer springs are arranged one above or below the other, mutually, without use of rubber, and act on the pitch or path length of the springs...	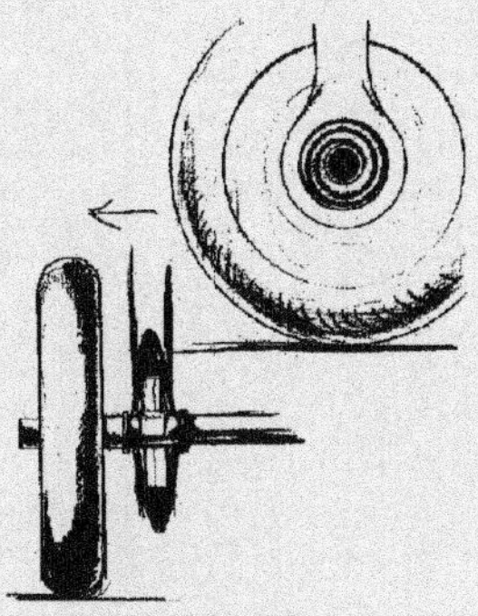
Regulation device for rotation engines in airplanes for the setting of the engine axis in latzeral, horizontal and vertical direction E. 22834/77 hGm 656 886	11.11.1916 (a) 14.11.1919 (l)	t.m.t. engine shaft is moveable on a crossbeam and pivotable hanged on a beam and can be adjusted by on any length adjustable beam struts by means of screw thread, nut or in another way laterally, horizontally and vertically.	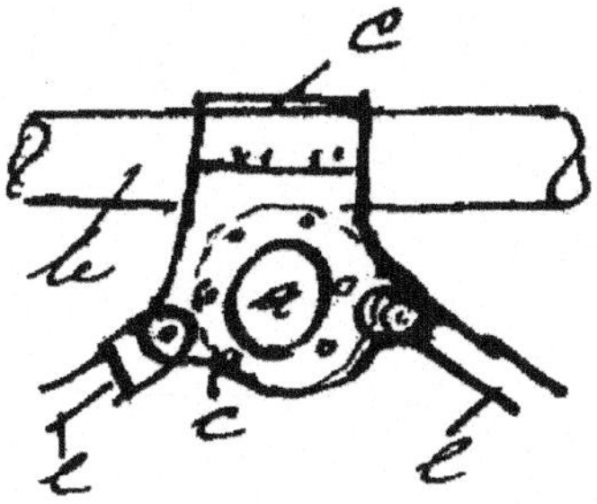
Revolution counter connection for airplanes E. 22331/42 r Gm 644 480	06.03.1916 (a) 08.03.1919 (l)	t.m.t. the end of the airframe, the dampening surface with height control and the rudder are rammed simultaneously with a thrust clasp and the rudder is mounted in square connections, which connect or clotures the parts of the controls with the end of the airframe and it links the rudder with the end of the airframe to move the tails shoe.	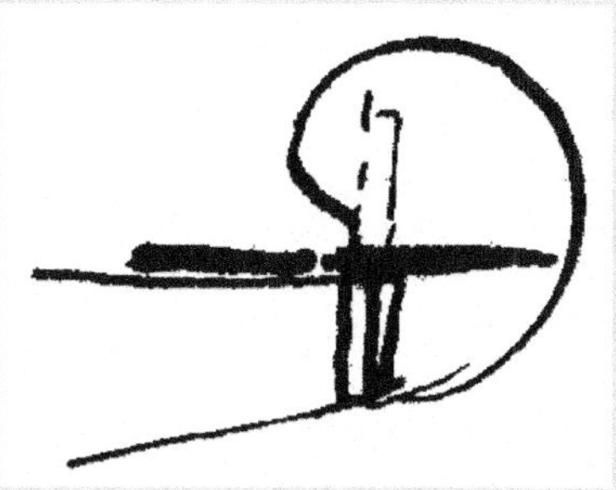
Revolution counter connection for airplanes E. 22331/42 r Gm 644 480	06.03.1916 (a) 08.03.1919 (l)	t.m.t. the spring between both engine parts of engine and revolution counter are so arranged in a sheath, that it transfers the impetus elastically on the revolution counter during turning on, the change of the number of revolutions and blowbacks of the engine.	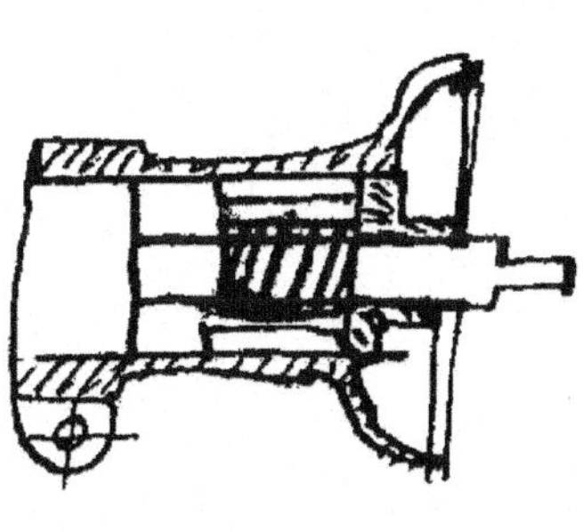

Utility Patent			
Content **Registered-number** **File number**	**(a) signed in** **(e) grated** **(zg) withdrawn** **(z) rejected** **(l) defunct**	**Description of the Claims** **("t.m.t." = " ... thereby marked that...)**	**Fig.** **(Remark: The drawings originate from a survey of the Euler-Werke, source: Bundesarchiv Koblenz, Signature N1103)**
Fuel regulation for carburettor, especially for rotating engines on airplanes E. 23019/46 bGm 690 210	10.03.1917 (a) 10.10.1918 (e) 14.03.1920 (l)	t.m.t. according to the different influences of the air and the weather the number of revolutions that is achieved with a certain amount of fuel is displayed on different scales so, that within the division of each scale the air and weather influences in question are accounted for.	see DRP 303 865
All-around guided moveable tail skid for airplanes E. 22366/77 hGm 672 089	15.09.1917 (a) 18.09.1920 (l)	t.m.t. tail skid shoe and the tail skid jolt tube are cushioned with one and the same spiral spring.	see DRP 309 219
Patents			
Airplane with machine-gunner DRP 248 601	24.07.1910 (e)	t.m.t. the machine-gun with its barrell is fixed installed in front of the pilot's seat in the chassis, so that the aiming merely occurs by the elevation and rudder of the airplane and the recoil acts in the direction of flight.	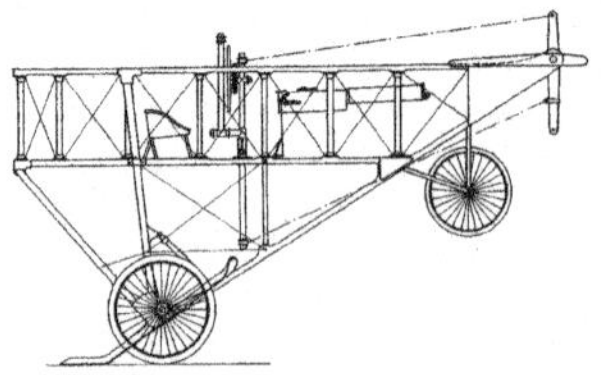
Airming device for airplane with fixed installed machine-gun after patent 248 601. addition to patent 248 601 DRP 258 918	02.04.1912 (e)	t.m.t. on the front part of the chassis are two aiming devices, each including rear and front sight, fixed installed, by which the upper one is adjusted to the higher and aft sitting pilot, the lower one to deeper sitting passenger, who has to operate the MG...	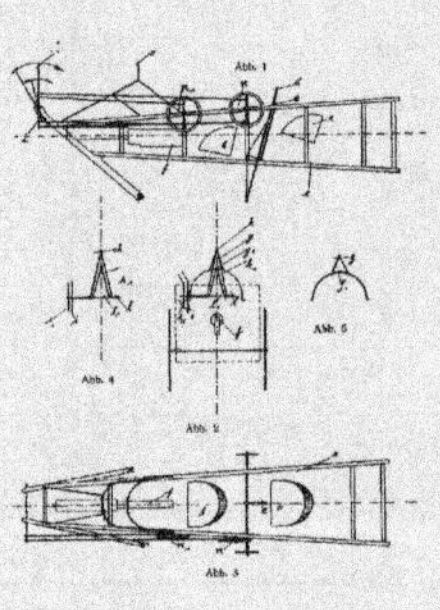

Patent			
Content **Registered-number** **File number**	**(a) signed in** **(e) grated** **(zg) withdrawn** **(z) rejected** **(l) defunct**	**Description of the Claims** **("t.m.t." = " ... thereby marked that...)**	**Fig.** **(Remark: The drawings originate from a survey of the Euler-Werke, source: Bundesarchiv Koblenz, Signature N1103)**
Bracing of aeroplane wings E. 16384 XI/77 h5 DRP 249 177	24.11.1910 (a) 02.03.1915 (f)	t.m.t. there are mutually directed little supports arranged one above the other and in the middle between two supported places of laying parts of two similar airplane parts, and their tips are not only connected with the next located stiffening points but also under themselves with tension wires.	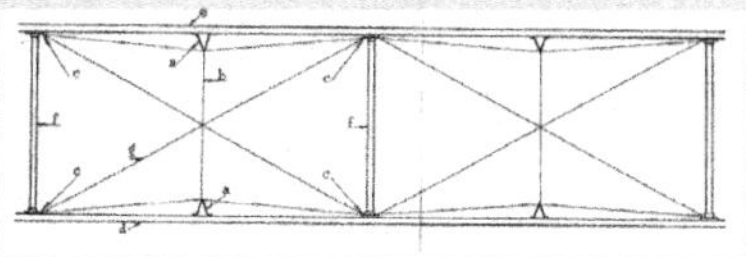
Onesided covered wings E. 16299 XI/77 h5 DRP 246 371	21.10.1910 (a) 21.03.1912 (e) 01.05.1915 (f)	t.m.t. they are covered between the curved woods and the rib-bands from the anterior to the rear carrying frame to relieve the the covering of the wings and to prevent their bulging upward. Bands across about one another or in a slanting line...	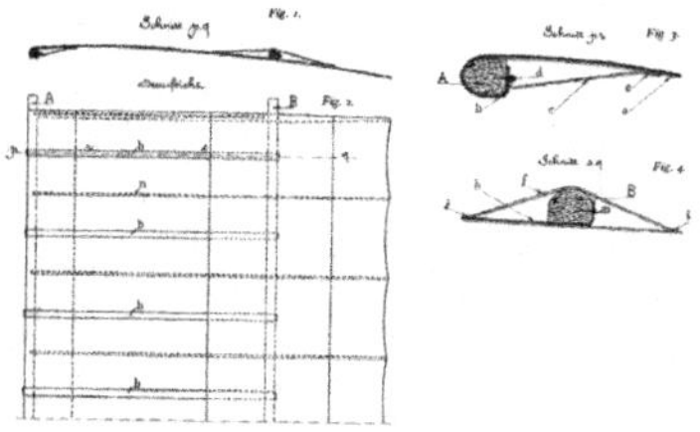
Controls for airplanes with an on all sides moveable lever that is causing the control of the elevation and banking E. 16139 XI/77 h5 DRP 249 176	04.05.1910 (a) 22.04.1914 (e) 10.12.1919 (f)	t.m.t. on one axis of rotation of this lever is a second lever that causes the steering to the sides arranged in a way that both levers can act independently from each other to cause steering to the sides and banking, but both together and each one alone can cause elevation.	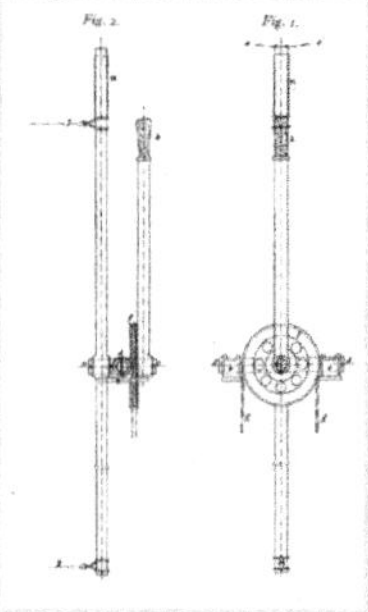
Device for the connection of tension wires, especially for monoplanes E. 17193 XI/77 h8	22.07.1911 (a) 24.05.1912 (z)	t.m.t. in particular various tension wires are fastened in a two-part metal clip, which reach around the strut serving as fixture or that kind and which both parts are connected by screws...	without

Patent			
Content **Registered-number** **File number**	**(a) signed in** **(e) grated** **(zg) withdrawn** **(z) rejected** **(l) defunct**	**Description of the Claims** **("t.m.t." = " ... thereby marked that...)**	**Fig.** **(Remark: The drawings originate from a survey of the Euler-Werke, source: Bundesarchiv Koblenz, Signature N1103)**
Starting-up rack for flight machines with traversing wheels E. 17187 XI/77 h4	28.07.1911 (a) 11.12.1912 (z)	... and in front of them auxiliary wheels, the auxiliary wheels are so arranged that they touch the ground in the same moment if the apparatus is rolling on the ground and tilting forward und they prevent further tilting, while the apparatus has reached the most favourable position of the main wings to achive the highest speed...	without
Starting-up rack for flight machines which can be easily separated from the wings E. 17833 XI/77 h2 DRP 267 072	27.02.1912 (a) 17.04.1913 (e) 04.02.1919 (f)	Airplane, its wing scaffolding on one hand and airframe of as well as chassis on the other hand in itself closed and from each other independent parts form the like, the chassis jutting forwardly is pushed from ahead in the wing scaffold and only the most forward of its 4 main longerons below in the centre is divided ... and is resting on the chassis...	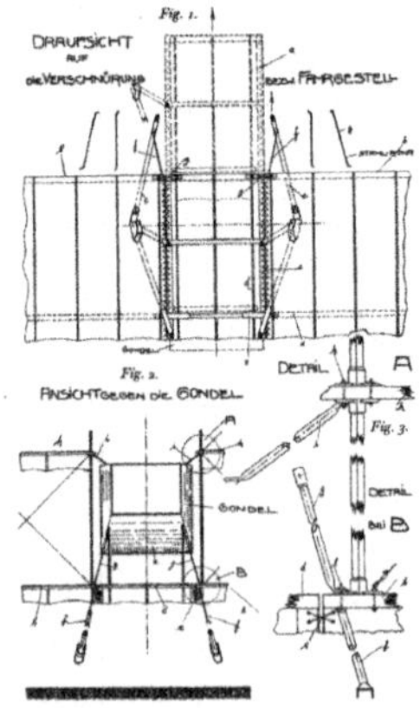
Combined height-, rudder- and banking control for flight machines E. 18284 XI/77 h5 DRP 275 825	26.07.1912 (a) 28.07.1912 (e) 31.10.1919 (f)	t.m.t. the control lever with two auxilary levers rests outside of the pilot's gondola b, b1 is connected like a joint parallelogram by the rods a, c connected in a manner that the auxilary levers, that are connected with the wire cables which lead to the control surfaces, join every vibe of the control lever in the same manner.	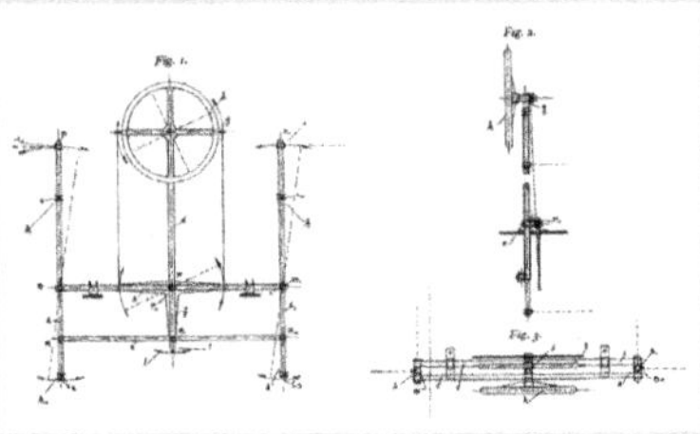

Patent			
Content **Registered-number** **File number**	**(a) signed in** **(e) grated** **(zg) withdrawn** **(z) rejected** **(l) defunct**	**Description of the Claims** **("t.m.t." = " ... thereby marked that...)**	**Fig.** **(Remark: The drawings originate from a survey of the Euler-Werke, source: Bundesarchiv Koblenz, Signature N1103)**
Combined height-, rudder- and banking control for E. 17944 XI/77 h 2	23.03.1912 (a) 26.08.1912 (z)	t.m.t. the hand wheel f stands vertically and is fixed on the upper end of the lever a. Lever a is fixed laterally moveable on the axis c, which is rigidly connected with the lever e on the sides of the apparatus that is directly moving the height control, so that the forward and backward moves of the first lever a are also made by the two sideward levers e, however the sideward move remains without influence.	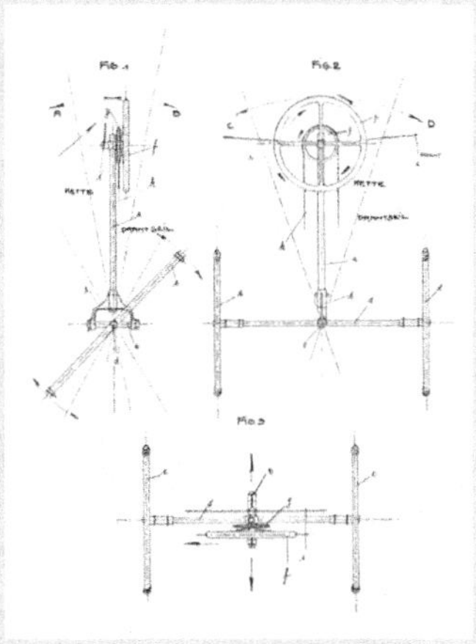
Multiplane with foldable ends of the wings E. 17726 XI/77 h 8 DRP 268 368 with addition DRP 272 770	22.01.1912 (a) 25.09.1913 (e) 12.05.1915 (f)	t.m.t. the uppermost folding surface is articulated connected with the one laying below by solid rods, while the second uppermost folding surface and by tension wires with the upper solid wing and the lowest solid part of the airplane as well as the deeper laying folding surfaces...	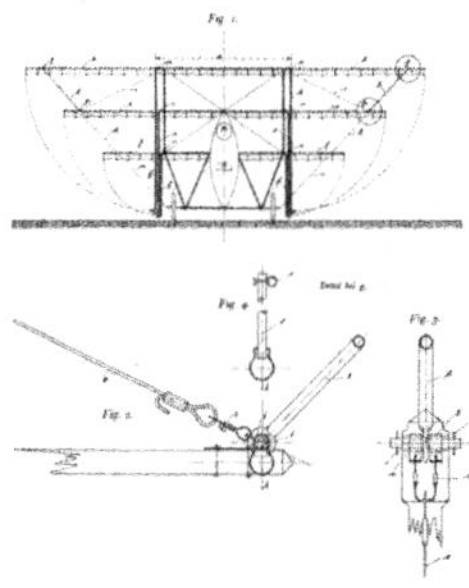
Banking control for aurplanes with onesided extension or shortening of the wings E. 18198 XI/77 h 5	26.06.1912 (a) 21.04.1914 (z)	t.m.t. the lifting of one side by the enlargement of the wing on this side and the reduction on the other side is caused and that the enlargement is caused by the shifting of the wing (for biplanes and multiplanes the upper wing b or the wings).	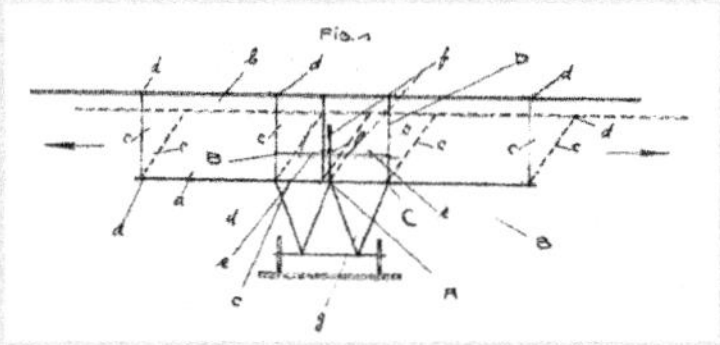
Seat upholstery for airplanes E. 18489 XI/77 h 8 DRP 272 786	28.09.1912 (a) 14.01.1914 (e) 1919 (f)	t.m.t. 1. one or several tyres d are laid around the pilot's or passenger seat, which carry pneumatic tyres c on the inner side and 2. these tyres are connected elastic by rubber bands e with the pilot's gondola, both with for the purpose to catch the pilot or passenger softly after a hard landing.	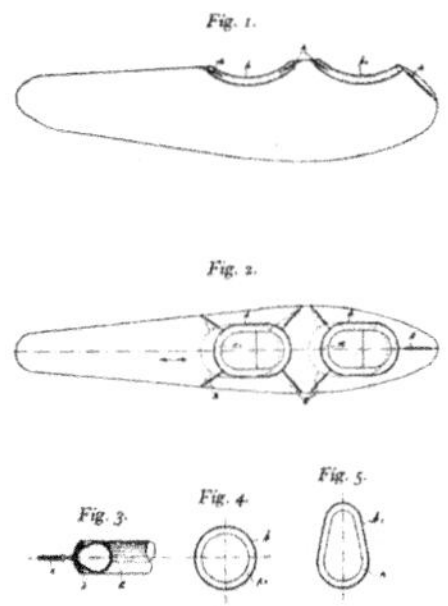

Patent			
Content **Registered-number** **File number**	**(a) signed in** **(e) grated** **(zg) withdrawn** **(z) rejected** **(l) defunct**	**Description of the Claims** **("t.m.t." = " ... thereby marked that...)**	**Fig.** **(Remark: The drawings originate from a survey of the Euler-Werke, source: Bundesarchiv Koblenz, Signature N1103)**
Radiator with shifted cooling ribs, especially for flight machines E. 19030 XI/77 h 8	20.03.1913 (a) 16.04.1914 (z)	t.m.t. die colling ribs are shifted for the purpose to achieve this form and all lay with the flat side parallel to the direction of the movement of the vehicle, so that the wind can freely flow between the plenum.	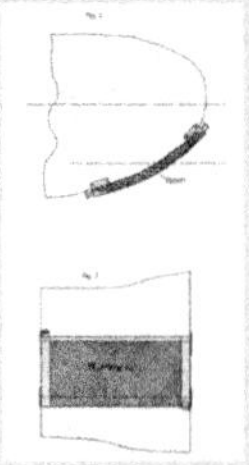
Frame for airplane's wings E. 19075 XI/77 h 8 DRP 281 299	04.04.1913 (a) 12.09.1914 (e) 02.06.1916 (f)	t.m.t. single incomparable thick struts can put through jumbled and the ends can be put in the rim struts and the coherence is achieved by diagonaly running tension wires. Tension wires run through the whole system, the ends are fixed on two rim struts each with grommets...	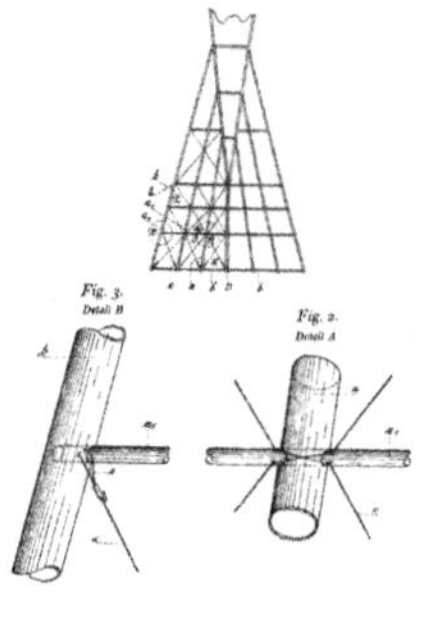
Pedal control for airplanes E. 19196 XI/77 h5 DRP 281 496	10.05.1913 (a)	... with which the pedal by means of an articulated fixed inter-lever is grasping an adjustable shaft, t.m.t. pedal that is built for the hosting of the whole foot is supported by a role, which is sliding on a support if the pedal is going up.	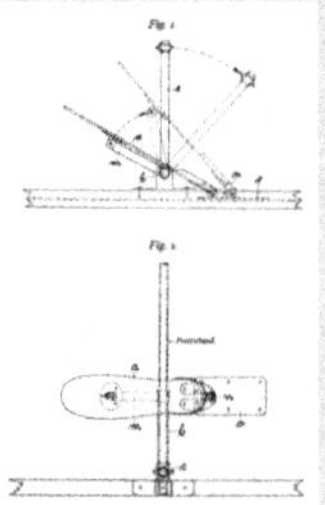
Turnbuckle, especially for flight machines E. 19642 XII/47 d DRP 288 619	30.09.1913 (a) 05.10.1915 (e) 12.09.1919 (f)	t.m.t. the fork screw of the slotted spring pin f, f1 which is touching the wire ends is divided and the ends of the bolts d, d1 which are provided with a counter thread are connected with each other by an auxilliary turnbuckle a, this permits a separation and composing of the span connection without change of the setting...	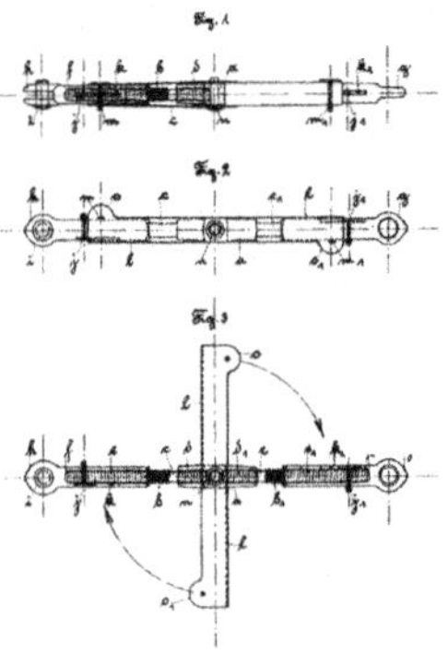

Patent			
Content **Registered-number** **File number**	**(a) signed in** **(e) grated** **(zg) withdrawn** **(z) rejected** **(l) defunct**	**Description of the Claims** **("t.m.t." = " ... thereby marked that...)**	**Fig.** **(Remark: The drawings originate from a survey of the Euler-Werke, source: Bundesarchiv Koblenz, Signature N1103)**
Hinge for the connection of airplanes surfaces E. 19692 XI/77 h8 DRP 276 062	15.10.1913 (a) 04.04.1914 (e) 09.12.1919 (f)	t.m.t. the edge cross-beam of one surface a has a channel d over its lenght and is shifted into a tube c in such a way that an hollow cavitiy is created between the mentioned channel and the wall of the tube, in which - through the slots of the cladding tube - lugs f rise up, that can be fastened in the known manner with screws g and nuts h or suchalike. At the cross-beam b of the other sureface are fastened...	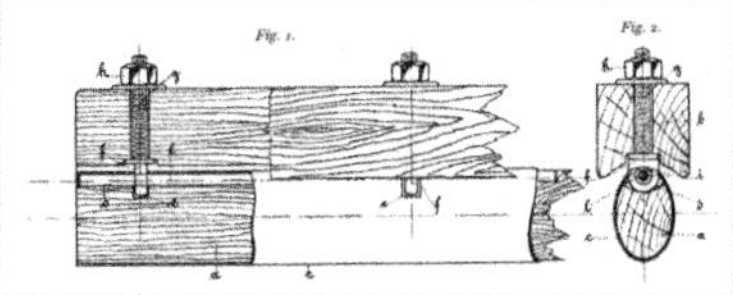
Machine-gun arrangement for airplanes E. 21289 XI/77 h8 DRP 299 699	04.10.1915 (a) 20.04.1916 (e) 01.12.1919 (z)	t.m.t. the machine-gun support is fixed – additional to a pivot – at the rim of the airframe on a shiftable and swingable to all sides arm of changeable length in the middle of the airframe in flight direction.	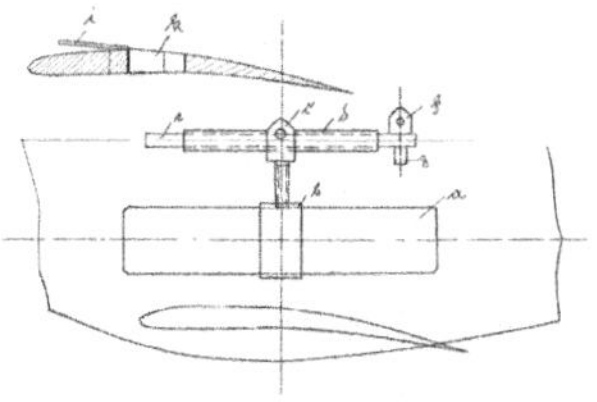
Machine-gun arrangement for airplanes, additional patent to D.R.P. 248 601 and auxilliary patent 258 918 E. 21637 XI/77 h8	19.04.1916 (a) 05.04.1918 (zg)	t.m.t. a fixed firing second, third etc. MG in an airplane is operated concerning the airming so as in the additional patent 258918. The fixed firing 2. and further MG, can according to the more growing or shortening distance to the target, be adjusted with the muzzle more to the MG operated by the pilot or away (from this men) and then be fixed. Aiming after the principle of patent 248 601.	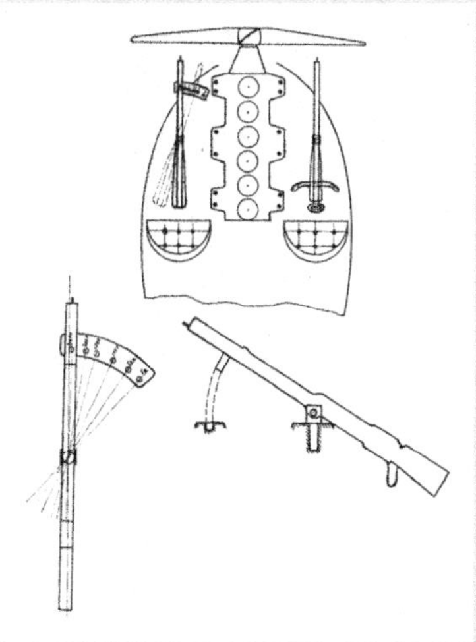

Patent			
Content **Registered-number** **File number**	**(a) signed in** **(e) grated** **(zg) withdrawn** **(z) rejected** **(l) defunct**	**Description of the Claims** **("t.m.t." = " ... thereby marked that...)**	**Fig.** **(Remark: The drawings originate from a survey of the Euler-Werke, source: Bundesarchiv Koblenz, Signature N1103)**
Fuel regulation for carburettor, especially for rotary engines of airplanes E. 22213 I/46 b2 DRP 303 865	10.03.1917 (a) 13.03.1919 (l)	t.m.t. according to the different influence of the air and the weather the achieved number of revolutions by a certain amount of fuel is displayed on different scales so that within the division of the scale the relevant air and weather influences are accounted for.	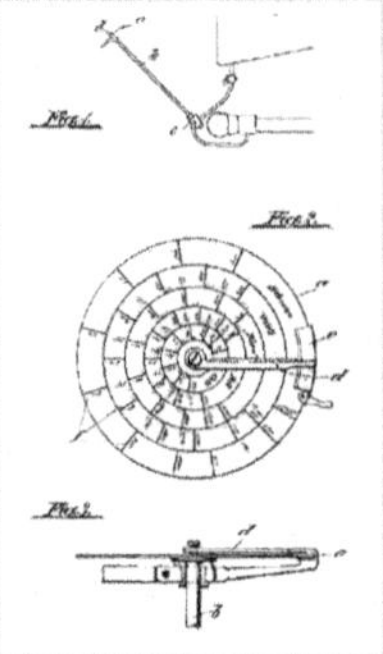
On all sides controlled, moveable tail skid for airplanes E. 22593 XI/77 h4 DRP 309 219	15.09.1917 (a) 17.09.1917 (e)	t.m.t. by means of one and the same spiral spring through a tube the slipping skid is spring-cushioned horizontaly and vertically.	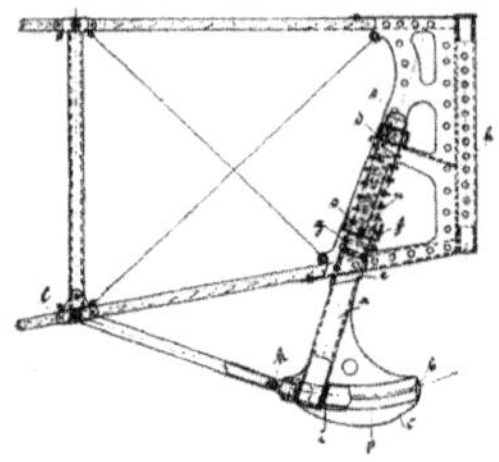
Airplanes, whose wings are adjustable on the horizontal level parallel to the engine axis E. 23180 XI/72 h8	07.05.1918 (a) 27.01.1920 (f)	t.m.t. cell shafts and tombstone stand firm, so that the tension cable experience no change of the shift of the wings, also during simultaneous adjustments of the angle of incidence. Shift of the wings is separately or simultaneously possible by hand in flight or when standing...	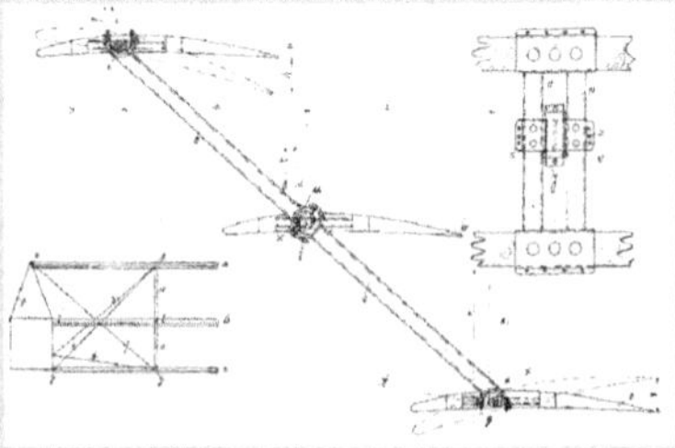

Appendix 3: Contract

... Pf. in Marken entwertet.
... zur Hauptausfertigung:
... a. M., den 15. JAN. 1913
... Hauptzollamt.

3 M. – Pf. in Marken entwertet.
Desgl. zur Hauptausfertigung: 68 M
Frankfurt a. M., den 15. JAN. 1913
Königliches Hauptzollamt.

Becker
z. N

B 74/12.

Es sollen als Stempel verwendet werden:

zur Hauptausfertigung .... M.

zur Nebenausfertigung .... M.

zur Sicherheitsleistung .... M.

The English translation for this starts on page 312.

Vertrag.

Zwischen der ~~Versuchs-Abteilung der Verkehrstruppen in Schöneberg-Berlin, Siegfriedstraße 2,~~ Fliegertruppe und den Euler-Werken Frankfurt a/M.

wird gemäß G. J. IIc 14683.12.v.19.10.12. / Jluk. IIc 11317.12.v.22.10.12.

vorbehaltlich der Bestätigung durch die ~~General-~~Inspektion des Militär-~~Verkehrs~~ Luft-und Kraftfahrwesens nachstehender Vertrag auf Grund freihändiger Vergebung

geschlossen.

1.

Die Firma Euler-Werke Frankfurt a/M.

verpflichtet sich, an die ~~Versuchs-Abteilung der Verkehrstruppen,~~ Fliegertruppe und zwar frei Flugplatz Darms

nachgenannte Gegenstände für die daneben gesetzten Preise zum 1.1.1913

zu liefern: Ein Euler-Flugzeug neueste Type komplett mit 100 P.S. Argus-Motor einschl. sämtl. motorischen Teile, Jnstrumente, Ersatzteile und Werkzeuge zum Preise von 20 000 Mark, in Worte „ Zwanzigtausend Mark ".

2.

Innerhalb von 14 Tagen nach Bestätigung dieses Vertrages durch die ~~General~~ Inspektion des Militär Luft- und Kraftfahr- ~~Verkehrs~~wesens hat die Firma eine Sicherheitsleistung von 1000 Mark, wörtlich: - Eintausend Mark ". bei der Kassenverwaltung der ~~Versuchs-Abteilung der Verkehrstruppen~~ Fliegertruppe zu hinterlegen.

3.

Die diesem Vertrage angehefteten allgemeinen, besonderen und technischen Vertragsbedingungen (Beil. 1— 3) haben dieselbe Kraft, als wenn sie im Vertrage selbst aufgeführt wären.

4.

Beide Teile haben den in zweifacher Ausfertigung aufgestellten Vertrag zum Zeichen der Genehmigung unterschrieben wie folgt:

Döberitz, ~~Schöneberg-Berlin,~~ den 30 ten November 1912.

Frankfurt a/M. den 21. ten November 1912.

Fliegertruppe

~~Versuchs-Abteilung der Verkehrstruppen.~~

Der Unternehmer.

[Signature]

Lohmann.

Major und Kommandeur.

Bestätigt!

Schöneberg, den 6. Januar 1913.

Inspektion des Militär Luft und Kraftfahrwesens.

KÖNIGL. PREUSS. INSPEKTION DES MILITÄR- LUFT- U. KRAFT-FAHRWESENS.

Messing

Generalmajor und Inspekteur.

Beilage 1.

Nationale.

I. Allgemeine Angaben.

1. Firma: Euler - Werke Frankfurt a/M.
2. Anschaffungsjahr und Tag: 1 Januar 1913.
3. Anschaffungspreis und Verfügung: M. 20 000 .-
4. Typ: Euler. Motor vorn angeordnet Höhensteuer hinten.

II. Motor.

1. Motortype: Argus.
2. Fabriknummer:
3. Anzahl der Zylinder: 4 Cylinder
4. Gewicht des Motors: 180 kg.
5. Nominelle Leistung bei Touren: 93 P.S. bei 1210 Touren
6. Betriebsstoff: Benzin
7. Art des Vergasers: Spritzvergaser
8. Art der Zündung: Magnetelektrisch
9. Größte Vorzündung:
10. Bohrung:
11. Hub:
12. Art der Kurbelwellenlager:
13. Art der Kolbenstangenlager:
14. Art der Schmierung:
15. Kühlung: Wasser
16. Wassermenge:

III. Apparate

1. Hauptzelle: Euler
2. Schwanzzelle: eine Fläche
3. Ailerons resp. Verwindung: Ailerons
4. Höhensteuer: hinten
5. Fahrgestell: „Euler"

Fliegertruppe

Lehmann.

[illegible signature]

Fliegertruppe

(Dienststelle)

Beilage 2

zum Vertrage vom 30./21.ten November 1912.

über Lieferung von einem Euler-Doppeldecker

Allgemeine Vertragsbedingungen.

Gegenstand des Vertrages.

1. Der Gegenstand des Unternehmens bildet die im Vertrage zu bezeichnende Leistung. Im einzelnen bestimmt sich Art und Umfang der dem Unternehmer obliegenden Verpflichtungen nach den besonderen Leistungsbedingungen, Zeichnungen und sonstigen als zum Vertrage gehörig bezeichneten Unterlagen. Kann die Menge der zu liefernden Gegenstände nur ungefähr angegeben werden, so hat die Lieferung zu den angegebenen Preisen nach Maßgabe des Bedarfs zu erfolgen, gleichviel ob in der angegebenen Zeit die bezeichnete Menge nicht erreicht oder überschritten wird.

Berechnung der Vergütung.

2. Die dem Unternehmer zukommende Vergütung wird nach den wirklichen Leistungen unter Zugrundelegung der vertragsmäßigen Einheitspreise berechnet. Diese Einheitspreise sind auch maßgebend, wenn der Unternehmer, mit dem ein Vertrag abgeschlossen ist, gleichartige, im Kostenanschlage nicht vorgesehene Leistungen ausführt. Abweichungen hiervon sind zu begründen.

   Die Vergütung für Tagelohnarbeiten erfolgt nach den vertragsmäßig vereinbarten Lohnsätzen.

Versäumnisstrafen.

3. Eine im Vertrage bedungene Versäumnisstrafe gilt nicht für erlassen, wenn die verspätete Vertragserfüllung ganz oder teilweise ohne Vorbehalt angenommen worden ist. Eine tageweise zu berechnende Versäumnisstrafe für verspätete Ausführung bleibt für die in die Zeit einer Verzögerung fallenden Sonntage und allgemeinen Feiertage außer Ansatz.

Güte der Leistung.

4. Die Leistungen müssen den besonderen Bestimmungen des Vertrages entsprechen.

Unterlassung von Geschenken usw. an Angestellte.

5. Der Unternehmer erkennt ausdrücklich als ihm bekannt an, daß die Annahme von Geschenken oder geldwerter Vorteile von Unternehmern oder Lieferanten sämtlichen Angehörigen und Angestellten der Heeresverwaltung, mit Einschluß der nur mittelbar Angestellten, verboten ist. Er verpflichtet sich, weder selbst noch durch andere Personen — Geschäftsteilhaber, Angestellte usw. — den Angehörigen oder Angestellten der Heeresverwaltung Geschenke oder geldwerte Vorteile zu gewähren oder anzubieten und im Übertretungsfalle den vierfachen Betrag des Geschenkes als Vertragsstrafe zu zahlen.

Entziehung der Leistung.

6. Die Stelle, die den Zuschlag erteilt hat, ist berechtigt, den Vertrag aufzuheben, wenn sich nach seinem Abschlusse herausstellt, daß der Unternehmer vorher mit anderen Verabredungen behufs Enthaltung von der Verdingung oder sonst zum Schaden der Heeresverwaltung getroffen hatte. Dieselbe Stelle ist ferner befugt, dem Unternehmer die Arbeiten oder Lieferungen ganz oder teilweise zu entziehen, sowie den noch nicht vollendeten Teil auf seine Kosten ausführen zu lassen oder selbst für seine Rechnung auszuführen, wenn der Unternehmer gegen die nach Ziffer 5 und 8 übernommenen Verpflichtungen verstößt. Von der verfügten Entziehung wird dem Unternehmer durch eingeschriebenen Brief oder Brief gegen Behändigungsschein Eröffnung gemacht.

   Abschlagszahlungen können im Falle der Entziehung dem Unternehmer nur innerhalb desjenigen Betrages gewährt werden, der als sein sicheres Guthaben unter Berücksichtigung der entstandenen Gegenansprüche ermittelt ist.

Alfred Unger, Berlin C.2, Spandauerstr. 48.

Verpflichtungen der Bewerber auf Grund der eingereichten Angebote.

7. Werden verschiedenartige Gegenstände oder Leistungen gleichzeitig ausgeboten, so bleibt der Mindestfordernde für jeden einzelnen Gegenstand an sein Angebot gebunden.

Das gleiche gilt, wenn ihm nur für einzelne Sorten sonst gleichartiger Gegenstände der Lieferung oder nur für einen Teil der Leistungen der Zuschlag erteilt wird.

Eine Zurücknahme des Angebots aus dem Grunde, daß ihm nicht die gesamte Leistung usw. übertragen wird, ist ausgeschlossen, wenn der Bewerber nicht den Vorbehalt gemacht hat, sich nur bei Übertragung der gesamten ausgebotenen Leistung usw. an sein Gebot gebunden zu halten.

8. Die Unternehmer sind zur Geheimhaltung aller zu verarbeitenden Rohstoffe und der zu fertigenden Fabrikate verpflichtet, deren Zusammensetzung oder Konstruktion nicht bekannt werden soll, ferner der Bestellungen, die für den Kriegsfall vorgesehen oder als geheim zu behandeln bezeichnet sind, sowie der Abnahmevorschriften, Zeichnungen usw., die nicht im Buchhandel zu haben und ihnen als geheim zu halten bezeichnet sind. Insbesondere ist auch die Lieferung von Mustern, die für das deutsche Heer geliefert werden, an das Ausland oder an deutsche Firmen als Zwischenhändler verboten. Zuwiderhandlungen unterliegen, abgesehen von der gemäß Ziffer 6 festgesetzten Entziehung der Leistung, der gesetzlichen Bestrafung nach dem Gesetz gegen den Verrat militärischer Geheimnisse vom 3. Juli 1893 (R. G. Bl. S. 205 bis 208).

9. Für die ihnen zur Ausführung der Aufträge von der Heeresverwaltung gegen Empfangsschein leihweise übergebenen Zeichnungen, Vorschriften und anderweitigen Gegenstände sind die Unternehmer haftbar. Abzeichnungen und Abschriften dürfen nur mit Genehmigung der vertragschließenden Dienststelle gefertigt werden und sind an diese oder an das Abnahmekommando nach Beendigung der Leistung usw. abzugeben.

Verpflichtung der verdingenden Dienststelle.

10. Die verdingende Dienststelle übernimmt die Verpflichtung, vor etwaiger Aufhebung der Verdingung die Leistung an keinen Unternehmer zu vergeben, der an dem Verdingungsverfahren nicht beteiligt ist.

Diese Aufhebung kann aber ohne weiteres und ohne Angabe von Gründen erfolgen, solange noch nicht der Zuschlag erteilt ist.

11. Die Annahme eines Gebots und die daraus für die Heeresverwaltung gegen den gewählten Unternehmer hervorgehenden Rechtsverbindlichkeiten treten daher erst mit Erteilung des Zuschlages ein.

Übertragbarkeit des Vertrages.

12. Ohne Zustimmung der Aufsichtsbehörde darf der Unternehmer seine vertraglichen Verpflichtungen nicht auf andere übertragen.

13. Die verdingende Dienststelle hat das Recht, von dem Vertrage zurückzutreten, wenn der Unternehmer vor Erfüllung des Vertrages in Konkurs verfällt.

14. Auch kann die verdingende Dienststelle von dem Vertrage zurücktreten, wenn das Guthaben des Unternehmers ganz oder teilweise mit Arrest belegt oder gepfändet wird. Wegen der in diesem Falle zu gewährenden Abschlagszahlungen finden die Bestimmungen in Ziffer 6 sinngemäße Anwendung.

Für den Fall, daß der Unternehmer stirbt, bevor der Vertrag vollständig erfüllt ist, hat die verdingende Dienststelle die Wahl, ob sie das Vertragsverhältnis mit seinen Erben fortsetzen oder als aufgelöst betrachten will.

15. Macht die Dienststelle von den ihr nach Ziffer 13 und 14 zustehenden Rechten Gebrauch, so teilt sie dies dem Unternehmer, dem Konkursverwalter oder den Erben des Unternehmers mittels eingeschriebenen Briefes mit.

Kosten und Stempel.

16. Briefe und Depeschen, die den Abschluß und die Ausführung des Vertrages betreffen, werden beiderseits portofrei gesandt. Portokosten für Geld- und sonstige Sendungen, die im ausschließlichen Interesse des Unternehmers erfolgen oder durch seine Schuld notwendig geworden sind (Mahnbriefe, Beanstandungen usw.), trägt dieser.

17. Die Kosten des Vertragsstempels trägt der Unternehmer nach den gesetzlichen Bestimmungen. Auch diejenigen Stempelbeträge sind von dem Unternehmer zu zahlen, die von der Steuerbehörde etwa nachträglich gefordert werden.

Die übrigen Kosten des Vertragsabschlusses trägt jeder Teil zur Hälfte.

18. Die Kosten der Verpackung trägt der Unternehmer.

19. Zur Sicherung der Erfüllung der vertraglichen Verbindlichkeiten und für jeden Nachteil, der der Heeresverwaltung dadurch erwächst, daß der Vertrag in irgend einer Beziehung vom Unternehmer nicht erfüllt wird, kann eine Sicherheitsleistung gefordert werden. Sicherheitsleistung.

Sicherheit kann in barem Gelde, mündelsicheren Wertpapieren, Sparkassenbüchern oder sicheren — gezogenen — Wechseln geleistet werden.

20. Zu den annehmbaren Wertpapieren gehören:

1. Schuldverschreibungen, die vom Reich oder von einem Bundesstaat ausgestellt sind;
2. Schuldverschreibungen, deren Verzinsung vom Reich oder von einem Bundesstaate gewährleistet ist;
3. Rentenbriefe der zur Vermittelung der Ablösung von Renten in Preußen bestehenden Rentenbanken;
4. Schuldverschreibungen, die von einer deutschen kommunalen Körperschaft oder von der Kreditanstalt einer solchen Körperschaft oder mit Genehmigung der staatlichen Aufsichtsbehörde von einer Kirchengemeinde oder einem kirchlichen Verband ausgestellt und entweder von seiten der Inhaber kündbar sind oder einer regelmäßigen Kündigung unterliegen;
5. die mit staatlicher Genehmigung ausgegebenen Pfandbriefe und gleichartigen Schuldverschreibungen einer Kreditanstalt der im Artikel 73, § 1, Abs. 2 des Ausführungsgesetzes vom 20. September 1899 zum Bürgerlichen Gesetzbuche (G. S. S. 177 ff.) bezeichneten Art;
6. die auf den Inhaber lautenden Schuldverschreibungen, die von einer Preußischen Hypotheken-Aktien-Bank auf Grund von Darlehen an Preußische Körperschaften des öffentlichen Rechts oder von Darlehen, für die eine solche Körperschaft die Gewährleistung übernommen hat, ausgegeben sind.

21. Eine Außerkurssetzung von Schuldverschreibungen auf den Inhaber findet nicht statt.

22. Mit den Wertpapieren sind die Zins-, Renten-, Gewinnanteil- und Erneuerungsscheine zu hinterlegen. Die innerhalb des Leistungs- usw. Zeitraumes fälligen Zins-, Renten- und Gewinnanteilscheine können dem Unternehmer belassen werden.

23. Reichs- und Staatspapiere sind zum Kurswert anzunehmen, wenn dieser den Nennwert übersteigt, die übrigen annahmefähigen Wertpapiere sind zum Nennwert zu berechnen, doch ist die verdingende Dienststelle befugt, in besonderen Fällen Sicherheitsleistung unter Berechnung des Kurswertes zu verlangen.

24. Wechsel bieten nur dann genügende Sicherheit, wenn sie die Unterschriften von mindestens zwei als zahlungsfähig bekannten, unbeteiligten Personen oder Firmen tragen.

25. Werden als Sicherheit Sparkassenbücher hinterlegt, so wird als Sperrvermerk auf das Buch gesetzt:

> „Es wird ersucht, auf dieses Buch außer Zinserträgen keine Zahlung zu leisten."

Bei Wiederherausgabe der Sparkassenbücher ist der Sperrvermerk wie folgt aufzuheben:

> „Sperrvermerk vom . . . . 19 . . wird hiermit aufgehoben."

Den Vermerken ist Ort, Datum, Bezeichnung der Dienststelle, Unterschrift und Dienststempel beizufügen.

26. Hinterlegtes bares Geld wird nicht verzinst.

27. Die Sicherheit wird in der Regel in der in Ziffer 41 bezeichneten Kasse hinterlegt und bleibt bis zur vollständigen Erfüllung des Vertrages in ihrem Verwahrsam.

Auf Verlangen der verdingenden Dienststelle ist der Unternehmer aber auch verpflichtet, Sicherheit in der Weise zu bestellen, daß er sie entweder zu dem Girokonto der

Reichsbank einzahlt oder Wertpapiere in dem Kontor für Wertpapiere bei der Reichsbank oder bei der Preußischen Zentralgenossenschaftskasse niederlegt.

Den ihm erteilten Hinterlegungsschein hat er der verdingenden Dienststelle mit einer an die Reichsbank usw. gerichteten, in zweifacher Ausfertigung aufgesetzten Erklärung zu übergeben, daß die hinterlegten Werte jener Dienststelle verpfändet und nur gegen ihre alleinige Bescheinigung auszuhändigen sind.

28. Dem Unternehmer ist auch gestattet, bei der General-Militärkasse in Berlin einen größeren Bestand an annahmefähigen Wertpapieren zu hinterlegen, um damit seiner Pflicht der Sicherheitsleistung gegenüber mehreren Dienststellen zu genügen. Er empfängt hierüber einen Hinterlegungsschein.

29. Ob der von der einzelnen Behörde in Anspruch zu nehmende Teilbetrag der Gesamthinterlegung für sie frei ist und für sie als haftbar erklärt werden kann, bescheinigt auf Antrag des Unternehmers die General-Militärkasse der Dienststelle durch die Erklärung, daß von der Gesamtsicherheitsleistung des Unternehmers ein Teilbetrag von . . ℳ für sie verpfändet ist.

30. Der Verkauf dieses Teilbetrages erfolgt auf Ersuchen der Dienststelle durch die General-Militärkasse.

31. Die Teilsicherheitsleistung oder ihr übrig gebliebener Teil wird verfügbar durch die Freigabe der Dienststelle. Der pfandfreie Teil der Gesamtsicherheitsleistung kann von dem Unternehmer durch Austausch des alten Hinterlegungsscheines gegen einen neuen erhoben werden.

32. Beschränkt ein Unternehmer sein Geschäft nur auf den Bereich eines Armeekorps, so hat die Gesamtsicherheitsleistung bei der Korpszahlungsstelle zu erfolgen. Im übrigen finden für diesen Fall vorstehende Bestimmungen dem Sinne nach Anwendung.

33. Die Zins- usw. Scheine werden so lange, als nicht eine Veräußerung der Wertpapiere zur Deckung entstandener Verbindlichkeiten in Aussicht genommen werden muß, an den Fälligkeitsterminen dem Unternehmer ausgehändigt, sofern sie ihm nicht bereits nach Ziffer 22 belassen sind. Den Umtausch der Erneuerungsscheine, die Einlösung und den Ersatz ausgeloster Wertpapiere besorgt die Kassenverwaltung auf Veranlassung des Unternehmers, der auch den durch Nichtbeachtung einer Auslosung entstehenden Schaden zu tragen hat. Für den Ersatz abgelaufener Wechsel hat der Unternehmer zu sorgen.

34. Wenn der Unternehmer in irgend einer Beziehung seinen Verbindlichkeiten nicht nachkommt, kann die Dienststelle zu ihrer Schadloshaltung auf dem einfachsten, gesetzlich zulässigen Wege die hinterlegten Wertpapiere und Wechsel veräußern oder einkassieren.

35. Wegen der Art des Pfandverkaufs verzichtet der Unternehmer auf die Beobachtung der Vorschriften der §§ 1234, 1236, 1237 Satz 2, 1238 und 1239 des B. G. B.

Die Rechte Dritter an der Sicherheitsleistung werden hierdurch nicht berührt.

36. Von dem Verkauf der Sicherheitsleistung und dem Ergebnis erhält der Besteller der der Sicherheitsleistung Nachricht.

37. Die Rückgabe der Sicherheit, soweit sie nicht für Verbindlichkeiten des Unternehmers in Anspruch zu nehmen ist, erfolgt spätestens 4 Wochen nach Erfüllung der ihm obliegenden Verpflichtungen oder, insoweit die Sicherheit zur Sicherung der Haftverpflichtung dient, spätestens 4 Wochen nach Ablauf der Haftpflichtzeit gegen Rückgabe des mit Empfangsbescheinigung versehenen Hinterlegungsscheines.

38. In Ermangelung anderweiter Verabredung gilt als bedungen, daß die Sicherheit in ganzer Höhe zur Deckung der Haftpflichtverbindlichkeiten einzubehalten ist.

ig. 39. Die Schlußzahlung erfolgt auf die vom Unternehmer einzureichende Kostenrechnung spätestens innerhalb 4 Wochen nach ihrer vollendeten Prüfung und Feststellung.

Abschlagszahlungen werden dem Unternehmer in angemessenen Fristen auf Antrag, nach Maßgabe des jeweils Geleisteten, bis zu der von der Dienststelle mit Sicherheit vertretbaren Höhe gewährt. Bleiben bei der Schlußabrechnung Meinungsverschiedenheiten bestehen, so soll dem Unternehmer das ihm unbestritten zustehende Guthaben gleichwohl nicht vorbehalten werden.

40. Vor Empfangnahme des als Restguthaben zur Auszahlung angebotenen Betrages muß der Unternehmer alle Ansprüche, die er aus dem Vertragsverhältnis über die von der Dienststelle anerkannten hinaus etwa noch zu haben meint, bestimmt bezeichnen und sich schriftlich vorbehalten, widrigenfalls die Geltendmachung dieser Ansprüche später ausgeschlossen ist. Verzicht auf spätere Geltendmachung aller nicht ausdrücklich vorbehaltenen Ansprüche.

41. Alle Zahlungen erfolgen an der Kasse der vertragschließenden oder der besonders bezeichneten Dienststelle. Verweigert der Empfangberechtigte die Annahme der Zahlung, so kann der Betrag bei der zuständigen Hinterlegungsstelle (Regierungshauptkasse) hinterlegt werden, um die Rechnungslegung nicht aufzuhalten. Zahlende Kasse.

In diesem Falle sind der Verwahrungsschein und die etwaigen Belege über geleistete Abschlagzahlungen vorläufig als Beleg für den Rechnungsbetrag anzusehen und der Kassenrechnung beizufügen.

42. Die in den besonderen Vertragbedingungen vorgesehene, in Ermangelung solcher nach den allgemeinen gesetzlichen Vorschriften sich bestimmende Frist für die dem Unternehmer obliegende Gewährleistung für die Güte der Leistungen beginnt mit dem Zeitpunkt ihrer Abnahme. Der § 460 Satz 2 und § 640 Abs. 2 des B. G. B. findet keine Anwendung, vielmehr haftet der Unternehmer für jeden Mangel unbeschränkt, auch wenn er infolge grober Fahrlässigkeit unbekannt geblieben oder bei der Abnahme nicht gerügt worden ist. Haftpflicht.

43. Die zu liefernden Gegenstände müssen von dem Unternehmer mit seinen Arbeitern und Einrichtungen im Inlande hergestellt sein. Auch ist inländisches Material zu verwenden, sofern nicht besondere Umstände dies ausschließen. Untersuchung und Abnahme der gelieferten und Bezahlung der abgenommenen Gegenstände.

Zivilarbeiter der verdingenden Dienststelle dürfen zur Erledigung von Leistungen usw. für die Militärverwaltung nicht verwendet werden.

Als Hersteller können nur solche Unternehmer angesehen werden, die geschlossene Fabrikationseinrichtungen als Eigentümer, Nießbraucher oder kraft eines sonstigen dinglichen Rechts oder als Mieter oder Pächter besitzen und für eigene Rechnung betreiben. Die Ermietung von Fabrikationseinrichtungen in Betrieben anderer gilt nicht als Beweis für die Eigenschaft als Hersteller.

Ein nachgewiesener Verstoß gegen diese Bestimmungen hat die Ausschließung solcher Unternehmer bei weiteren Vergebungen zur Folge.

44. Die Beschaffenheit und Menge wird von der Abnahmekommission geprüft.

Zu diesem Zweck und zur Beurteilung der Güte der verwendeten Rohstoffe und Einzelteile sind die mit der Untersuchung usw. beauftragten Personen berechtigt, in alle Stufen der Anfertigung Einsicht zu nehmen, wozu ihnen von dem Unternehmer das Betreten seiner Arbeitsräume usw. zu gestatten ist, wenn ihm nicht zur Wahrung eines Fabrikgeheimnisses besondere Vorbehalte zugestanden sind, die im Vertrage zum Ausdruck kommen müssen.

45. Bei Abnahme in der Fabrik usw. des Unternehmers hat dieser den entsprechend ausgestatteten Abnahmeraum, die erforderlichen Kräfte und Einrichtungen zur Handhabung, sowie den für Aufbewahrung des gesamten Materials benötigten Raum kostenlos zur Verfügung zu stellen. Bei abgeschiedener Lage der Abnahmestelle ist auch für vorschriftsmäßige Unterbringung und Verpflegung des Personals gegen Erstattung der für Quartier- und Naturalleistung gesetzlich vorgeschriebenen Gebührnisse durch die Unternehmer zu sorgen. Ist durch Verschulden des Unternehmers eine wiederholte Abnahme notwendig, so trägt er die Kosten.

46. Der Unternehmer kann zur Wahrnehmung seiner Interessen der Prüfung und Abnahme beiwohnen oder sich durch einen Bevollmächtigten vertreten lassen. Er kann hierbei Abstellungen unwesentlicher Mängel mit Zustimmung der Abnehmenden veranlassen. Seine Sache ist es, sich durch Anfrage darüber zu unterrichten, wann und wo die Prüfung stattfindet.

47. Wenn die Prüfung der Gesamtmenge einer Leistung usw. mit bedeutenden Kosten oder zu großem Zeitaufwand verknüpft ist — wie die chemische Untersuchung von Metallen und die Prüfung von Flüssigkeiten in verschiedenen Gefäßen —, so ist die Beurteilung eines Teils der Leistung usw., dessen Umfang die verdingende Dienststelle bestimmt, für die ganze Leistung usw. maßgebend.

48. Für die als brauchbar abgenommenen Gegenstände und Leistungen erfolgt die Bezahlung, ohne Abzug von Zwischenzinsen, bar oder im Wege des Giroverkehrs gegen vorschriftsmäßige und mit Empfangsbescheinigung versehene Rechnungen.

Auf die Reichsbank ausgestellte weiße Schecks sind von den Unternehmern als Zahlung anzunehmen, sofern es sich um Beträge von mindestens 300 Mark handelt und Überweisungen mittels roter Schecks oder Postgiro nicht Platz greifen. Die Reichsstempelabgabe für weiße Schecks hat der Unternehmer zu tragen.

Zahlungen über höhere Beträge als 800 Mark an auswärtige Unternehmer, die kein Girokonto bei der Reichsbank haben, werden im Wege des Postanweisungsverkehrs mittels mehrerer Postanweisungen auf Gefahr und Kosten der Empfänger bewirkt.

Über die Zahlungen sind besondere Empfangsscheine zu erteilen.

Unterläßt ein am Ort wohnender Unternehmer trotz ergangener Aufforderung die Abholung des fälligen Betrages an der Kasse, so muß er sich bei Zusendung durch die Post den Abzug des Portos gefallen lassen.

49. Beanstandete Stücke sind sofort nach endgültiger Unbrauchbarkeitserklärung, je nach den getroffenen Vereinbarungen, entweder gänzlich oder derart unbrauchbar zu machen, daß eine Wiedervorlage oder Weiterverwendung ausgeschlossen ist, oder sie sind durch deutliche Anbringung des Unbrauchbarkeitsstempels an einer oder mehreren Stellen zu kennzeichnen. Die Stempelung ist so anzubringen, daß sie ohne Änderung der Abmessungen des Stückes nicht entfernt werden kann.

50. Wenn diese Maßnahmen allein nicht genügende Gewähr gegen Wiedervorlage bieten, so sind die unbrauchbaren Stücke nach der Stempelung bis zur Beendigung des Abnahmegeschäfts vom Abnehmenden unter sicheren Verschluß zu nehmen.

51. Auf Antrag des Unternehmers kann die Unbrauchbarmachung oder Stempelung unterbleiben, wenn er die verworfenen Stücke, wie Ortscheite, Eisenbeschläge usw. anderweit verwenden kann.

Diese Stücke sind aber in ihrer Form leicht sichtbar und so zu verändern, daß sie für den ursprünglichen Zweck keine Verwendung mehr finden können, oder sie sind bis zur Erledigung des Abnahmegeschäfts vom Abnehmenden unter Verschluß zu bringen.

52. Werden gelieferte Gegenstände von der Abnahmekommission für unbrauchbar erklärt, so ist der Unternehmer verpflichtet, sie innerhalb der durch die besonderen Vertragsbedingungen festgesetzten Frist aus den ihm zur Ablieferung angewiesenen Räumen zu entfernen.

Unterläßt er dies, so werden nach Ablauf der Frist die zurückgestellten Gegenstände für seine Rechnung und Gefahr einem am Orte befindlichen Versandgeschäft zur Aufbewahrung oder Rücksendung übergeben.

53. Den Ersatz verworfener Gegenstände hat der Unternehmer innerhalb der durch die besonderen Bedingungen festgesetzten Frist zu leisten. Geschieht dies nicht, so ist die verdingende Dienststelle befugt, die Gegenstände zu jedem Preise auf Gefahr und Kosten des Unternehmers anderweit in Bestellung zu geben oder anzukaufen. Das gleiche Recht, und zwar ohne Mahnung und ohne Gewährung einer Nachfrist, steht der verdingenden Dienststelle zu, wenn die im Vertrage festgesetzten Lieferfristen von dem Unternehmer nicht innegehalten werden. Findet eine Ersatzbeschaffung statt, so ist für die entstehenden Mehrkosten die hinterlegte Sicherheitsleistung zu verwenden.

Es ist nur eine Ersatzleistung zulässig.

54. Werden für Rechnung des Unternehmers Gegenstände beschafft und sind sie billiger als zum Vertragspreise angekauft, so hat er keinen Anspruch auf den Unterschied zwischen diesen Preisen.

55. Über die aus dem Vertrage entspringenden Streitigkeiten entscheidet zunächst die General-Inspektion des Militär-Verkehrswesens. Der Entscheidung hat möglichst eine mündliche Erörterung mit dem Unternehmer vorauszugehen. Die Entscheidung gilt als anerkannt, wenn der Unternehmer, der bei der Mitteilung hierauf ausdrücklich hinzuweisen ist, nicht binnen 4 Wochen vom Tage der Zustellung ab schriftlich Widerspruch erhebt. Erst gegen die Entscheidung der General-Inspektion des Militär-Verkehrswesens können die ordentlichen Gerichte angerufen werden. Austrag von Streitigkeiten.

56. Der Streit berechtigt aber den Unternehmer nicht, die weitere Erfüllung seiner Vertragsverbindlichkeiten zu verweigern oder zu verzögern.

57. Für die aus dem Vertrage entspringenden Rechtsstreitigkeiten hat der Unternehmer als Kläger wie als Beklagter bei dem zuständigen Gericht, in dessen Bezirk die den Vertrag abschließende Dienststelle ihren Sitz hat, Recht zu nehmen.

Döberitz, den 30. November 1912. Frankfurt a/M., den 21. November 1912.

(Dienststelle:) Fliegertruppe

Der Unternehmer.

[signature]

Lehmann.

Major und Kommandeur.

Beilage 3.

B E S O N D E R E B E D I N G U N G E N.

I. Zelle: 1.) Das verwendete Material muß von erstklassiger Qualität sein; die gesamte Bauart muß dem augenblicklichen Stand der Technik entsprechen. Vor der Bespannung findet daher zur Prüfung eine Rohbauabnahme durch einen Offizier der Fliegertruppe statt.

2.) Die zerlegbaren Teile sind zu numerieren; entsprechend einer in doppelter Ausfertigung als Blaupause mitzuliefernden Skizze.

3.) Betriebsstoffbehälter dürfen nicht über den Motor angebracht sein.

4.) Windschutz ist anzubringen; besondere Sorgfalt ist auf Anbringung von Tourenzähler, Barometer, Uhr, Kartenrollapparat, Schauvorrichtung für Stand von Betriebsstoffen und Kühlwasser zu verwenden. Sämtliche Jnstrumente sollen vom Führer, Kartenrollapparat auch vom Bassagier zu beobachten sein.

5.) Am Bord des Flugzeuges ist das in der Anlage I aufgeführte Werkzeug unter zu bringen.

6.) Es sind 2 Sitze anzubringen.

7.) Auf Beobachtungsmöglichkeit ist sehr großer Wert zu legen; der Führer muß unmittelbar unter oder neben sich den Erdboden erblicken können.

II. Motor: 1.) Die Wahl des Motors bleibt der Firma überlassen; vor endgültiger Wahl des Motors ist das Einverständnis der Jnspektion einzuholen.

2.) Der Motor wird auf dem Versuchsstande der Firma in Gegenwart von Vertretern der Fliegertruppe einer 3 stündigen Bremsprobe unterworfen. Er muß hierbei 1.) 2 Stunden laufen. Die Tourenschwankungen dürfen 10 % nicht übersteigen. 2.) 1/2 Stunde mit 10 Grad Steigung und Vollgas. 3.) 1/2 Stunde mit 10 Grad Neigung und der geringsten

ihm

ihm möglichen Tourenzahl, die jedoch 500 Touren nicht übersteigen darf, unter sonst normalen Verhältnissen laufen. Jn das Bremsattest aufzunehmen sind die alle 15 Min. zu notierenden Angaben über:

a.) Tourenzahl, b.) Zugkraft, c.) Kühlwassertemparatur.

Vor und nach dem Versuch ist genaue Wägung des Benzins und Öls vorzunehmen, derart, daß völlige Klarheit über den Betriebsstoffverbrauch des Motors gewonnen wird. Das Spezifische Gewicht von Benzin und Öl ist zu messen. Während der Versuche müssen Öl- und Benzinzufuhr genau den Betriebsbedingungen und Einrichtungen des im Flugzeug eingebauten Motors entsprechen.

3.) Während der Versuche darf kein Aussetzen, keine Unregelmäßigkeiten und keine Veränderung der einzelnen Teile stattfinden.

4.) Nach Beendigung wird der Motor auseinandergenommen und genau geprüft. Hierbei sich zeigende Fehler oder Mängel sind vor endgültiger Abnahme durch den Fabrikanten zu beseitigen, können auch wenn der Motor den Anf-orderungen genügt hat, seine Abnahme ausschließen.

5.(Die Firma hat die Fliegertruppe eine Woche vorher von dem Zeitpunkt und Ort der Bremsprobe zu benachrichtigen und Vorsorge zu treffen, daß die Versuche in der angegebenen Weise ohne Zeitverlust ausgeführt werden können.

6.) Standmotore müssen besonderen Anlaßmagnet oder Batterie besitzen. Die Jnspektion behält sich vor, die Anbringung eines doppelten Kerzensatzes zu verlangen.

7.) Die Öl- und Benzinleitung muß völlige Sicherheit gegen Brüche durch Vibration gewähren. Reiner Gummischlauch darf nicht verwendet werden.

8.) Der Benzinbehölter muß Querwände und ein dem Führer zugängliches Ventil für augenblickliches, völliges Ablassen des Drucks besitzen. Druckventile und Manometer müssen den höchstzulässigen Druck entsprechen. Die Betriebsstoffbehälter werden einer Probe für 3 fachen Druck unterzogen.

9.)

9.) Sämtliche Hähne müssen gegen unbeabsichtigte Öffnen gesichert sein; die Sicherung darf absichtliches Öffnen nicht erschweren.

10.) Bei Tauch- und Schleuderschmierung muß eine Kontrolle des Ölstandes im Kurbelgehäuse, sowie Ölzufuhr während des Fluges möglich sein.

11.) Der Motor muß Auspuffstutzen und Vorwärmer besitzen.

12.) Über die Motorprüfung ist eine Verhandlung in dreifacher Ausfertigung aufzunehmen.

13.) Bei Motoren ausländischen Fabrikats ist ein Bremsattest beizubringen; die angegebenen Werte werden vor Abnahme auf dem Versuchsstande der Fliegertruppe nachgeprüft

III. Leistungen des Flugzeuges:

1.) Nutzlast einschl. Besatzung und Ballast: 200 kg.

2.) Aktionsradius : 250 km.

3.) Eigengeschwindigkeit: mindestens 80 km./Std.

4.) Steigfähigkeit: 500 m. in 15 Min. im Kreisflug gemessen.

5.) Anlauf nicht über 60 m.

6.) Auslauf nicht über 70 m.

IV. Abnahme des Flugzeuges:

1.) Vor dem Anstrich und dem Beziehen findet eine Rohbauabnahme statt; eine Verhandlung hierüber ist aufzunehmen.

2.) Der Ort der endgültigen Flugabnahme ist Darmstadt. Die Transportkosten sowie die Kosten für die Montage trägt der Fabrikant.

3.) Die Abnahme erfolgt durch eine Kommsission, das Beisein eines Vertreters der Firma ist freigestellt.

4.) Bei der Abnahme muß das mit einer Militärsteuerung ausgerüstete Flugzeug eine Stunde fliegen, gesteuert durch einen Piloten der Firma. Die Höhe von 500 m. muß in höchstens 15 Min. nach dem Start erreicht sein, und von den an Bord befindlichen 2 Barometern angezeigt werden. Unmittelbar nach Erreichung der 500 m. ist im Gleitflug auf ca. 100 m. herunterzugehen. Bis zur Landung darf nunmehr das

Flugzeug

Flugzeug eine Höhe von ca. 200 m. nicht mehr übersteigen. Die Landung hat im Gleitflug aus mindestens 100 m. Höhe mit abgestellter Zündung zu erfolgen.

5.) Falls das Flugzeug die geforderten Bedingungen innerhalb 30 Tagen seit der ersten Vorführung nicht erfüllt, behält sich die Jnspektion vor, die Anforderungen entsprechend dem Fortschritt der Technik zu erhöhen.

6.) Der Zeitpunkt der Vorführung ist 2 Tage voerher der Jnspektion und der Fliegertruppe mitzuteilen. Bei ungünstiger Witterung kann auf Wunsch des Unternehmers die Abnahme verschoben werden.

V. Das beigefügte Nationale ist von der Firma verant(wort)lich auszufüllen.

VI. Die Firma übernimmt die Verpflichtung einen bereits im Fliegen ausgebildeten Offizier auf Wunsch der Fliegertruppe auf neuen Typ im Fliegen auszubilden. Die Kosten hierfür sind im Kaufpreis einbegriffen.

VII. Jnstrumente: Es sind mitzuliefern:

1 Barometer

1 Uhr

1 Kartenrollapparat

1 Tourenzähler

Eine Vorrichtung zur Verständigung zwischen Führer und Passagier

VIII. Ersatzteile und Werkzeuge:

1 Laufrad (normal für Flugzeuge der Heeresverwaltung)

1 Laufachse

2 Federn

1 für den Motor ausprobierte Luftschraube

1 Satz Schuhe für das Fahrgestell,

Ventilfedern für 4 Ventile

1 Einlaß- und 1 Auslaßventil

8 Zündkerzen

1 Satz sämtl. Dichtungen

1 Satz Kolbenringe

1 Ersatzteilkasten für den Magnet,

1 Satz Kabel mit Schuhen fertig zum Einbau

1 Satz Schlauchverbindungen mit Schellen

12 Ersatzspannschlösser für jeder am Flugzeug vorkommender Gattung

1 Satz Schuhe für die Zelle

2 Zuggummi oder Federn für den Sporn

6 Ersatzschaugläser für Benzin

6 desgl. für Öl

50 m. Spanndraht

50 m. Stahldrahtkabel für die Steuerung

1 Kolben mit Kolbenbolzen und Pleuelstange

1 Satz sämtl. Lager einschl. Kugellager

b. Eine sicher und unter Ausschluß von Behinderung für die Besatzung auf dem Flugzeug anzubringende Bordtasche mit einer Nachweisung des entsprechenden Jnhalts. Die Nachweisung ist mit Kupfernieten im Jnnern der Bordtasche geschützt und gut lesbar zu befestigen. Etwaige der Eigenart des Motors oder Flugzeuges entsprechenden Teile sind erforderlichen Falls in die Bordtasche außerdem aufzunehmen:

<u>Jnhalt der Bordtasche:</u>

1 kl. Engländer „ Saturn "

3 m. Spanndraht

1 Zwickzange

1 Kombinationszange

3 kl. Schlichtfeilen

1 Heft dazu

1 Schraubenzieher

1 kl. Benzinlötzeug

1 Rolle Jsolierband

1 Ersatzschwimmer in Schachtel

1 Stck. Gummischlauch 50 cm.

4 gr. u. 4 kl. Spannschlösser

3 m. Spanndraht

1 m. Messing-Bindedraht

0,25 kg. Weiße Putzwolle

4 Zündkerzen in Holzbüchsen

0,5 qm. Flugzeugstoff

2 Kombinationszangen doppelt

1 Schraubenzieher — " —

1 Pneumatik-Reparatur-Kasten

1 Büchse Gummilösung

1 Spritzkännchen für Öl

1 desgl. für Benzin

1 kl. Luftpumpe für Pneumatik

Außerdem: 1 Werkzeugkiste verschl. (2 Schlüssel) und feldbrauch-. bar enthaltend:

Die erforderlichen Motorschlüssel (einschl. Kerzen- Magnet und Spulenschlüssel.)

1 Abzugsbügel für den Propeller

1 Beißzange

1 Brennerzange

1 Rundzange

1 Flachzange

1 Winkelreibahle

1 gr. Engländer

1 Ösenzange

1 kl. u. 1 gr. Handhammer

2 Meißel

2 Durchschläge

1 Schlichtfeile ▭ □ △ ⌀

1 ▭ Strohfeile

2 ▭ ⌀ Holzraspeln

1 Lötzeug mit 2 Lötkolben

1 verschließbare Messingspritzkanne

1 Handbohrmaschine

1 Bogensäge

1 Satz Spiralbohrer (für Holz und Metall)

1 Ölkanne

1 Feilkloben

1 Satz Steckschlüssel für das Motorgehäuse

1 Körner

1 Federzollstock 2 m.

1 Benzinpinsel

1 Handfeger

1 Holzhammer

1 Schraubenzieher

Ferner alle durch die Eigenart des Motors oder Flugzeuges erforderlichen Werkzeuge oder Ersatzteile.

II. Die Firma hat etwa zu leistende Lizenzgebühren für die Benutzung von Patent- oder Musterschutzrechten allein zu tragen, bezw. die Gewähr dafür zu übernehmen, daß die zu liefernden Gegenstände frei von Patent oder Musterschutzrechten dritter Personen sind, bezw. daß sie berechtigt ist, die dem Jnhaber dieses Patents oder Musterschutzes gehörende Rechte auszuüben, und verpflichtet sich, dem Reichsmilitärfiskus für alle von dritter Seite wegen Verletzung solcher Rechte erhobenen Ansprüchen schadlos zu halten, vorbehaltlich aller sonstigendem Reichsmilitärfiskus aus der übernommenen Gewährleistung zustehenden Rechte.

Nachtrag:

Die Heeresverwaltung besitzt das Recht, vom Vertrage zurückzutreten, falls der Vertragsgegenstand nach 4 Wochen nach dem Lieferungstermin nicht zur Anlieferung gelangt ist.

Döberitz, den 18. November 1912. Frankfurt a/M., den 21. November 1912.

Fliegertruppe

Lehmann

Major und Kommandeur.

Contract

Between the Inspektion des Militär-Luft- und Kraftfahrwesens in Schöneberg-Berlin and the company August Euler, Frankfurt a/Main the followig contract will be concluded based on free-handed placing according to General War Department Nr. 364.12.11 A. 7.IIc 13126.11 from 21.12.1911, under reserve of the confirmation by the General-Inspektion des Militär-Verkehrswesens.

1.

The company August Euler, Frankfurt a/Main undertakes to deliver postcalled objects for the prices sedated to the Inspektion des Militär-Luft- und Kraftfahrwesens on 2 April 1912 to airfield Döberitz:

One Euler biplane military type 1912 with 70 HP Gnôme-engine including spare parts and reserve parts as well as physica instruments at a price of

—— 24000.- M, ——

in words: "twentyfourthousand Mark".

2.

Within 14 days after the confirmation of this contract by the General-Inspektion des Militär-Luft- und Kraftfahrwesens the company has to deposit a security of

—— 1200.- M, ——

in words: "onethousandtwohundred Mark" at the cash management of the Luftschiffer-Bataillons No. 1, Reinickendorf.

3.

The general, special and technical contract conditions attached to this contract (Appendix 1 – 3) have the same strength, as if they were performed in the contract themselve.

4.

Both sides have signed the contract in double issue as sign of approval as follows:

Schöneberg-Berlin, 30 March 1912
Frankfurt a/Main, 11 March 1912

Inspektion des Militär-Luft-
The Contractor
und Kraftfahrwesens

Messing

August Euler
Major General

Confirmed:
Berlin, 12 April 1912
General-Inspektion des
Militär-Verkehrswesens

Lyncker
LeutnantGeneral

Appendix 1
for the contract from 11 March 1912
about delivery of 1 biplane

Nationale

I. General data

1. Company: August Euler, Frankfurt a. Main,
2. Year and day of acqusition: 1912
3. Cost price and disposition: 24000 M
4. Type: Euler biplane

II. Engine

1. Engine type: "Gnôme" Original
2. Factory number: 1139
3. Number of cylinders: seven
4. Weight of engine: 83 kg
5. Nominal performance at revolutions: 70 HP at 1250 revolutions
6. Fuel: Gasoline
7. Type of carburetor: Original Gnôme
8. Type of ignition: magneto-electric
9. Biggest pre-ignition: no adjustability of the ignition time
10. Bore: 120 mm
11. Stroke: 130 mm
12. Type of crankshaft bearing: Gnôme
13. Type of piston rod bearing: similar
14. Type of lubrication: similar
15. Cooling: air
16. Water quantity: no water

III. Devices

1. Main airframe: 14 m x 1.500 m
2. Tail airframe: 3 m x 1.000 m
simple, no airframe
3. Ailerons resp. warping: Ailerons
4. Height control: aft
5. Running gear: "Euler"

Inspektion des Militär-Luft-
The Contractor
und Kraftfahrwesens

Messing

August Euler
Major General

Supplement 3
To the contract from 11 March 1912 about the delivery of 1 Euler biplane

I. Cell

1. The used material must be of high-class quality, the whole design must correspond the current state of technology. Before the stringing a check with acceptance of the framing by an officer of the teaching facility takes place.
2. The devisible parts are to be numbered according to a blueprint sketch that has to be provided with two copies.
3. Fuel tanks may not be fitted over the engine.
4. Windbreak is to be attched, special care must be applied to the fixing of revolution counter, barometre, clock, map rolling device, display for the state of fuels and coolant. All instruments should also be observeable by the passenger.
5. Aboard the airplane the tools listed under figure V are to be accomodated.
6. There are 2 seats with controls to be attached, the control organs for the passenger must be easily to engaged the clutch and to disengaged.
7. A very big value is laid on opportunities for observation, the pilot must be able to look directly below and next to himself to the ground.

II. Engine

1. The choice of the engine remains left to the company, before the final choice of the engine the consent of the inspection is to be caught up.
2. The engine is subjected a three hours long break test on the servicing state of the company in presence of representatives of the delivering facility. Here it must 1.) run 2 hours with the propeller destined or it and the number of revolutions which is described as normal in the conditions determined under III. The touring variations may not exceed 10 %. The propeller used during the break test will be stamped by the delivering facility. 2.) ½ hour with 10 degrees of inclination and full throttle. 3.) ½ hour with 15 degree inclination and the lowest possible number of revolutions, which may not, nevertheless, exceed 500 revolutions under usually normal conditions. The following information is to be taken down in the break certificate at each 15 minutes a) number of revolutions, b) attractive force, c) temperature of the coolant. Before and after the test an exact weighing of petrol and oil is to be carried out, so that complete clarity is won about the consumption of engine. The specific weight of oil and petrol is to be measured. During the test s oil and petrol supply must exactly correspond to the operating conditions and equipment of the engine built-in the airplane.
3. During the tests no exposure, no irregularity and noc change of single parts may take place.
4. After completion the engine is taken apart and checked exactly. On this occassion appearing mistakes or defects are to be removed before the final acceptance. They [the mistakes] can - even if the engine has satisfied the demands - exclude its accpetance.
5. The company has to inform the delivering facility 1 week before about time and location of the brake test and to make provision tha the tests can be made in the explained way without time delay in the given way.
6. In-line engines must have a special starting magneto or battery. The inspection reserves itself to demand the fixing of a double set of spark plugs.
7. The oil and petrol lines must guarantee complete safety against breaks by vibration.
8. The petrol tanks must have partitions and a valve that allows the pilot instanteneous, complete jettison of the pressure. Pressure control valves and manometer must correspond the biggest allowed pressure. The fuel tanks are tested with tripled pressure.
9. All cocks must be protected against unintentional opening. The protection may not complicate intentional opening.
10. With circulation- and dry-sump oiling system a control of the oil state in the crankshaft as well of the oil supply must be possible in flight.
11. The engine must have an exhaust carbine and an economizer.
12. A report with three copies must be made about the engine check.
13. For engines of foreign production is an brake certificate required and the given values will be tested on the test stand of the training facility before acceptance.

III. Performance of the Airplanes

1. Pay load incl. aircrew and ballast: 200 kg
2. Range of action: 250 km
3. Airspeed at least: 80 km per hour
4. Take-off distance not more than: 60 m
5. Landing run not more than: 70 m

IV. Acceptance of the airplanes

1. Before the .... and the covering an acceptance of the framing will happen, a negotiation about that are to be taken up.
2. The location of the final airplane acceptance is Döberitz. The manufacturer carries the costs for transport and costs for assembly.
3. ....
4. During the acceptance the airplane must fly one hour, piloted by a pilot of the company. The height of 500 m must be reached at most 15 minutes after the start and be registered by 2 barometres on board. Immediately after reaching 500 m is to be gone down to ca. 100 m with a gliding fight. Now up to the landing the airplane may not fly above a height of ca. 200 m. The landing has to occur in a gliding flight from at least 100 m height with put down engine.
5. If the airplane is not fulfilling the demanded conditions within 30 days since the first demonstration, the inspection reserves itself to raise the demands according to the progress of the technology.
6. The time of the demonstration is to be reported two days earlier to the inspection and the training facility. In unfavourable weather conditions the acceptance procedure can be shifted after request of the enterpriser.

V. Spare parts and tools:

Besides the engine and other items in the airplane are to be delivered:

a) Spare parts:
1 wheel,
1 running axle,
2 springs,
1 air-screw tried for the engine,
1 set shoes for the chassis,
valve springs for 4 valves,
1 intake valve, 1 outlet valve,
8 spark plugs,
1 set of all seals,
1 set of piston rings,
1 spare part box for the ignition magnet,
1 set cables with shoes ready for installation,
1 set of hose connections with clamps,
12 spare turnbuckles from every type used on the airplane,
1 set aluminium.... for the cell,
2 pull rubber or springs for the tailskid,
6 spare inspection glasses for petrol,
6 dto. for oil,
50 m tension wire,
50 m steel wire cable for the controls,
1 piston with piston bolt and connecting rod,
1 set of all bearings,

b. A safe board bag with attestation of its content that can fixed at the airplane with exclusion of any hampering of the aircrew. The attest is protected with copper rivets in the inner space of the board bag and must be fastened well legible. Moreover, any characteristic parts of the engine or airplane should be taken up in the board bag if necessary.

Content of the board bag:

1 little Engländer [monkey wrench] "Saturn" 3 m tension wire
1 pincer 1 m brass binding wire
1 combination pliers 0.25 kg while cleaning wool
3 mill files 4 spark plugs
1 heft thereto 0.5 qm of airplane fabric
1 screwdriver 1 pneumatics repair.....
1 little petrol soldering device 1tin elastic solution
1 role isolating tape 1 oil squirt
1 spare swimmer in box 1 squirt for petrol
1 rubber hose (50 m) 1 little airpump for pneumatics
4 big and 4 little turnbuckles

c. Moreover:

1 Toolbox closeable (2 keys) and field-useable containing:
The necessary engine spanners (incl. spark plugs)
Magnet and reels spanner 1 trigger guard for propeller
1 pincer 1 roundnose pliers
1 flat-nose plier 1 big. Engländer [monky wrench]
1 big and 1 little hand hammer 2 chisels
1 square-, round-, half round-, flat mill file 1 screwdrivers, big.
1 straw file 2 round-, flat-wood graters
1 closeable brass oil squirt 1 blowtorch with 2 soldering irons
1 set spiral drills (for wood and metal) 1 center punch

1 hand vise 1 oilcan
2 punches 1 hand drilling machine
1 yardstick 1 petrol brush
1 hand brush 1 wooden hammer
Furthermore all necessary tools and spares for the characteristics of the engine or airplane.

VI. Instruments

There are to be delivered as well:
1 barometre 1 map
rolling apparatus
1 clock 1
revolution counter
1 device for the communication between pilot and passenger.

VII. The enclosed "Nationale" is to be filled by the company.
VIII. The company takes over all obligations to train an officer in flying. The costs for this are included in the purchasing price.

IX. The company has to carry possible payments of royalties for the use of patents or registered patents alone or to garantee that the delivered items are free of patent rights or registered patents of third persons or that it is entitled to execute the rights of the owner of these patents or utility patents and is obliged to pay the Imperial Military Exchequer for all infringements of such rights by third parties, provisory of all other rights, appertained to the Imperial Military Exchequer resulting from inhereted warranties.

Inspektion des Militär-Luft-
The Contractor
und Kraftfahrwesens

Messing

August Euler
Major General

Above: Euler pusher combat aircraft with open gunner's cockpit. (P. M. Grosz Collection/STBD)

Appendix 4: Examination Rules

Examination rules
for the one-year voluntary service

1. Engine Construction and Operations

a. Scientific knowledge to prove during verbal examination:

I. Knowledge of the general construction of internal combustion engines and their essential components with both engines with standing and with rotating cylinders. Mainly also knowledge about

- the four stroke and two stroke operating principle,
- the crank engine: pistons, connecting rods, crankshafts and their mounts;
- the cylinder: with water coats and with air colling, their kind of connection;
- control organs: valves, valve linkeages, cam wave, drive;
- crank case: construction and fixture;
- ancilliary apparatuses: radiator, water pump, coolant circulation, the cooling process, carburettor, magneto apparatus, spark plugs, ignition circuit circle, the lubrication device.
- fuels: their types and feed line.

II. Knowledge of the most common engine systems (N.A.G., Argus, Daimler-Mercedes etc.) concerning their general construction and details of the engines according to the points of view given in segment I.

III. Operation and treatment of the engine

- Preparations of the engine and its check before the start-up;
- the start-up of the engine;
- the maintenance of the engine during operation;
- fuels and their gasification, oils and lubrication, ignition, cooling, general points of view.

IV. The operational disturbances of engines and their individual parts.

- Which signs point to disturbances of the going of the engine?
- How happens the search for the source of mistakes?
- Which are the most common distrubances and its causes?
- How does the removal of mistakes happens in single cases?
- Which repair works may be carried out by airmen, which require the removal to the factory?

b. Practical knowledge to prove at the examination engine

- The check of an engine before start-up;
- the start-up of an engine and its adjustment;
- detection of causes of operational disturbances;
- removal of the mistakes that can be removed by the airmen;
- dismantling of single engine parts for the purpose of simple, in practice often occuring little repair work.

2. Aircraft Science (verbal examination)

I. General points of view about the air drag as a weight-bearing and restraining strength in aeronautical engineering and its causes. The size and direction of the air drag with different shapes of surfaces and bodies.

General points of view concerning the amount of work involved in floating.

The flight work in horizontal flight and climbing flight.

The basic knowledge of the balance position of an airplane in the 3 levels. About the middle point of pressure and its wandering, about the barycenter and the different barycenter situations and its influence on the balance position in flight with running engine and in gliding flight.

The influence of changing weights and screw forces during the flight.

II. The individual parts of the airplane and their meanings: the wings, the chassis, controls and control facilities: the side controls, height controls and ailerons.

Description of proven modern airplanes (monoplanes and biplanes) and comparative judgements of their constructions.

III. Explanation of the easiest laws of the strength theory: stress by pull, push, bend and thrust and the most important cases of stress in the airplane.

The primarily used construction materials, their firmness, mutual advantages, suitability and usability on the single airplane components. Examples of the application of the strenght theory during improvised repairs of airplanes by airmen.

3. Science of Flight (verbal examination)

I. The flight

- move of controls and its mutul influence;
- sluggishness of the airplane and damping;
- Starting and climbing;
- descending and landing;
- the flight in the curve;
- the gliding flight;
- influences of the engine, the engine torque.

II. Flying under complicated condition
- wind and shifting by wind;
- climbing and descending airflows, gusts and difficult weather conditions;
- conditions in bigger heights;
- flying with strong load;
- rise and landing on difficult terrain.

III. General remarks
- fire, crash, averages;
- the psychological.

4. Assembly Work and Maintenance Work on Airplanes (practical examination at the airplane)

- The check of an airplane in all parts before the flight.
- Removal of mistakes that an airman can repair himself.
- Assembly and dismantling works at airplanes.
- Easy maintenance works with simple means in the field.

5. Meteorology (verbal examination)
I. The air movements and their streams
- ohorizontal air movements and its causes;
- okinds of terms for wind regarding strength and direction;
- omeasurement of wind and estimation of wind strength;
- othe wind conditions on Germany, upward and downward directed air movements and their causes;
- othe influence of the ground unevennesses, the ground vegetation and ground cover, the solar radiation, the time of day and seasons on these moves;
- oconclusions for the piloting of the airplane;
- othe characteristic of the air movement near the earth's surface and its influence on start and landing;
- oguests, thunderstorms and funnel clouds, its origin, nature, dangers and indications;

II. The clouds
- otypes of clouds and their heights.
- ocauses of origin and dissolution of clouds;
- ohints, which the different types and shapes of clouds can give the airman regarding vertical and horizontal streams of air, in and over the clouds.

III. The weather
- The formation of high pressure and low pressure areas;
- airstreams in high pressure and low pressure areas and in different heights;
- cloudiness: temperatur and precipitations in high pressure and low pressure areas;
- the direction of travel in low pressure areas;
- the foundations of weather predictions;
- the weather map;
- evaluation of weather conditions regarding cross-country flights with the help of weather maps and the use of local observations, especially concerning clouds and the indications of meteorological instruments;
- othe weather service for aviators.

6. Map reading, orientation, driving gear (verbal examination)
The basics about the depiction of terrain on the map:
- The graduations, measuring and estimating of distances on the map, the common display modes of the vegetative soil cover and plants (signatures) and the ground shapes (layer lines and mountain lines).
- the reading of ground levels;

Skills in the reading of atlases
- 1 : 100 000 (ordnance survey maps)
- 1 : 200 000 (topographic survey map of the German Reich)
- 1 : 500 000 (Vogel's map of the German Reich)
- Evaluation of flight distances on the maps 1 : 100 000 and 1 : 200 000 regarding orientation and possibilities of landing;
- the preparation of the map for the cross-country flight;
- the principles for the application of the map as helpful means for the orientation under different conditions (orientation with points, lines of direction etc.).

7. Compass teaching and astronomical aids for orientation (verbal examination)

Knowledge of the construction and the installation

of compasses common for airplanes (Fluid- and dry compasses);

- the influence of the earth-magnetic forces on the compass;
- the term Missweisung [abberation of the magnetic needle].
- the influence of the iron parts of the airplane on the compass;
- the concept of deviation;
- the determination of the Missweisung after latitude and its annual change;
- the practical determination of deviation in the airplane with running engine;
- the compensation of the compass with the purpose of the removal of the affects of the Missweisung and deviation;
- explanation of terms: right-pointing course, missweisender cours and compass cours;
- The use of Missweisung and deviation for the cours to be steered;
- the principles after which the pilot without the use of special instruments of measuremet, merely with the help of a good watch, the nautical yearbook and maybe a star map can make a general orientation with the help of the stars;
- knowledge about the starlit sky.

8. Instrument teaching (verbal examination)

Knowledge of the anaeroid barometer and barographs for air pressure and height measurement, the variometer, anemometer, revolution counter, manometer and inclination gauge.

The general construction and the mode of operation of these instruments, their use treatment, check and correktion.

9. Medical schooling (verbal examination)

- Points of view about a personal hygiene and clothing suitable for airmen;
- first help in accidents;
- knowledge of the mainly occuring accidents and illnesses in aviation in the air and on the ground as experience teaches.
- Which measures are to be taken in particular cases up to the appearance of medical help?

Three-Month Special Courses for Airmen

Nr. Subject Weekly class hours	Lecture	Exercises
1. Engine construction and operations	4	6
2. Aircraft science	3	–
3. Science of flight	1	–
4. Assembly and maintenance work on airplanes	–	6
5. Meteorology	4	–
6. Map reading and driving gear	3	–
7. Compass teaching and astronomical aid	2	2
8. Instrument teaching	–	1
9. Medical schooling	1	–
10. Police regulations	1	–
Total	19	15

Left: Close up of the Euler triplane trainer prototype landing gear. (P. M. Grosz Collection/STBD)

Appendix 5: Reliability Prices of the National-Flugspende

THE ADVISORY BOARD OF THE NATIONAL-FLUGSPENDE
City and Benefit Flights of the National-Flugspende 1914.
A. City flights

Under abolition of the present call for bids the following prizes are put out by the National-Flugspende:
I. Every German pilot receives a prize for an uninterrupted flight which is accomplished on an airplane which was manufactured in Germany with a German or foreign engine beyong other competitions:

1,000 M. for 2 hours,
2000 " 3 "
3300 " 4 "
4900 " 5 "
6800 " 6 "
9000 " 7 "
11,500 " 8 "
14,300 " 9 "
17,400 " 10 "
20.,800 " 11 "
24,500 " 12 "
etc.

II. The above prices are paid only if the whole flight except start and landing occurs outside of an airfield and one goes away during

a 2-hours flight for 60 km,
a 3-hours flight " 90 "
a 4-hours flight " 120 "
etc.

from the airfield and the same distance is not flown two times. The flying over the turning points has to be proven by the dropping of messages and the uninterrupted flight durance must be proven by two barographs* which were checked and sealed before. The proof of the start must be made in a kind admitted by the Deutscher Luftfahrer-Verband. Concerning the place and time of the landing officers, reserve officers, head officals and community leaders etc. can serve as sports witnesses.
III. During flights with seaplanes the regulation named under II sentence 1 comes to discontinuation; however, during every application flight a minimum distance of 60 km in a straight line must be traveled.

* For the free check of the used heights measuring devices volunteered:
Physikalisches Institut der Universität Marburg,
Physikalischer Verein in Frankfurt a. M., Kettenhofweg 136,
Meteorologische Landesanstalt für Elsaß-Lothringen, Straßburg, Illtorstaden 1,
Drachenstation am Bodensee in Friedrichshafen,
Königl. Bayerische Meteorologische Zentralstation, München.

IV. Such pilots who neither have been trained with support of the National-Flugspende nor have received a flight donation from her up to now, do not need to go away from the airfield for the acquisition of prizes for the second and third hours, if they have kept during a 2-hours flight at least 15 minutes long and during a 3-hours flight at least 30 minutes long a height of 250 m which has been proven by the barogram.
V. Such pilots, who have already received donations from the National-Flugspende, must outperform their earlier awarded performances and receive for that part of their new achievement, for which they have received a donation earlier, only half the prize put out for this bid; for the part of the flight that is outperforming the old achievement the set out prize must be paid completely.
VI. The prize gained by an application flight becomes paid half to the pilot, the other half to the airplane owner.

B. Benefit flights

The pensions written out until now by the National-Flugspende for the in each case longest German duration flight without stopover and the farthest cross-country flight within 24 hours persist unchanged. The regulations are:

I. That German pilot, who has flown respectively the longest time non-stop, at least six hours, gets a monthly pension of 2,000 M from the National-Flugspende up to the maximum total amount of 10.000 M., until another outperforms his flying time. The pension is paid at the end of every month for the time while the pilot holds the record. The first day is paid fully, the last is not calculated.

II. That pilot who flies through the measured longest distance over the country within 24 hours between rise and landing location, receives as premium a monthly pension of 4,000 M up to a maximum amount of 20,000 M., until another German pilot outbids this achievement. The pension is paid at the end of every month for the time while the pilot holds the record. The first day is paid fully, the last is not calculated. As minimum performance a total distance of 500 km is required.

III. The prizes named under I and II should be paid in the future to the German pilot who beats the respectively existing German record by 15 minutes or by 15 km for at least the duration of a month as full amount even if his achievement is already outbid by another German pilot before this time around just as much. A surpassing by less than 15 minutes or 15 km is not recognized as outbid of the earlier achievement. The entrainment of a passenger or the suitable load is not necessary anymore.

IV. The control of the flying achievements has to be made in the way described under A. II.

C. Common Regulations

I. The National-Flugspende holds back an amount up to 150 M from the acquired premiums for the payment of the running insurance sum, if the pilot has not completely paid the insurance amount for the running year.

II. It is requirement for the application for cash prizes that every applicant was insured during a premium flight on grounds of the insurance police provided by the National-Flugspende, if he can prove that he had insured himself in a different way with the same amount before the 1 March 1913 and during his application for a price.

III. For all disputes arising from this general offer an arbitration board is created under exclusion of the legal process, its chairperson is the managing curator of the National-Flugspende or one representative ordered by him and in this administrative committee of the National-Flugspende one committee member is elected from

1. the Luftfahrer-Verband,
2. the association "Deutsche Versuchsanstalt für Luftfahrt",
3. the aircraft factories,
4. the German pilots.

IV. The acceptance of a premium obliges the pilot to make himself unrestrictedly available in case of war and in peace during the following year after the receipt of the premium for a special three-week exercise of the army administration.

V. The committee reserves itself to exclude applicants from the participation in this bid who have not done justice to the regulations of the National-Flugspende.

VI. German female pilots receive the same premiums for the same achievements without take-over of the under IV called obligations.

VII. Military pilots receive additional honor prizes instead of cash prizes.

VIII. Every applicant receives afore mentioned prizes and additional prizes only once, the pension arbitrarily often.

IX. The entitlement to payment of a prize is not given anymore, as soon as the reserved 400,000 M for this puspose are disbursed.

THE ADVISORY BOARD OF THE NATIONAL-FLUGSPENDE
Reliability Prizes of the National-Flugspende

I. The National-Flugspende pays German pilots who fly in the time from 1 March to 31 December 1913 on in Germany made, with German or foreign engines equipped airplanes beyond other competitions one hour without stopover, a prize of 1,000 M. and for every next hour flown without stopover an additional prize of 1,000 M each.

II. If the flight with passenger – if necessary under supplement of the passanger's weight by ballast of 65 kg – or with ballast of 65 kg is accomplished, then an additional prize of 500 M. for every hour additonal to the above prizes is paid if the following conditions are fulfilled:

1. During an 1-hour flight the flight has to go from the place of the rising to a point in at least 30 km distance and back, and, besides, within 15 minutes a height of at least 500 m must be reached and be maintained during the flight 15 minutes long with a minimum height of 500 m.
2. During a 2-hours flight the flight has to go from the place of rising to a point in at least 30 km distance and back and then again to a point in at least 30 km distance from the place of rising and at least 10 km sidewise from the first turning point, and, besides, a height of at least 500 m must be reached within 15 minutes after the start and during the flight 30 minutes long a minimum height of 500 m be kept.
3. During a 3-hours or 4-hours flight accomplished in the same way additional to the present requirements a height of 800 m must be reached during the flying time and be maintained for 30 minutes. All turning points must be at least 10 km distant from each other. In flights of five hours and more must be reached a height of 1,000 m besides the present requirements and be maintained for 15 minutes.

III. That pilot who has flown the longest time during the application for earlier mentioned prices, however, at least 6 hours without pause, receives so long a monthly pension of 2,000 M. Up to a total amount of 10,000 M.from the National-Flugspende until another outperforms his flying time. The pension is paid at the end of every month for the time, while a pilot holds the record. The first day is calculated completely, the last is not calculated.

IV. The participation in the 1-hour flight is only open for such pilots, for whose training was not paid a premium from the National-Flugspende.

V. Furthermore it is requirement for the application for cash prizes that the applicant was insured during the execution of the premium flight on the base of the insurance policy provided by the National-Flugspende, if he is not proving that he was insured elsewhere with the same amount before 1 March 1913.

VI. The control of the flight performances occurs through an air force officer or two sports witnesses approved by the Deutscher Luftfahrerverband according to its general regulations. Employees of the same company are neither allowed to be witnesses among themselves or for the owner and the latter can not be sports witness for his employees.

VII. For all disputes arising from this general offer an arbitration board, whose chairperson is the managing curator of the National-Flugspende or one representative ordered by him, will be founded under exclusion of the legal process, and there is one committee member each elected in the administration commission of the National-Flugspende

1. from the Luftfahrer-Verband,
2. from the association "Deutsche Versuchsanstalt für Luftfahrt",
3. from aircraft companies,
4. from German pilots.

From the acquired premium the National-Flugspende is holding back an amount of 135 M for the payment of the running insurance sum, if the pilot has not completely paid the insurance amount for the running year.

VIII. The acceptance of a premium obliges the pilot to make himself unrestrictedly available in case of war and in peace during the following year after the receipt of the premium for a special three-week exercise of the army administration.

IX. German female pilots receive the same premiums for the same achievements without take-over of the obligations called under VIII.

X. Military pilots receive additional honor prizes instead of cash prizes.

XI. Every applicant receives afore mentioned prizes and additional prizes only once, the pension arbitrarily often.

National-Flugpreis

That German pilot who flies through the measured longest distance over the country in the time from 1 March to 31 December 1913 on in Germany made, with German or foreign engines equipped airplanes beyond other competitions with passenger or with ballast according to the regulations under figure II of the Reliability prize within 24 hours from the rise in the airline between starting and landing place the measured longest distance over land, receives as premium so long a monthly pension of 4,000 M. up to the maximum amount of 20,000 M., until another German pilot excels this flight achievement.

The control of the flight achievements occurs in the same manner as it is prescribed for the reliability price; moreover, however, officers, reserve officers, head officals and heads of the district county can serve concerning the location and the time of the landing as sports witnesses. Possible disputs can be decided by the same arbitration board which is envisaged for the reliability prize.

For military airmen honor prizes are scheduled.

Concerning insurances compare above under V. and VII. paragraph 2.

Insurance

Since the insurance in the manner described above under No. V is precondition for the application for preceding mentioned cash prizes, it is advisable to conclude a contract of insurance with the managing insurance society Victoria in Berlin on grounds of the police provided by the National-Flugspende as soon as possible. With the business deal the pilot must pay the first insurance rate of 45 M., whereupon the National-Flugspende pays its share of the annual premium of 200 M. to Victoria. For the other quarterly payments of 45 M. Each the pilot alone remains juridically obliged. If the airman receives a cash prize for his flight achievements then the not yet paid rest of the annual insurance premium is kept back by the National-Flugspende and is led away to Victoria.

The benefits of the insurance are in the case of an unfitness to work after a flight accident in a daily sickness benefit up to 5 M. and n the case of invalidity in an annual pension of up to 1,600 M.

Above: Euler quadraplane D 4 prototype. (P. M. Grosz Collection/STBD)

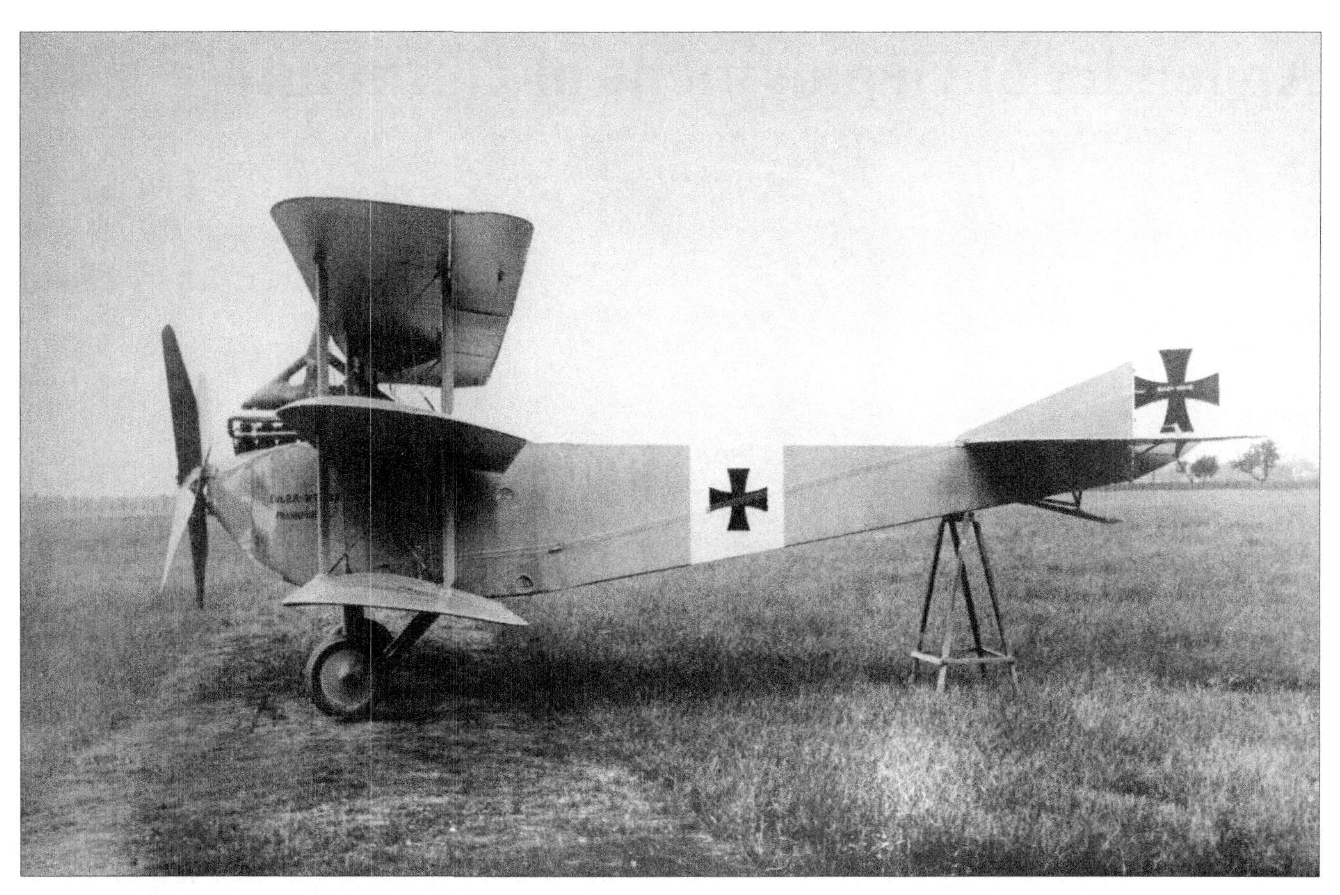

Above: Euler triplane trainer. (Peter M. Bowers collection/MOF)

Above: The Euler D I D4000/16 fighter prototype, work number 300. The extended forward fuselage was used on the prototype fighters only; all production D I and D II aircraft had no fuselage extension. The D II fighter prototype was D4001/16.

Appendix 6: Deployment of German

Aviation Industry in 1915

Appendix 7: Photograph Gallery

Above & Below: ILA postcards.

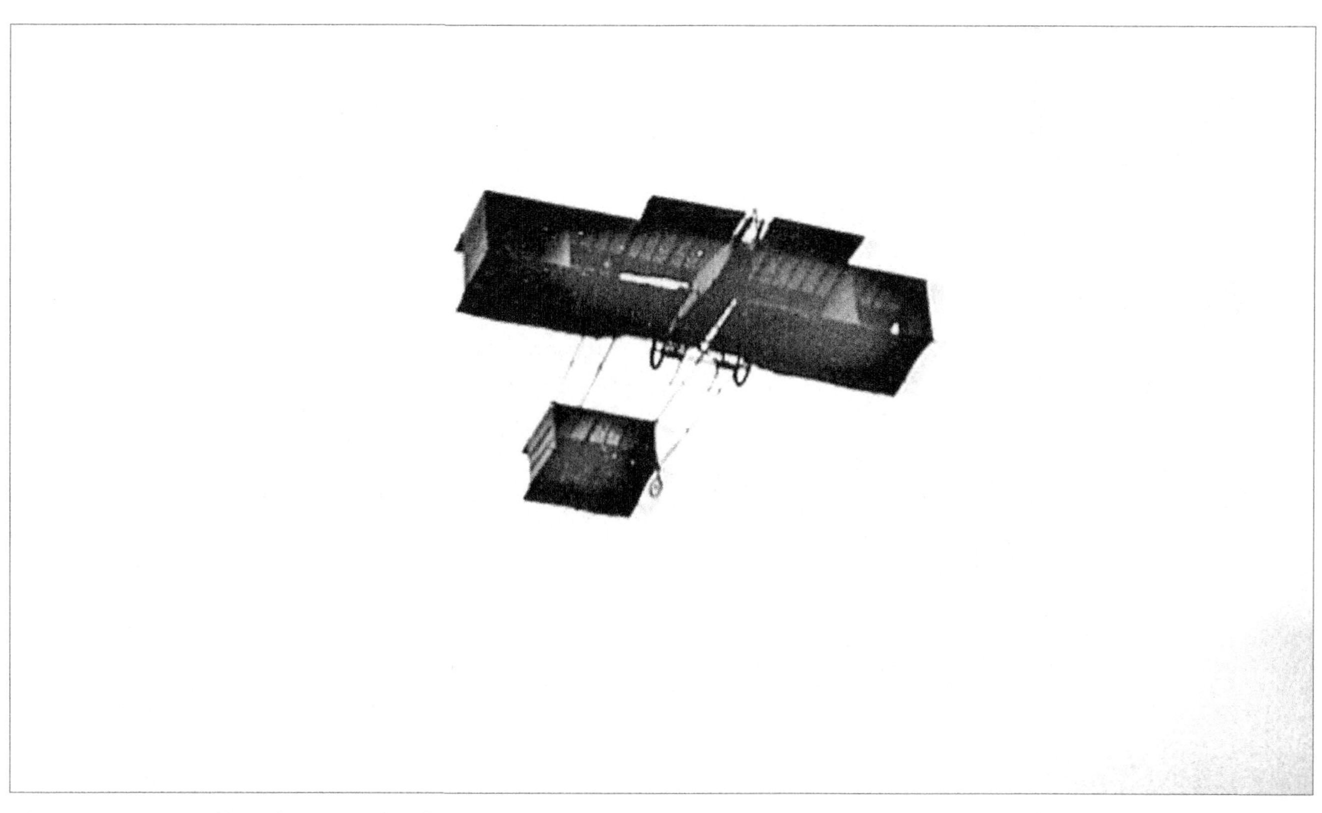

Above & Below: Early Euler aircraft in flight, 1909/1910.

Above: Euler in flight with nose wheel and two spur wheels aft, 1909. **Below**: ILA exhibition building, 1909.

Above: 1910, Euler with helpful team during the preparation of the take-off.
Below: 1910, contemporary picture postcard.

Above: 1910, Leutnant Hiddessen ready for take off.

Below: 1910, crowd of people in front of an Euler airplane in Karlsruhe.

Above: 1910, Euler biplane with forward elevator and without skids.
Below: 1910, educational trip to the Griesheimer Sand.

Above: 1910, Euler biplane, Kleiner Gelber Hund (Little Yellow Dog) from behind.
Below: 1911, August Euler with spouse on 1.12.1911.

Above: 1911, An older Euler with skids and head wheel.
Below: 1911, One-Year-Volunteer Reichardt in Euler flight machine.

Above: Euler monoplane similar to a *Taube*. (P. M. Grosz Collection/STBD)

Facing Page, Top: 1911, engine installation of a Gelber Hund.

Facing Page, Bottom: 1911, Euler in conversation with Hiddessen, Gelber Hund. (Stechmann, private)

Below: 1912, silhouette of a Kleiner Gelber Hund (Little Yellow Dog) in flight.

Above: Two Euler airplanes in the air.

Below: Repair of the tail skid on Gelber Hund (Yellow Dog) in Darmstadt (10 June 1912).

Above: Demonstration of an Euler biplane, 1912.

Above: Worknumber 42 (with B12/12 on the rudder). (Stechmann, private).

Above: August Euler with guests in Frankfurt, 1913.
Below: Crash of a Gelber Hund (Yellow Dog), military type, 1913.

Départ d'un Aéroplane Allemand ayant atterri à ARRACOURT (arrt de Lunéville)

Above: Military-Euler B.12/12 (Wnr. 42) during a visit to France, 1913.

Below: Greetings from Adolphe Pegoud to August Euler, 1913.

Above: Airframe forepart of a B I airplane in metal light-weight construction, 1914.

Below: Visit of a military delegation, 1914.

Right: Details of the landing gear suspension, wooden wheel, 1916.

Below: Fuselage forward section, landing gear axis, 1916.

Above: Triplane, probably the D.R. 7, 1918.

Below: B I airplanes of different manufacturers (LVG, Albatros, Euler), 1917.

Above: Euler military biplane type 1914 in front of the Euler Werke. Note the nose wheel. (P. M. Grosz Collection/STBD)

Above: Euler B I trainer draws a crowd. (P. M. Grosz Collection/STBD)

Above: Euler B I trainers, perhaps at the Euler Werke. (P. M. Grosz Collection/STBD)

Above: Euler B I trainer in the snow. (P. M. Grosz Collection/STBD)

Above: Euler Werke photo of an Euler military biplane type 1914 with nose wheel. (P. M. Grosz Collection/STBD)

Above: Euler Werke photo of an Euler military biplane type 1914. (P. M. Grosz Collection/STBD)

Above: Euler military biplane type 1914 with nose wheel. (P. M. Grosz Collection/STBD)

Below: Euler B I trainer. (P. M. Grosz Collection/STBD)

Above & Below: Euler B II trainers. (P. M. Grosz Collection/STBD)

Above & Below: Euler B II trainers. (P. M. Grosz Collection/STBD)

Above & Below: Euler B II trainers. (P. M. Grosz Collection/STBD)

Above & Below: Euler B II trainers. (P. M. Grosz Collection/STBD)

Above: Euler B II trainer B 413/14. (P. M. Grosz Collection/STBD)

Above: Euler B II trainer B332/15 tactical number 33 after a landing accident. (P. M. Grosz Collection/STBD)

Above & Below: Euler B II trainer B332/15 tactical number 33 after a landing accident. (P. M. Grosz Collection/STBD)

Above & Below: Euler B II trainer B332/15 tactical number 33 after an accident. (P. M. Grosz Collection/STBD)

Above: Euler B II trainer B334/15 tactical number 35 after a landing accident. (P. M. Grosz Collection/STBD)

Facing Page, Above: Euler B II trainer B1361/15 with an Albatros B-type at left. (P. M. Grosz Collection/STBD)

Facing Page, Below: Euler B II trainer B.343/15 tactical number 41. (P. M. Grosz Collection/STBD)

Above: Euler B II trainer B342/15 after a landing accident. (P. M. Grosz Collection/STBD)

B.1361/15

Above: Euler B II trainer flying over the flying school flight-line of other Eulers. (P. M. Grosz Collection/STBD)

Above: Euler B III trainer. (P. M. Grosz Collection/STBD)

Above & Below: Euler B III trainer. (P. M. Grosz Collection/STBD)

Above: Euler B III trainer. (P. M. Grosz Collection/STBD)

Above: Euler B III trainer. (P. M. Grosz Collection/STBD)

Above: Euler C I aircraft. (P. M. Grosz Collection/STBD)

Above: Euler Werke photo of an early Euler C I with observer and gun in front cockpit. (P. M. Grosz Collection/STBD)

C 3609/15

Above: Euler C I aircraft. (P. M. Grosz Collection/STBD)

Facing Page: Euler C I C3609/15 having a bad day. (P. M. Grosz Collection/STBD)

Above: Euler pusher combat aircraft. (P. M. Grosz Collection/STBD)

Above & Below: Front and rear views of the Euler single-seat pusher fighter *Gelber Hund*. (P. M. Grosz Collection/STBD)

Above: Euler pusher combat aircraft with open gunner's cockpit. (P. M. Grosz Collection/STBD)

Facing Page, Above: Structure of Euler pusher combat aircraft with nosewheel. (P. M. Grosz Collection/STBD)

Facing Page, Below: Euler pusher combat aircraft with open gunner's cockpit. (P. M. Grosz Collection/STBD)

Above: Euler pusher combat aircraft. (P. M. Grosz Collection/STBD)

Above & Below: Euler pusher combat aircraft with open gunner's cockpit. (P. M. Grosz Collection/STBD)

Above & Below: Euler D I prototype work number 300 with extended cowling. The production D I had the 100 HP, 9-cylinder Oberursel U I without fuselage extension. The production D II had a strengthened airframe, especially the landing gear, for training use. There is no visual way to distinguish between the D I and D II except serial number. Production D II engines were either the 80 HP, 7-cylinder Oberursel U 0 or the 100 HP, 9-cylinder Oberursel U I; both were used within the same D II series for Work Numbers 325–351 and 352 401. Euler D II aircraft in the series Work Numbers 402–431 used the 100 HP Oberursel U I. (P. M. Grosz Collection/STBD)

Above & Below: Euler D I prototype work number 300. (P. M. Grosz Collection/STBD)

Above & Below: Euler D I prototype work number 300 with fuselage extension. (P. M. Grosz Collection/STBD)

Above: Euler D I prototype work number 300 with fuselage extension. (P. M. Grosz Collection/STBD)

Above: Euler D I prototype work number 301 without fuselage extension. (P. M. Grosz Collection/STBD)

Above & Below: Euler D I prototype work number 301 without fuselage extension. (P. M. Grosz Collection/STBD)

Above & Below: Euler D I prototype work number 301 without fuselage extension. (P. M. Grosz Collection/STBD)

Above & Left: Euler D I prototype with fuselage extension. (P. M. Grosz Collection/STBD)

Above: Euler D I prototype work number 301 without fuselage extension. (P. M. Grosz Collection/STBD)

Above: Euler D II prototype with fuselage extension. (P. M. Grosz Collection/STBD)

Above & Below: Euler D II prototype with fuselage extension. (P. M. Grosz Collection/STBD)

Above: Euler D II 2352/17. (P. M. Grosz Collection/STBD)

Above: Euler D II 274/17 closeup with Gotha WD14 in the background. (P. M. Grosz Collection/STBD)

Above: Euler D II aircraft under production in the Euler Works. (P. M. Grosz Collection/STBD)

Above & Below: Euler D 6 biplane fighter prototype. (P. M. Grosz Collection/STBD)

Above & Below: Euler D 6 biplane fighter prototype. (P. M. Grosz Collection/STBD)

Above & Below: Euler D 6 biplane fighter prototype. (P. M. Grosz Collection/STBD)

Above & Below: Euler D 5 biplane fighter prototype. (P. M. Grosz Collection/STBD)

Above & Below: Euler D 5 biplane fighter prototype. (P. M. Grosz Collection/STBD)

EULER-WERKE
FRANKFURT A/M

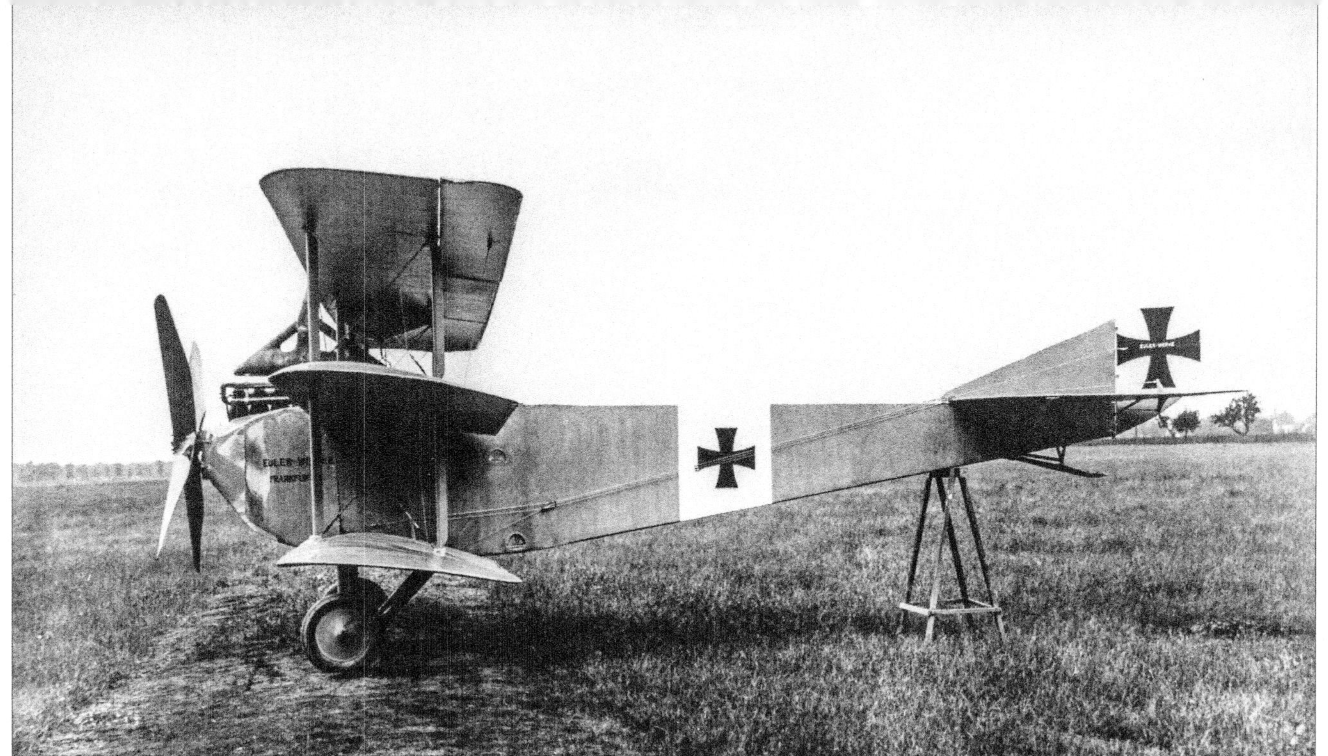

This Page & Facing Page: Euler triplane trainer prototype. (P. M. Grosz Collection/STBD)

Above & Below: Euler triplane D.R. 4 prototype. (P. M. Grosz Collection/STBD)

Above & Below: Euler triplane D.R. 4 prototype. (P. M. Grosz Collection/STBD)

Above & Below: Euler triplane D.R. 4 prototype. (P. M. Grosz Collection/STBD)

Above, Below, & Facing Page: Euler triplane D.R. 5 prototype. (P. M. Grosz Collection/STBD)

Above, Below, & Facing Page: Euler triplane D.R. 5 prototype. (P. M. Grosz Collection/STBD)

Above & Below: Euler quadraplane D 4 prototype. (P. M. Grosz Collection/STBD)

Above & Below: Euler triplane D.R. 9 fighter prototype. (P. M. Grosz Collection/STBD)

Above, Below, & Facing Page: Euler triplane D.R. 7 fighter prototype. (P. M. Grosz Collection/STBD)

Above & Below: Euler triplane D.R. 7 fighter prototype. (P. M. Grosz Collection/STBD)

Appendix 8: Memorandum

Memorandum on the occassion of the accidents during the training of flight trainees in the Military Aviator's Schools in the years of war 1915/16/17 and 18.

An astonishingly high number of accidents and deaths seems to occur during flight lessons on the military training area Darmstadt and also other military aviation schools.[1]

The known figures deviate considerably from each other.

However, if even only one third of the given cases were a fact these would also have to be looked at as an extraordinary high number of accidents.

I do not need to assure that I am not driven by ambition to play a role.

It is also not my thing to intervene in single cases and their causes.

If I still deal with the flight training in the present memorandum so this happens merely to serve unselfishly the fatherlandish aviation because as oldest German expert of pilot training I feel qualified to write down my opinion in the following lines and offer the military authority in charge most respectful to to use what seems to be useful.

Maybe also the whole work is suitable under omission of things which are unsuitable for the military service and attribution of the required military moments to be handed over to the leaders of the Fliegerstationen for their information or as directive.

I am convinced that based on my explanations the competent authoritative military places will find out what the present extremely high accidents and death figures are due to without it would be necessary to involve me in the evaluation of the single questions and accidents and their causes. However, I expect with pleasure a competent criticism of my remarks.

In 1908 I have founded the Fliegerstation Darmstadt and there I flew personally for three years and namely, as the relations lay at this time, to test unfinished test machine this means dangerous new constructions at a time when aircraft construction was still in the children's shoes.

One had to consider wind, weather, the arrangement of the place, bad airplanes, defective constructions. As result of the weaker engines one had to compute much more careful than today. As well questions of the teaching principle are solved today and more safe than in the past and the teaching personal is including trained and experienced instructors and airmen today.

I have trained pilots, either civiians or pilots of the Royal Prussian and Bavarian army administration during the above mentioned time in Darmstadt. The airplanes did not carry two persons and the flight trainees had to make their first flights alone without instructor and alien help after their theoretical training.

I mention here that during my activity and the training of officers, NCOs, and civil pilots during the training activities at the military training ground in Darmstadt in spite of the bad machines and incomplete means in the first three years not a single pupil or aviator crashed to his death or merely injured himself. I am only mentioning this because of the reason, to say that I keep the opinion that this extraordinary number of incidents was not caused by the local conditions of the airfield as some apparently assume.

However, from an aerotechnical point of view the airfield in Darmstadt has been obstructed completely by the military authority meanwhile. It was expanded and enlarged under consideration of all other points of view except the aviator's point of view. So today one can also say that the airfield in its current condition in connection with manufacture and hall arrangement is not so perfectly suited for the training of aviators as before. The Militär-Bauamt, the garrison administration, and other constructional military institutes mostly win a bigger influence on the production and enlargement of the airfield's arrangement than the aeronautical experts.

However, on the other hand also the extraordinary high number of fatal crashes can not only be founded by the needs which the war itself brings because if during a slower training the aeronautical qualities and the number of trained pilots would be bigger in a certain period of time then one would not be able to hold against this that the war made the faster training and bigger number of accidents unavoidable.

I also point at the risk which a training method with such a high number of accidents is carrying for the future military aviation. The enthusiasm for flying is big in Germany, one should not think it is lower in other countries or that we might afford too much at the expenses of the big enthusiasm. It is unavoidable that parents of the young flying enthusiasts get to know about the lethal accidents. The ready airmen and trainees also show off with pleasure about the great danger and if the son is coming home with the wish to volunteer for the aviation troops then the parents enquire with the most detailed questions at many places. Moreover, the communications coming to the parents are blown out as a result of the really occuring high numbers of accidents and it develops bit by bit an aversion and compassionate worry with a troop which seems to be so extraordinary dangerous already during the training of the young people in the homeland. Even if the imagination is allowing to consider the case of emergency and the activity of the airmen in the field and the safe death, in the long run this must severely damage the military interests of aviation because every brave man goes with pleasure in the war for his fatherland but one should not deny that the most people hope as one says not every bullet hits and the decision to become an aviator will not result with the own death. However, if this is becoming the general assumption one day then we will experience our "blue wonder" with the general enthusiasm for the aviator's profession.

I have always been close to the sportive and youthful circles in question in Germany. I know abilities, disposition, courage, perseverance, enthusiasm, and the limits of our people from my 25-year long uninterrupted work in all modern areas of the German sport.

The voluntariness of the report to the aviation troops plays an important role. Without this voluntariness of the Fliegertruppe one can not preserve its performance and its excellent fresh mind for a longer time if we don't find means and ways to reduce the number of accidents in training.

Maybe one has to train 5 to 10 times more aviators slowly, carefully, and cautiously to cover the need without such high numbers of accidents, to protect the best forces of these troops, otherwise the very important and necessary plentiful choice falls away here. According to my experiences from hundreds of trainee pilots unavoidably only 15–20 people become really high-class pilots, the more one must keep of the remaining 80–85 pilots in the Fliegertruppe the more they load the troop with disadvantages in mind and effeicency.

Alone with courage, guts, and defiance of death one can not achieve a lot in flying, other qualities are equally necessary and even more necessary. Sports activity with physical strength and agility to harden the body to support the countries' defence are not maintained since a very long time by our nation. So we have no final judgment when the bow of demands is overstretched. In any case it is certain that our human material has some good qualities which the enemy nations doesn't own, not in the same amount as necessary for aviation.

Orders, strict regulations, and acceleration against the weather and objections of the aviator cause the opposite of what is intended with it. With orders from the safe place in administration is therefore done less than with guts and courage of the aviator alone. One can nearly say about flying that courage and guts alone are dangerous, just as one can claim here that who needs courage to fly wants to cover other defects related to necessary abilities; such a courage has as cause worry and fear of the probably felt insecurity and inability.

The airmen who needs the most courage is in the biggest danger and mostly also the least able one. This world does not belong to the most courageous, but that airman who thinks he has all aeronautical abilities. It does not come into his mind that he needs courage and guts very different to the brave soldier who is following orders without being able to oppose something special to the individual danger threatening him. Therefore one should order so little as possible during flight training. So that later nothing must be ordered to the ready airmen regarding flying because he is not encompassed by his superior or instructor then.

The teaching and learning of flying is not even a fight with an armed opponent, so the more the protrudingly said applies.

In my practice those airmen and trainee pilots had most courage and guts which performed at least, especially among officers, they aways tried to replace lacking skills by force and energy, risked more than the most talented, to save the aviatic honor. They were always in the greatest danger because their courage and ambition stood in no relation to their abilities. If such men with little practical and aeronautical skills get goals set and get orders with the threat of replacement then their ambition strikes them dead soon.

To possess care, skill, and thoroughness, to control and limit ambition, courage and high spirits are qualities which one should expect from a trainee pilot; on the other hand the training method should work on the education of such aeronautical qualities. However, often it is the other way around, training becomes often a courage and guts competition and the competent, proficient, and capable man becomes eclipsed within a short time of training by the dashing, less skilled with his lucky accidental success of the reckless. A aviation troop trained this way has no qualities in the long run, it is playing va banque with lucky hits.

Here can be said almost properly: better once cowardly than the whole life dead to the harm of the future aeronautical performance.

One can not apply the same principles on the training of aviators, which one applies on on the other purely military disciplines, it concerns here in the central issue something completely else.

Particularly one may not determine the replacement of seemingly less capable airman after time and a system from the distance. Without knowledge and approval of the instructor one may not remove subnormal aviators or even force subnormal aviators by term settlement. If this time is also connected with bad, for training inexpedient weather then accidents happen especially with usually careful and sensible trainees.

The instructor must remain decisive under all circumstances, he knows the man and the causes of his skill or non-skill best. If the instructor can not be decisive for further training or replacement then the instructor, but not the trainee, must be removed or substituted.

The opinion of the instructor about the mental state of the trainee plays a quite important role here. A flying instructor who can only fly is no suitable flying instructor. Flying instructors need a very special training, they must be people of the highest possible objectivity and intelligence. I would create a special taining establishment for the military training of flying instructors with all necessary means to make the instructors first class mind people in a scientific sense. In my opinion the most capable flier is not an instructor for the purpose of my view without a certain high degree of intelligence.

Before an airman is made instructor or trainees are entrusted to him, he should have to make a teacher examination after a careful offical preparation, this is equally necessary as the trainees examination. It is not enough that an instructor is only an officer since the instructing or leading officer must own human and psychical qualities, to which one should make the biggest demands, if a certain extensive big training result should be connected with low or suitable accident figures.

One could write volumes of tragedy about many lethal crashs which have their cause in wrong positions of the instructor to the trainee or from person to person. It is better that they remain buried in penitent hearts of the concerned instructors. The instructor is also not always responsible that he became an instructor, often not even the person who selected him but the applied system of appointment of teacher staff carries ofthen the guilt here.

Apart from all these moments the machine material will have of course also a decisive influence on the occurence of mistfortunes; however, this influence is not as big as the earlier mentioned aspects.

A machine which is discarded from the field and is made a teaching machine, must be checked under all circumstances, whether it is owning the characteristics, which one must demand of a school machine for the hand of an unskilled, sometimes even incapable trainee. For example if such a machine is tail-heavy then it is maybe possible for a skilled experienced pilot to tickle the highest climbing performance from this machine but it is a very dangerous instrument of training in the hand of a trainee. A front-heavy machine is equally dangerous and if the military repair shops are tempted to compensate this front-heaviness by the placement of weights in the tail of the machine, thus the wing areas of the controls are not enough any more to limit the additional weights accelerated to one direction; such machines become gradually killer machines by similar improvements. So modified machines are more frequently in use than one is believing, a periodical check of all school machines in this direction is necessary; it is also necessary to check outbalanced machines after a use of some periods again and especially after bad landings. Additional weights for balancing must be forbidden as well as counterbalancing by inclined damping fins. I would prohibit adjustable and inclined damping fins already in aircraft factories. Also such machines are in use.

There are of course still a lot of such and similar aspects to be considered, as soon as a machine is manufactured of adjusted for training: it should own especially big payload and uplift, the wings should not be too little, the dead load not too big. It would have to fall back automatically into normal flight position after pilot errors, this is nearly impossible with machines which have 30–50 kg lead in the tail, and especially if the pilot errors occur in curves.

It is also cheaper and more succesful for the training to advance step by step with the use of machines and instead of immediately shooting with live ammunition to let exercise the first flight exercises at first with big and flimsy exercise machines in very calm weather and with very well suited machines until one knows if the trainee has the quality and skill at all to become a pilot.

School machines should be repaired always only by the original factory if the breakage is so big that the airfield's repairshop can not fix the damage because what is not possible for this airfield workshop is impossible for a carpenter's workshop, a piano factory, or furniture workshop aerotechnically as well. There are in general much fewer people who understand something from aeronautical engineering in the sense of construction and relevant effects in the air as one believes. It is often the opposite of what many amateurs imagine for the practical case in the air, the expertness is often too young, in the best case 7 years old, in the most cases 2–4 years old.

Often authoritative persons also sit at the most influential positions which only believe to understand something of areonautical engineering and the training of airmen, but who miss every training and individual experience. This is also the result of the development stage in which flying is; at such mass training one should clear up with it.

In my humble opinion only half of the young people in accepted aviation is useful for the time as pilot trainee. There is not much achieved by the examination of of eyes, heart, lung and kidneys; nervous people and also men who are not free of alcohol, have sometimes the most brilliant aeronautical characteristics, while by no means the best healthiness conditions alone should be basic conditions for the acceptance in the pilot training. This should be understood particularly in the regard that the judgement of the health of eyes, heart, lung, and kidneys must be set in a temporary relation to the not repudiable danger in aviation, in so far as heart, lung, and nerves are not required to be judged in flying for an estimated time of life of 80 years. Intelligence, nervousness, artistic vigour, and skill go very often hand in hand. If self-control, being moderate, careful, critical spirit of enterprise is added then the best qualities for a pilot are given, if the latter is nervous, then it is paying a role like other illnesses, which one can keep under control.

All airmen are nervous in the long run on the ground while the most nervous people are often the most calmest and quitest people in the air under difficult conditions. One must believe it because it is in such a way, also the judgment of a neurologist who has mostly leased the relevant reason, changes nothing in it, one ask the old high-class aviators about this.

It is also of special importance that one does not limit himself to simply prohibit the consumption of alcohol at the Fligerstation; it is better on the contrary to organise it unseen in friendly meetings and to limit the relevant consumption on this way. Nevertheless, people drink, and in particular if it is forbidden.

The excessive use of cigarettes is a much bigger enemy for the airman than alcohol, a custom, which rages just in the aviation troop in a frightening manner; it causes a specific type of nervousness, particularly, since the cigarette-smoking airman smokes the more if he faces flying fearful and needs courage and before the start he is sometimes formally devouring 10–20 cigarettes, namely because he wants to fly and has to fly. However, he is not always knowing this cause for his cigarette smoking.

I would not like to omit to confess that I have also drunk with my trainees at the right time and have discovered that the aeronautical mind has had always use from this. Here one has the best opportunity to take away the catastrophic side from aviation, to create a happy self-denying mind without condition, which predominates with a certain strength and cheerfulness and proud calm all nerve destroying moments and dominates and controls all nervousness. If one drinks at an aviation station or outside among trainees that one can hardly avoid if one has the right people and wants to keep them in the right mood then one should not let fly and one should also supervise all holidays and drinking days and should arrange that they fall on days with bad weather, where one can possibly not fly at all. So one can also influence the pilots disciplinatory in this direction for later times when they are left to themselves. Finally he will also only fly based on his own decision and perform well if he is really skilled and has himself completely in his hand. The people who do not drink at all and commit no excesses will seldom become aviators in big enough numbers.

If the purely military aspects suffer from these points of view in favor of the total situation in this peculiar special troop, this has in my humble opinion no great importance. Here is more than anywhere a bigger freedom in place and lies founded in the matter itself since personality is everything, obedience little, because in the case of emergency the pilot alone is responsible for his devotion to duty without any companion and control, also if he is flying with company. He can do or let what he wants, without being able to be controlled regards cause and effect. His personal free qualities are decisive for his actions and achievements, he is conducting war on his own fist, in aircombat he is commanding General and acting soldier at the same time. Moreover he is hanging in the air, from which he can find – beside the soldier's death – his death by crash.

Endnotes

1 Such a troop can be bred in the long run only in bigger freedom, particularly because various artistic qualities are also demanded and the purely technical aspects are the artistic aspects for these laymen.

One must find and remove skivers with other means, so that the other airmen are not bothered by the measures taken against the first group and disadvantaged in their personal qualities and striving for independence.

Furthermore it has to be considered that for each different training purpose, e.g., giant airplanes, fighter airplanes, bomb-dropping airplanes, other principles, other training machines, other instruction methods must be applied. Also during the retraining for another type it is necessary that one knows the previous course of training of the trainee in the new school. If for example a high-class pilot who was trained up to now with flight machines with an engine aft was set on another airplane type with a tractor engine then one can not point enough to the fact that the flight machine must be operated regarding the controls completely reversed in landings. This is not so easy in practice as it sounds because people do also in the air often and easily from mechanical habit not what he wants to do. A quite good pilot who has learned to fly with an engine in front will nearly never become a pilot on airplanes with the engine aft. The same will judge airplanes with engines aft always worse and use the most hair-raising reasoning for this.

For this reason until now airplanes with engines aft could not stay in the German army, although they have unusual advantages for military purposes. However, this is also connected with the skill-qualities of our German man.

If for example one is not considering the previous training of a man during the retraining for another type of airplane, e.g., giant airplanes with engines aft, then it is nearly unavoidable that bigger damages, accidents, and crashs occur. It is necessary that the instructor knows and has flown both types, the one flown earlier by the pilot trainee and and the new one that he should fly now. Otherwise the teacher can not give the necessary instructions.

Furthermore one has to point out that aerobatics which are liked at all times and are flown especially with joy without any special occasion or need in the homeland over cities because of ambition and high spirit, should be forbidden on the strictest. With this machine one can make a certain trick, with the other not. What one pilot is able to do regading this, is the other not able to do. In both cases the trick is imitated without making sure that the available skills and means are sufficient. Such tricks lead to the fact that the pilot becomes more and more reckless without every purpose and cause and he gets an excessively big trust in himself which the machine is not bearing in certain situations. Such enterprises become a ladder with a predetermined end.

I have had trainee pilots who were so obsessed by this trick illness that they said to me on related confrontations: "I know that these tricks will cost me the neck one day I feel it when I execute them and try new ones. On the ground I plan to do it never again but then in the air and if spectators and companions seem to me so small I do not control myself and become more and more unreliable to me and my decisions which I have caught on the ground."

It does not need many small, unlucky moments to let a trick end with a fatal crash; in any case the best trick is not very useful if it is damaging and they serve rather as bad examples for the lesser talented.

In such attempts sometimes the height over the earth is underestimated, the pilots tend to make tricks especially in low heights, especially, if they want to appear over the audience, their companions and visitors over the airfields. This is always dangerous and useless, and, nevertheless, it happens over and over again.

These and many other questions play here in and and are in my opinion one cause for the big number of accidents because they are not appreciated accordingly. The moments mentioned above as causes of flying accidents and these themselves reduce not alone the voluntariness of the entry in the aviation troops in the future but are also a big danger for the training period if several serious accidents occur one after another on one airfield. This always effects the trainees and instructors suchlike that the next accident are often only the the result of the preceding without the need for a specific cause, and a neverousnesss originates among the airmen which is equally dangerous for training as already existing shortcomings in organization, instruction course and machine material.

Then the numbers of acidents and multiply itself, the causes of the accidents are searched with nervousness at the wrong places and allegedly found. In such cases a new series of trainees should not bypass into the next, but there should lie a short trainee-less time between two periods of training. Left good trainees should be transfered to another station, maybe such a station with accidents temporarily closed for reconstruction or other purposes.

In many cases I have observed on different airfields in France and Germany that after the meeting of many misfortunes with lethal results within some days the next week brought an even bigger number of accidents which then had its cause merely in the first incident and the resulting mental constitution of instructors and trainees.

In peace this has often gone so far that pilots of the same station got put together and denied to fly for days. This proves best at all how opposite orders and regulations can bring damage to the mental constitution of flyers and flying teachers.

In such cases long technical discussions and consultations about aeronautical, constructive, and weather opportunities arise in which the trainees outbid each other concerning the possibility of accidents, so that there are finally only accidents left that make the best man in such an environment incapable.

Crash and break commissions should not discuss accidents and their causes in front of trainees so that no unnecessary fears and cowardice are caused. One should not unnecessarly bring scientific aeronautical construction moments in the pilot's discussions. They will not understand them in the relatively short time, understand a lot wrong, feel a certain insecurity against their aircraft factories what makes them finally distrustful and this is always of extraordinary influence on the mental state of the airman.

Excellent designers and professors of aeronautical engineering are in general bad fliers because they know all opportunities of accidents and do hardly come to fly because of all the considerations. One should eleminate such theorists among the trainees or turn them into designers or use them in suitable offices at other places in aeronautical engineering.

By the way the trainee is much longer in training than he himself and many instructors think. In fact he learns if he can already fly and in my opinion it lasts at least 1½ years until the pilot is completely at home in the air. An aviation troop which must and will send its young aviators already after 6 months in the field, does not scoop from the full, has no iron reserve, it lacks the rest for a sensible careful training, everything rushes and must come in such a way as it is.

Many of the achievements prescribed currently do not stand in a suitable relation to the expected success. This applies here for the training just as for the practical flying. For example I would not send three Zeppelins and a number of airplanes to England, to risk 50 first-class people, which were sorted out from 350 people, and Zeppelins, airplanes, and airmen with a material of some millions to destruction in wind and weather, to, what can be assessed before, to annihilate a little number of women and children, some soldiers, and finally also some buildings in England by bombs. The expenditures are much higher, in military means like aeronautical qualities, compared to the successes which are seen militarily. They have no big importance and with which, after all, nothing further is reached, as that one makes it easier for the Englishmen to maintain the war mood. Even in retaliatory measures one should ask oneself in aviation: Does the opponent or us have more damage by retaliation? I mention this only as example in connection with the question that one must calculate the flying qualities under all circumstances in comparison to the presumable achievement, an aviator is the Queen of the chess board of war, this will prove the longer the war is lasting as one can produce only find a few first-class aviators. If the enemy is doing the same, so it is for him not always in the long run the same as for us.

Only after this war one will get an overview concerning the fact, how big the input is in the air and how little in many cases the success of this input, how difficult the different armament and combat means in the air are to produce and to create, and then soon a scale of measurement will be created. Then we know what can be seen ais a success in the air, purposeful and paying, in relation to the actual costs and the input of human material and aeronautical qualities.

If these experiences are concluded with the respective figures in comparative charts and graphical illustrations lie in front of us, then in my opinion we will know that the airplane and the aviator are in general much higher to evaluate and in some fields much lower than today. About this a special work should be authored and the necessary material should be already collected and arranged today.

March 1918
Orderly room

Versuchsabteilung der Verkehrstechnischen — Berlin Schöneberg, 25.2.1914

Note 1. Reason for this memorandum was among others the death of 18 officers at the Fliegerstation in Darmstadt within one week in March 1918. (means the period from 18 to 24 March 1918; see BA Koblenz, estate Euler, Signature N1103-273). The real number of aviators killed in crashes is not definitive to clarify. The local press, here the "Griesheimer Anzeiger" from March 1918 registered one report. A research in the register of death of Griesheim for the months March and April 1918 revealed:

On 12.3. the Reserve Infanterie Ersatzbataillon Nr. 80 reported four deaths by airplane crash; on 22.3. the acting 49. Infanterie Brigade Darmstadt, Flieger-Ersatzabteilung 9 reported four deaths by airplane crash; on 8.4. the acting 49. Infanterie Brigade Darmstadt, Flieger-Ersatzabteilung 9 reported two deaths by airplane crashs.

These are ten deaths within less than 30 days. Another airmen still died in May because of his combustions, which he suffered in the crash.

Above & Below: Euler triplane D.R. 9 fighter prototype. (P. M. Grosz Collection/STBD)

Appendix 9: Excerpt of a Letter from the V.P.K. to the Euler-Flugzeugwerke[2]

Prüfungskommission

Strictly Confidential

To the
Euler Flugzeugwerke
Frankfurt a.M.

After the discussion on 16.2. the examining board has decided after repeated hearing of the works and on condition of higher approval to base the next prize competition for aircraft on the demands that are listed in the attachment.

The commission does not misjudge the demands at all that – increased pay load in connection with 6-fold security by keeping of the characteristics of the single airplane type – is exceeding the instantaneous state of technology and the skills of the different works. However, it has won the conviction in the last consultations that it is most useful for the aircraft works and the development of the military aviation if the <u>steadier, actual need of the troop</u> is laid out as leitmotif and goal of all work instead of the restless, permanently changing "compromises" between the current efficiency of the works and the greatest possible compliance of the troop.

The fuel amounts and special characteristics of the 3 types are determined by the intentions for it's use and therefore to see so long as constant until the practical use demands other points of view.

The pay loads are calculated (in) a form that they can be acknowledged for a long time as sufficient.

For work and invention is also a big and firmly framed field of activity given.

Concerning the pay load is noted in detail:

For every passenger is about 100 kg set which are distributed on:

1. body weight,
2. firearm and ammunition,
3. instruments and board pocket,
4. map equipment, baggage, engine cover and propeller cover.

The pay load is even more reduced for the tactical post reconniaissance (type II) to make the aircraft leighter and so easily transportable as possible.

With type I the pay load increases by 50 kg for dropping ammunition and photographical and telegraphical devices.

The pay load of type III grows beside the weight of the 3 passengers (300 kg) about 150 kg for 2 machine guns with equipment or dropping ammunition.

1. the weight of the armour platings is set "of necessitiy" for the calculation of the pay load instead of the weight of a passenger. A support of this absolutely important question is particularly welcomed. An airplane which is able to carry in addition parts of the armour plating on observance of the other rules will have to count with an extraordinary preference in the coming competition.
2. The prize distribution should occur after minus- and plus points, depending on wether the airplane is achieving the demands or is leaping it.
3. The test of the armour plating on usefulness is a matter of the test company Adlershof which keeps the works informed about the results.
4. The same is valid for possible orders in the storage of the dropping ammunition and other further inquiries.
5. the procurement of engines for attempts remains a thing of the works.
6. In the future it is intended to demand the delivery of silencers together with orders.
7. The full month November (1914) is taken in view as time of the competition (Adlershof-test company).
8. The airplanes in the works or in order at the time are to be delivered according to the present conditions. On this occassion it is noted that the currently used types (biplanes and Tauben) in their current state of development are all categorized as types of class I.
9. They already have to expect an increase of fuel to 6 hours and a pay load of 220 kg with the next order while other conditions remain constant.
10. In the future after the competition 1914 the size of the orders will depend on to what extent the airplane is coming closer and closer to the demands in the attachment.
11. For the competition in November 1914 it is intended to suggest the following prizes:

	Type I.	Type II.	Type III.
1. Prize	75.000	100.000	100.000

2. Prize	50.000	50.000	50.000
3. Prize	25.000	25.000	25.000

…………

1 attachment

sign. Roethe
Major

Attachment

Demands for Aircraft type I.
suitable for long flights, equipped with tools of destruction or photogr. device or radiotelegr.

Wing span	not more than 14 ½ m
Engine power	about 125 HP
Transport ability	very well
Assembly	one hour with 5 men
Number of seats	two
Start	100 m
Landing	70 m
Natural stability	excellent
Climbing ability	800 m in 15 min
Observation opportunities	so good as possible (as before)
Angles of shooting	lesser important (self-defence)
Agility	as good as possible (as before)
Quietness	very desirable
Speed	about 120 km
Amount of fuel	for 6 hours
Size of tank	for 6 hours
Pay load	250 kg
Armour plating	desirable (counts as pay load)
Machine guns	no
Acceptance flight	1 hour (high-altitude flight can be included)
Security	6-fold

Demands for Aircraft type II.
suitable for short flights, for low level attacks in enemy fire, equipped with the most necessary self-defence (perhaps hand grenades)

Wing span	preferably not more than 12 m
Engine power	about 100 HP
Transport ability	excellent
Assembly	15 minutes with 5 men
Number of seats	two
Start	50 m
Landing	50 m
Natural stability	less important
Climbing ability	excellent, 800 m in 5 min
Observation opportunities	excellent also sidewards below
Angles of shooting	lesser important (self-defence)
Agility	excellent
Quietness	desirable (less important)
Speed	about 90 km
Amount of fuel	for 1½ hours
Size of tank	for 4 hours
Pay load	180 kg
Armour plating	very desireble (computes as payload)
Machine guns	no
Acceptance flight	1 hour (high-altitude flight can be included)
Security	6-fold

Demands for Aircraft type III.
suitable for long-distance flights, for low-level-flights

in enemy fire, equipped for attacks.

Wing span ability	The limit lies in the transport
Engine power	about 200 HP
Transport ability	good
Assembly	1½ hours with 5 men
Number of seats	three
Start	100 m
Landing	100 m
Natural stability	desirable
Climbing ability	good, 800 m in 10 min
Observation opportunities	excellent also sidewards below
Angles of shooting	excellent (hemisphere forward and preferably also backwards)
Agility	excellent
Quietness	desirable
Speed	more than 120 km
Amount of fuel	for 6 hours
Size of tank	for 6 hours
Pay load	450 kg
Armour plating	very desireble (computes as pay load)
Machine guns	two (computes as pay load)
Acceptance flight	1 hour (as in the margin)
Security	6-fold

Reason for this memorandum was among others the death of 18 officers at the Fliegerstation in Darmstadt within one week in March 1918. (means the period from 18 to 24 March 1918; see BA Koblenz, estate Euler, Signature N1103-273). The real number of aviators killed in crashes is not definitiv to clarify. The local press, here the "Griesheimer Anzeiger" from March 1918 registered one report. A research in the register of death of Griesheim for the months March and April 1918 revealed:

On 12.3. the Reserve Infanterie Ersatzbataillon Nr. 80 reported four deaths by airplane crash; on 22.3. the acting 49. Infanterie Brigade Darmstadt, Flieger-Ersatzabteilung 9 reported four deaths by airplane crash; on 8.4. the acting 49. Infanterie Brigade Darmstadt, Flieger-Ersatzabteilung 9 reported two deaths by airplane crashs.

These are ten deaths within less than 30 days. Another airmen still died in May because of his burns, which he suffered in the crash.

Endnote

1. Bundesarchiv Koblenz, estate Euler, signature N1103-55

Appendix 10: Copy of a Letter of the Euler-Werke[1]

EULER-WERKE, FRANKFURT AM MAIN

Frankfurt a. M., 2 December 1914
Niederrad

To Königliche Inspektion der Fliegertruppen,

Berlin-Schöneberg

I hand over to the Royal Inspection enclosed a protocol about the exam flight of a new type of flight machine, which correpondes to the new conditions demanded by the Royal army administration.

The flight machine shows the following changes compared to the present type:

The airframe is pressed from his front point up to behind the wings and the pilot's seat from a closed sheet steel.

This frame is nowhere welded together.

This steel frame takes up in itself:

the engine,

the oil tank for 6 hours,

the fuel tank for 6 hours,

the seats for pilot and observer also made of steel,

the controls,

all levers for the operation of the engine,

all instruments.

Furthermore the steel frame is connected with:

the steel undercarriage and

the steel spanning tower.

Furthermore this steel airframe takes up in itself the wing longeron in massive steel construction, so that neither a movement nor a distortion of the wing can happen at this point and a change of the angle of inclination of the wing against the engine is completely excluded. Within this steel airframe wood is used at no place. Consequently the space within this steel airframe is substantially bigger and more free and finally absolutely flameproof.

It is impossible that from the propeller to behind the pilot's seat any object can start to burn or overflowing fuel can burn more than itself. Consequently this kind of disagreeable results and dangers are excluded for these reasons.

The longitudinal support and the crossbar in this airframe are completely pressed steel sheet till aft the wings, so that shots and such like can not cause any adverse damages for the aircraft itself.

The whole steel frame from the propeller till aft the pilot's seat respective behind the wings contains absolutely no tension wires, turnbuckles, lugs, safeguards or alike, therefore it can not warp. The short tail end is removable from the real steel sheet frame by unscrewing 4 cross-beams, so that it can be separated within some minutes from the main frame. Therefore it is possible to load at least two frames on one rail car. The same are to be connected at their most external rear ends by pushing together a little piece of wood, so that two frames stand like a four wheeled vehicle on one rail car.

The cooler, which has provided the best results in long tests during a cold of 10° up to a warmth of 40° in the shadow, is also inserted in the steel frame. So it holds the engine case in winter on a steady warmth, in summer the warmth is derived from the engine downwards in a drain.

The cylinder heads which outstand from the steel frame, are completely closed by a bonnet, so that very essential warm differences on the cylinder jackets might not occur during cold. On the floor in front of observer the same is easy to open by a rope train, so that the observer can look directly on the earth.

The floor in the steel frame is made from strong aluminium metal and is provided with an oil deductive device, which collects all oil splashing around in the gondola and leads it to the earth by six small deduction tubes.

The small tail end which is holding the damping area and the control areas, shows in comparison to earlier machines and the LVG biplane, that served as model, a very essential strengthening of the cross section.

The chassis shoe experienced a change so that a pushing of the applied elastic rings or a scrubbing of the same is excluded. By a peculiar but simply arranged tin is it possible to pull out the start axis from the chassis without the need to touch or dismantle the elastic rings.

The tail end is tightened round aft and the end bind together by a piece of pressed steel frame.

A change is also met there that the up to now prescribed weight of the elevator control is not noticeable in the hand anymore, namely without the application of a retreat feather or elastics not a balance weight. Also this weight is not removed by the inclination of the damping area of the tail against the crankshaft. The damping area stands completely free of every pressure during the flight with the engine axis in the horizontal as well as the elevator area.

The machine was – as the enclosed protocol proves – flown today in the morning in very bad weather. It was very bumpy. The wind swayed in low heights between 8–16 meters, in bigger heights it was very windy and bumpy, the sky was covered.

The machine had 6 hour-tanks. The excess weight of the 6 hour-tanks is not subtracted from the load. It would add approximately 4½ kg on the pay load, so that the pay load would have amounted to 224½ kg then.

Under these conditions the machine shows the enclosed registered flight characteristics. A better climbing was impossible because of the covered sky. The gliding ability, which existed already in an excellent manner with the present type, became even bigger with this machine and the machine glides with shut down engine remarkably flat and very slow. From the barograms enclosed in the protocol exist 3 pieces because the machine flew under control of three Goerz' barographs No. 3019, No. 3045 and No. 3898.

For the rest, reference is made to the contents of the enclosed protocol and most respectfully left to you to inspect the flight machine with an expert commission and to test and fly it with a military pilot. In the latter case the breakage must go at the expenses of the Royal army administration.

I would like to note at the same time that the machine can not be produced with the currently paid price. It will be a bit more expensive than the machine delivered up to now. The machine and its single constructions are the result of a diligent test work in the last six months. I still note that the prototype is a factory machine which represents until the production of a new machine an extraordinary value, so that this machine can not be delivered to a regular price because this first machine has a three times higher cost price than a machine in regular serial production and is a kind of factory hand sample.

Respectfully
sign. August Euler

1 protocol
Factory No: 148

Negotiated Frankfurt a/Main the 2 December 1914.

The signed commission trialed on 2 December 1914 according to figure ......of the special conditions of the contract from .... biplane with 100 HP Mercedes engine Type 1246 No. 21132 of the Euler-Werken to be delivered to the Army administration in flight test.

Pilot of the airplane Wald, ... weight 74½ kg.
passenger .... Deville, >=.. weight 75 kg
ballasting 70½ kg
Sa. Weight 220 kg
Propeller (brand) Integral Nr. 4132
Operating materials were on board for all 4 hours, namely:
160 ltr fuel
12 kg oil
The start measured 60 m.
The landing measured 50 m
Air temperature in shadow 10 ° C
Air temperature in sun
Special weather conditions 8–16 meters bumpy wind, clouds at 1500 meters.

The height of 800 m was reached in 10 min after the takeoff. The achieved height was indicated by barographs of the factory Goerz No. 3019, No. 3045 and No. 3898.

Takeoff to the high-altitude flight 10 o'clock 02 min. before noon
Landing 10 o'clock 35 min. "
Departure to the 1 hour flight Uhr Min. "
Landing Uhr Min. "

The landing occured in a glide from 1650 meters with put down ignition.
Impregnate mass Aviatol

The airplane was checked in all parts with a detailed investigation, especially the points of soldering and welding, screw connections, control cables and its mobility in the guiding roles were checked in detail. The airplane was sealed.

Remarks:
This protocol is a private acceptance protocol of the Euler-Werke. The Euler-Werke guarantee for the correctness of the noted achievements and remaining information.

For the factory

Pilot Euler-Werke

H.W. Wald August Euler, Horter, Dr. Eulau

Endnote

1. Bundesarchiv Koblenz, estate August Euler, signature N1103-254

Appendix 11: The Case Daimler – Memorandum for the History of Aviation

The Case Daimler,
Memorandum for the History
of Aviation
by
August Euler

Frankfurt a. M., in April 1918

The purpose of this memorandum is to judge the case Daimler also from the other important viewpoints which lie in national interest as the ones already done by the Reichstag and the Royal army administration.

The judgement of the Reichstag and measures taken by the military against the Daimler-Motoren-Gesellschaft [Daimler Motor Company] have already caused a harmful judgment in the public opinion against the national interests by its one-sidedness.

The war has already caused so strong defeats of the objective judgment of authorization, achievement, compensation, and merit in the material and moral sense by the violent strength of the conditions that after the up to now known notifications about the case Daimler it means a jump into millions of open swords if one wanted to defend Daimler.

Nevertheless, the jump happens in national interest and for the protection of our German inventors and industrialists whose abilities and activity is inevitably connected with our national war and peace achievements.

With the following statements I represent the contrary point of view to the public opinion which is suffering under the current war psychosis and I will explain my view of the case with moralistic, industrial, technical, historical, legislative, national, and political reasons and moments.

The representative of the Royal Prussian War Ministry has said in the relevant Reichstag meeting to the justification of the Royal Army administration that Daimler delivered the best material, the best engines, and the factory had only received the considered orders when it really was the cheapest among all competitors.

This alone should be enough for the army administration, the Reichstag and the public opinion.

Everything, what has been said besides, turns upside down the up to now valid views, hurries ahead of the efficiency of our state and its remaining economy; how should other industries with less good products and higher retail prices be judged?

There is a big number of army suppliers who did neither own any noteworthy property before the war nor relevant factory equipment. They got the factory model of a grenade, a prototype airplane, etc., and related cash in advance and earned as single persons many millions during four years of war.

I give this example only to put it into contrast to Daimler and the following statements.

I think it is natural that the statements of the representative of the Royal War Ministry in the Reichstag were only made, to protect the army administration against the reproach that it did not work with greatest care regarding the price acceptance during the distribution of orders. However, this is rather incomprehensible at the same time, since one can not expect of the Royal army administration that it gives other enterprises, which deliver lesser good engines, the orders for higher prices, than such were demanded by Daimler. However, if it still happened, then it must have reasons.

What can be still said against Daimler then?

Only maybe that Daimler has economized so penny-wise and with business care earlier and today that such high earnings are the result from this.

Decisive for the judgement of the so-called adequate price will be also in war the free play of all into consideration coming competitive forces which result in the performance of the affected national industry; another scale of measurement does not exist under our valid legislation.

I won't to have said that the profit, which was made by the Daimler-Werke in the war, was not high enough; what I try to prove is, that it is rightly high, and that the terms of abuse, which rain down on the enterprise from all other sides as a result of the discussions in the Reichstag, are wrongful.

Merely for the completeness of this writing I state these terms of abuse here once again:

Fraud, usurer, traitor to the fatherland, sabotage, trickster, hobo, war profiteer hoodlums, profiteers, completed deception, treason, scandalous highway robbery against the Reich, blackmailers, cheating of the nation, beside of much worse comparisons, in which the heaviest insults were hidden.

The principles of the economy of our states or the

different communities and the justified self-interests have resulted from the historical development of the things in the world, also the valid legal concepts and customary equipment and authorizations.

The history of the development of the private property gives here the authoritative clues for what must be considered without fail as usual and rightly existing for today's relations, in so far as this arises from the valid right and the latter is the concentration of all collected relevant experiences from the above discussed history of development.

All these experiences there face strange, never before existing war fabrication relations with the only balancing moment, the fiscal registration of unexpected and too big profits, which result form the sudden mass production and the simplification of the working procedures.

However, if one considers the possible balance by taxes, then a scale of measurement derived from Daimler does not fit to the performance of the remaining and therefore Daimler can not be judged disparagingly for extraordinary good achievements.

Let us assume the case that the Daimler-Werke would have been guided by the reasons and points of view which now are represented in the press, by the Reichstag and by other important authoritative places, then the following should have happened:

The Daimler-Werke would have sold – as a result of its big efficiency in the technological, business, factory-organizational areas, and modern working methods and division of labor – an engine not for 20,000 – Mark but for 12,000 Mark, thus the result would have been that the whole remaining industry would have been forced to work for the same price if they wanted to receive orders.

However, the most German industrial factories have begun the manufacture of engines in the war or have made bad experiences with the profits of this production in the last years of peace.

The Daimler-Werke had big relevant experiences from the peace, the biggest technical success and the most luck in this respect because they brought out engines with which the German military mechanics got along best.

Should now the remaining industry work with losses or get higher prices than Daimler in spite of less good engines for military purposes, or should only Daimler be employed with flight engines?

This would probably be regretted – apart form others – by the Inspektion des Kraftfahrwesens, as it should be regretted for the war and peace performance of our motor vehicles and other articles in general.

On the said way Daimler would have undoubtedly avoided the nationalization, and from here the highest efficiency would have made the way down on the other side or Daimler would have made the same way, if not nationalized, or finally the army administration would have had, after all, no competitor for Daimler.

The whole performance of the German flight engine industry would still have stayed behind accordingly during the war compared to other states, since it is not certain, that seen internationally Daimler is making the best flight engine. Therefore the remaining industry had to be pulled in this competition of factories and to be kept there. From this, however, arises not only in peace but also in war a market price which resulted as involvement of all interests and within this frame Daimler has surely not demanded too much.

Up to a certain performance every industrial enterprise has an interest not to wake up the impression of lower material quality and labor, etc., in the public by a cheaper than usual price, particularly for articles, from which a high quality and reliability must be expected, as it is the case in the highest degree for flight engines.

Now it is further considered that the Daimler-Motoren-Gesellschaft could have taken rightly higher earnings than some other industrial enterprises.

It is unquestionable that the Daimler-Werke were among the pioneers concerning engine and flight engine production in Germany.

The Daimler-Werke have spend considerable sums [of money] for suitable facilities and experiences in peace time for such efforts, which were deducted over years from the profits in peace made by other peace products in favor of the future performance in war.

The founders of the company have used their lives together with other German technicians to give the world the tool to use the valuable good, the time, more efficient; this has succeeded with the biggest success in thinkable short time.

The company continued to work on this way and namely for years without earnings in its hands; its first income or the first rewarding sales was found exclusively and over years abroad.

The company is not one of the countless war companies which could freely scoop from the full results of the pioneer's work of others to gain the means for war mass production and profits.

Daimler and a few others enterprises were the creators of the technology being considered here and can not be compared to occasionally war multiplicators of alien intellectual property.

Capital, workforce, complete manufacturing plants, long experience as inventors, division of labor, and modern organization, technical and business experience, all with Swabian care, ambition and diligence accumulated in peace, have presented itself favorable and ready in war.

In addition long experiences came from the purchase.

The possibility for the correct judgment of the best fitting material quality were given in a form that losses were nearly impossible. No time-consuming new tests arose, no insecurity in the fabrication, material procurement, business, and technical dispositions; everything combined gapless in the most ideal manner.

This all would prove itself tangible, if one would gather the engine stocks of the army administration and would separate the useless flight engines from the useful ones, if one would take the engines with the same number of kilometers or time flown, would detect its further usability and then compare the so won result of its quality with the paid price.

In this higher quality are the costly tests made in peace which are written off from the earnings in peace by other products and which now let the war profit appear higher.

The current manager of the company has to take up the merit for himself that he has organized and melted the high technical qualities of the Daimler-Motoren-Gesellschaft by his organizational talent with the other industrial and commercial moments so useful that he deserves the merit as the organizor of the so greatly added value as a result of the collective effects of the different values.

He is neither an owner of the factory nor a sole proprietor, but only an employee of the company; he has duties from his employment and has only to answer to the appropriate legislation and to his supervisory board.

If such a technically very capable company as the Daimler-Motoren-Gesellschaft would not have such a capable businessman who melted technical abilities with the remaining business and industrial abilities so profitably then the so high appearing profits would have been lost in expenses and worse exploitation of technical abilities and not run again with such a large part in the governments coffers as taxes.

The Daimler-Motoren-Gesellschaft has paid 46 million war taxes from the businesses being considered here and distributed 7 million dividends.

Inventors and engineers are rarely alone realizing their mind products in manifold deeds.

However, the war has shifted in considerable measure the amount of salaries. If for example sport and luxury articles became mass articles; an aircraft engine was a little piece of art in peace or a luxury sportive tool, which was produced in little numbers.

During the war the airplane became a mass-produced article.

Who already had the necessary production facilities and other equipment, installations and experiences at the outbreak of war, had it from peace business-capital and peace work.

It turns out that the judgment of the height of the price has been put in general on unsafe feet by the war, since not only the industrialists take incomprehensibly high prices and profits, but also the war societies and other institutions, which are not army suppliers, sell rubber, oil, printed matter, machines and machine parts, raw materials, and thousands of other things for prices, which set others who have to pay for it, in astonishment. At that many of these institutions do not sell from their own manufacture, but only resell, know their purchase price before, their other costs, the wages and salaries, etc., are often covered by the military and Reichs budget, while the industry knows not even the delivery deadline and the opportunity to get the raw material, much less the price of the raw materials and the semi-manufactures at the time of the acceptance of the orders.

Mostly the sub-supplier quotes no price and suggests to give the order without price agreement because he can not evaluate or calculate the price of the last call.

Cases can also be stated where even the determined top prices were considerably overrun by the official sales prices because of unawareness.

The industry calculated up to now in the war concerning the order acceptance quasi from the wrist, without knowledge about the numerical documents of the often later occurring purchase, primarily with the absolute unsafe future, in addition with the possible drawback of the orders and the potential worthlessness of the for peace conditions unusable raw materials and half finished parts, tools, machines, buildings, often even the later sudden conversion of the whole personnel and all means on other articles, which are unknown like its marketing area.

The most careful and able so-called well-arranged businessman in the sense of the commercial law has the biggest profit not always from the intention of usury but for the reason of the use of higher care compared to his business duties; for the rest he lets the state take care, while he gives the state what the state needs and what it is asking him for.

By the way, an industrialist can not calculate if he is accurately following all the laws in war about the release and confiscation of material, its mandatory acquisition, and if he is not punishable and contrary to regulations storing material since the application for and the release of material may be carried out only on the base of occurred orders for the finished product.

Therefore the related exact costs become known only many months after the order under today's conditions.

If one has read the German papers about the case Daimler, one should think that Germany has nothing to owe to her industry.

The fact that the whole industry has been quiet up to now is equally incomprehensible.

The remaining engine industry has been fertilized in the conceivably highest measure by the Daimler-Motoren-Gesellschaft.

Army suppliers, which were only created in the war or converted to war production, receive the ready manufacture model by the army administration. They pay nothing for patents and utility patents in the most cases.

They also have not to make the related costly attempts and expenditures, which are for the most part and often only ways to the goal.

Where is the relevant protection of patents and utility patents considered in the evaluation of Daimler's profits? How high are the related achievements in peace included in the too highly found war profits?

As is generally known only very, very few from thousands of utility patents and patents are effective and in use for mass production.

The valid patent law also limits the usefulness of such patents and utility patents or such intellectual property accordingly, on the other hand it protects the relevant property in a very sharply restricted form.

A patent expires after 15 years or becomes a common property of the public or the state, a utility patent after six years.

Should the patent law be lifted?

Which law should take over its place?

On this occasion I must say with all deference which I have for the Reichstag:

Reichstag! If laws should not become passed, they must be given at first in every case.

For the case Daimler no law is written in the sense of today's view of the German Reichstag.

However, one can not call something deception, usury and treason, for which existing laws give the amount and limit for such merits and performances safely in form of a compensation.

Patent Law and Commercial Law

Nevertheless, one often has the impression as if with us and in particular during the war the patent rights and the intellectual property are disturbing. One thinks snidely about the personal achievement of the inventor and little about the industrial organizer. This all goes well for a short time in consideration of the accumulation of intellectual production but finally, in the long run one scoops here also in depth, instead from the full because such values run down in international competition and steady progress.

In a Bolshevist state such achievements as they are given with Daimler, are impossible, now such a government would maybe say:

"Yes, what one needs to make war?"

However, one can also say apart from the war: "Aviation, car driving, etc., is equally necessary, as agriculture, the telegraph, the railway, and shoes are for the modern human, without them we can not live anymore.

Already in primeval times the human beings could creep and climb, later they went barefoot upright, then they ran with better and better shoes, went over the water with strength of the hand, the sail and, finally, with steam and internal combustion engine.

They went over the land with bicycle, railway, automobile and now they want to fly.

Therefore flying, automobile, railway driving, et cetera, is necessary; however, the life without these achievements is not.

I would not like to have said that I forecast [airline] aviation already for a close and general future today, it maybe lies as far from today to the future as the general barefooted running lies backward.

If we want in Germany, as was expressed in the Reichstag, want to feed the inventor and industrialist like a mortgagee with 5% profit, then no possibility remains to encourage and use the creative forces of Germany. On the other hand the question arises, why an efficient war industry enterprise should be put on the same level or be judged even worse than a pensioner who personally is not contributing to the war effort?

During this opportunity it should be also tried to find out the causes of the judgment of the Reichstag, today's press and the public opinion. They lie in the political relations of our fatherland.

If in an industrial state the legislative body and its commissions in consultations can establish judgments about the industry, without the industry itself can represent its interest in such consultations, it is, as happened, condemned unheard to the damage of the national interests.

An industrial state should also work industrially and the related interests should be protected and heard also. Therefore it is necessary in the first line that the industry itself can represent its interests in the legislative body and not begging and bowing and scraping on detours at the doors of the Royal War Ministry, the Reich and state authorities and leaving it in each case to the available expertise, special and practical knowledge of the people in the office to represent the industrial interests according to the views of the legislative body with or without success or not at all.

The big boom which the German industry has taken without own Reich representation may be to blame that it has done nothing until now to remedy this lack. Abilities, diligence and the resulting big exports made it possible until now to work without a lobby in the legislative body.

After the war this will probably have to change for various reasons if the industrial abilities should be preserved as decisive factors in our national economy with its present importance. However, for this the industry needs more than ever before also money after the war, to be able to procure the necessary materials and only the industry itself will be able to do this with a related success to some degree.

If, after the war, the industry is only left with the (only from the war needs resulting) stationary brick heaps, machines. and factory equipment if maybe the tax screw has even inscribed mortgages, then the solution of the question of the acquisition of labor and material becomes more and more difficult.

The state and the war offices will be hardly able to bring in raw materials and orders from all over the world.

The case Daimler should be lighted up further, in so far also the order-awarding authority should be considered here as well.

In many cases the article whose manufacture is not mastering the difficulty of the acquititon of the materials and its qualities under today's conditions and prices for easy to understand reasons results all to easy by overeagerness in demanding too little pieces from this side. On the other hand, consequently for other articles, where the situation and people with their views are facing each other more comfortable, higher prices are approved.

There is also a big number of army suppliers that did not earn anything or even have lost all.

The royal army administration mostly has biggest haste if it gives an order since before weeks-long arguments are necessary with the delivering factory about the construction of the object and which demands can be made to it. So that usually the decision to give the order is made very late.

Then the company sometimes receives suddenly an order for a type or object for which it did not expect an order anymore.

Also changes enter in the course of manufacture for easily explained reasons which are often connected with tremendously big costs and difficulties. Therefore one can not expect that the army administration or the order-giving people have the right view for an appropriate judgement.

Then the cheapest prices are sometimes found very expensive but to avoid trouble with the principal the supplier in question is forced to change the order sometimes for free since an additional price increase for militarily prescribed changes is only pressed through very hard and with big time delay at the higher military authorities by the ordering military office.

Sometimes more and more orders for changes are given, so that the whole price calculation is blurred or shifts to other articles and is incorrect in relation to the first article.

So sometimes 5–6 manufactures for which different opinions and changes originated, create a mess.

The military authority often does not manage technical objects at the same time; costly trips and information on location are necessary to bring the objects to a right function again.

Then it turns out very often that lacking special knowledge of the army administration and their executive people or unavoidable haste carried the guilt for the complaint.

For groundless complaints it is never paid because such complaints are not planned with capital in the Army budget.

The company is forced to start or to cease the manufacture day-to-day after such objections. State of emergency works are made, sometimes many weeks long since decisions about the criticism can not be hurried up.

It is not thought about the payment of the caused expenses; related complaints are fruitless from the very beginning.

Since the industry can not know the amount of the upcoming differences in opinion and complaints, which are raised rightly or wrongly, but, in any case, has to consider them with a considerable percentage in the calculation, naturally higher prices are demanded for the different articles and with consideration of the experiences which the company in question has made in the last years with unjustified complaints, sudden changes, so-called factory blocking measures.

For example an airman falls from the air to the ground and is dead. One supposes that a mistake of the engine or the airplane or a single part is the cause.

The blame for the accident is pinned on the machine by the pilots for easy to understand reasons.

In such cases the factory is suspended by telegram, i.e., it is not allowed to deliver any airplane from this moment on, until the complaint is finished. This is often synonymous with work stoppage.

In peace times, when airplanes were not so urgently needed, operating an aircraft factory was often a desperate va banque game for these reasons.

The industrialist nearly always worked for all given orders under reserve of the belated approval for the order in work by the war ministry.

The orders are so urgent that they must be executed immediately; during the whole manufacture the approval of the war ministry floats as sword of Demokles over the head of the relevant industrial enterprise. It is often only given when the order is already delivered.

The situation dissolves itself legally when the acceptance of the object definitively occurred and the provisory approval of the war ministry lapses by itself.

However, during the manufacture it establishes a handle for the war ministry to withdraw from the contract for any disposed reason.

If one is adding to all these moments, which can be enumerated in similar manner to the thousands or a lot more worse one, the present state of war, the difficult acquisition of material, the unsafe prices of the different materials, the increasing wages and furthermore considers that the workforce declines with its abilities more and more during the war since the most competent and healthiest people are needed in the field and that the quality of the material is also declining, thus also related to this the actual costs are rising.

However, all this has an always increasing number of spoilt work pieces as a result.

All this results in the fact that a price calculation, which by the way can not follow the given order, is constantly not existing in war, and a law, to give orders on the base of reliable price calculations is simply not manageable as today with the best knowledge no industrialist can present a price calculation which corresponds to the real conditions of the delivery.

A law, which makes the submission of a calculation a regulation before the ordering will finally impose only duties on both parts which can not be fulfilled or the whole system of ration coupons and allocation methods as the base of the ordering must be lifted completely.

Final Review:
Therefore, for said reasons an industrial representation should be created in the Reichstag and an organ between Reichstag, industry, and war ministry which takes over the business, industrial, technical, scientific works being considered here and their execution and responsibility for the army administration.

The military authorities themselves should be stripped of the ordering work; this would lie in the interest of the state, in the interest of a serious industry which does not want to take a shopkeeper's position and in the interest of the military authority itself.

Today's highly sophisticated relations in technology, the banking business, science and the business occupation require such a comprehensive knowledge for the judgment about the overall situation of an industrial enterprise that one may think short that a military authority could purposeful distribute orders about so many billions and judge regarding the price.

One imagines that one would expect of a high-class industrial enterprise, that its business would be managed in technical and business respect of those representatives who assign them the relevant orders today.

Nobody would lay his money in the hands of people who have been trained their whole life merely for the practical military service or have at best a military administrative activity without any examination and without proof of an industrial and technical training according to today's conditions.

It is inevitable in the long run here that remedial action must be taken since the need for armament demanded by the army administration under the current conditions interferes with all modern branches of science and technology and for their evaluation is a complete, many years requiring study and practical experience necessary.

I imagine the organization of such an administrative purchasing department as follows:

Example for the Fliegertruppe:

1. Inspektion der Fliegertruppen
2. War ministry (Military department)
3. War ministry (Civil department)

To 1.) Inspektion der Fliegertruppen.

This command authority makes only demands for the required objects, which arise from the needs of service, and furthermore works with the complaints resulting from practical use and passes it to the military department of the Royal war ministry.

To 2.) War ministry (Military department, aviation)

This department procures the business communication between troops and civil department.

To 3) Kriegsministerium (Civil department, aviation)

a) Engineer's department,

b) Business department,

c) Scientific department,

d) Juridicial department,

e) Department for the management of the military budget,

f) Order department,

g) Department for Approval,

h) Department for the execution of complaints.

The officials of the civil department are employed and paid according to purely civil experiences and principles.

The responsible leader of the civil department should be hired and paid according to the principles for the leader of a big first-class industrial enterprise, as for example the company Ludwig Löwe u. Co. A.-G., Berlin, Huttenstr.,

the company Robert Bosch A.-G., Stuttgart,

the company Daimler Motoren-Gesellschaft, Untertürkheim.

The civil department resides the while communication with the industry, the suppliers or the business and technical directors.

Over the civil department presides a supervisory board which is appointed by the Reichskanzler from the most successful leaders of the biggest and oldest industrial enterprises of the German Reich. To the same all arrangements and books of the civil department of the war ministry lie open for inspection.

The supervisory board is responsible to the Reich (Reichsamt des Inneren).

In the case of problematic questions there is only one connection between the war ministry's military department and the war ministry's civil department through the honorary working supervisory board. So it can be avoided that purely military views get the upper hand over the alone decisive business and technical view and so the civil department can operate economically generous and completely technical and industrial.

Possible complaints of the industry would come through the Reichsamt des Inneren to the competent supervisory board, nothing could be made under the hand, because the people activity in the supervisory board would stay competitors and the interests of the Royal army administration, the interests of the Reich and the industry would fall into the weighing pan and balance each other.

The performance of the industry would technically and regarding the price unimagined increase for the army supplies, the costs of the military budget would be reduced in a suitable relation with higher and faster performances and better quality of the objects at the same time.

The stimulus for the technical perfection of the armament would be given in a completely different size than today.

A competition of the engineers and technicians would originate in the competent civil department of the war ministry, while today a competition of businessmen in technical armament means is existing and these armament means are finally and authoritatively awarded by professional soldiers with orders.

The salesperson would not come together with the using military pilot and the practical office, in which situation the salesperson even as a businessman ist mostly superior even in technical things.

All partners, who want to achieve and to prove their highest efficiency on a strictly juridical, technical and commercial way, would get one's money worth; an existence of laymen and occasional engineers as manufacturers and suppliers and principals would be impossible.

Appendix 12: Memorandum about the Tasks of the Reichsluftamt

Memorandum No. 1

The Undersecretary of the Reichsluftamt.
No. 136/19

Berlin, 9 January 1919

Many mistaken views about the activity and the sphere of activity of the Reichsluftamt are spread.

The activity of the former Luftamt of the soldier's council of the Fliegertruppen has let arise furthermore the erroneous assumption that a Reichsluftamt is an office for the placement of jobs, airplane sales or air travel agency.

Herewith I feel prompted to direct the following explanation to the public and the places interested in aviation:

The sphere of activity of the Reichsluftamt is the following:

Certification of airplane and airship pilots, registration of air vehicles and airlines for air traffic.

The cooperation in legal measures, which are remitted as a juridical base (the aerial law and its implementary regulations) for the allowance to air traffic.

The Reichsluftamt mediates the business dealings between all Reichs-, state and military authorities, the working circles, the aircraft industry, the air transport companies, etc., interested in aviation.

Furthermore its major task includes

the handling of the questions, which concern the future peace development of the national and international aviation;

the skilled and expert consultation of our negotiators for the peace negotiations;

the processing of appropriate questions with the federal states of the German Reich;

the support of flight competitions and airplane exhibitions with the purpose of the development of traffic and trade airplane types and aircraft engines, likewise the promotion of promising inventions , which concern the aviation and the aeronautical engineering.

The Reichsluftamt is not responsible for questions of the job mediation of the staff that worked earlier in aviation, also not for matters of the demobilization,but the demobilization office.

The Reichsluftamt is not responsible for questions of the utilisation of of the army devices of aviation but the Reichsverwertungsamt.

Since a nationalization of the air traffic is not yet considered by the government, the Reichsluftamt is not training pilots, does not employ pilots and is not operating any air traffic.

It must be pointed out that one can not assume, especially not in the next time, an extent of aviation as it was necessary during the war for military reasons and it will last until the people oriented themselves and their interests on international aviation.

The available means of war aviation are not competitive to the current peace aviation and the other means of traffic and transport.

If for the military aerial means of transportation immediately intended purposes were searched, this would lead - especially now in the winter - with few available fuels of rather low quality in connection with the carburettor question to unreliability which only would shake the trust of the public and strongly disadvantage the development of aviation for a longer time.

Therefore, it is inevitable that the biggest part of the staff schooled for aviation in war moves away in his former occupations.

It is hopeless to give the hope space that 100.000 and more pilots who had learnt to fly during the war, could reckon in the next future to see their professional existence in aeronautical existence; completely apart from the fact that the material and especially the fuel question, even if other pre-conditions would exist, would make a bigger professional aeronautical activity impossible for the next months.

The most pilots have learned to fly during the war at the expenses of the state. Already for this reason they have no higher right to claim their military service activity as their civil job like the other military persons. Pilots qualified during the war are mostly of juvenile age. They must search for another occupation as pilot is always only a job for at most 4 to 5 years as the present experiences have shown.

Furthermore, if the aerial legal issues are judged by national points of view, for the present Germany the important question of rentability comes into consideration.

It bumps into great difficulties to use the existing means of air transport in the German air traffic useful and profitable in the interest of the national economy, this should mean, profitable for the German air traffic enterprises and especially profitable for the purpose for which the air traffic is. If the latter is not possible then the purpose and therefore the application of air traffic for this purpose is lost.

During the war it became not known to the public in which relation the application of means stood to the aeronautical achievements, which, if one has to use them economically and considers the profitability in quite another light than in the light of national war enthusiasm would appear.

In the peace years from 1910 to 1914 the industry was occupied for the war expected at least from the world. If the war had not broken out, it would have had years long for this reason, that one had expected a war, a considerably bigger possibility of employment given than it is the case today after the war.

Consequently the extent that the aircraft industry and aviation has grown into before the war, was bigger than it can be today for the next future.

During the war the amount of the available means of aviation multiplied, so that we stand before an entire over-development compared with the ranges of application in peace.

Therefore, the industry just as the pilots will have to adapt to the by far biggest part to another activity.

A business success of the future aircraft industry will be only in the range of possibilities, if the aviation is unwinding internationally in the air without consideration of cities, villages, borders, duties, nationalities and water crossings and if all organizational national moments on the ground during start, landing and emergency landing can be done, so that the airplane gets a superiority for certain purposes and distances compared to other means of transport.

The airplane factories will become test workshops again and the breeding of new types for traffic purposes will be the tool for the economic construction of a later international competitive German aviation.

Aeronautical engineering and aviation are still, seen as a whole, in the stage of development.

The airplane system, with which we fly, has come to the end of its possibilities of development in today's totality.

Probably one can not make such an airplane bigger, faster, more load-bearing, smaller, more climbable, more controlable, more labile, more solid.

However, the single moments said here depend so on each other and balance themselves as values so mutually that, relatively seen, wind and weather have a certain degree of influence which limits the possibilities for an application of the system in the regular traffic.

In the competition with other means of transportation still the essential disadvantage must be considered for the airplane that the other means of transportation on the ground also have the night to its disposal.

Everything, that is ready in the evening after a written daily work, can, for example from Frankfurt a. M. or Munich, arrive in Berlin by rail and can be assigned to the prospective customers.

The airplane would be only in Berlin at the next afternoon, because it can only fly on the next morning.

Night flights of the public reliable transport belong into the realm of wishes; even for big distances over the land the airplane will be preliminary non-competitive where other modern means of transport like railway, automobile etc. are available. If, moreover, one adds the time for the arrival on and the departure from the airfield and furthermore assumes that the air passenger and the leader must also sleep after a 12-hour flight and the railway passenger get up from the railway equally well rested and can bring his big suitcases along, then the competitive ability of the airplane can not be considered as very big.

As well it may not be overlooked the fact that the air transport can not be a regular one after a timetable.

As well it can only be an accidental air transport, which can happen from case to case in fairly good weather.

With a statistic about the costs of training, the accidents and lethal crashs during the training of pilots in the four war years it would be easy to prove that the expenditures alone for the training of pilots stand in a rather unfavorable relation to the result which seems to be desirable for peace and economic purposes. This seems to be important if the state should take over the costs for a nationalized aviation. Furthermore it must be considered that new airman's staff must be trained every two to three years.

If one demands that I as an enthusiastic sportsman write a memorandum to the glorification of aviation for a rich land, then this memorandum will be carried by optimism and enthusiasm for our aviation.

However, as leader of the Reichsluftamt I feel obliged to put on the chains of the national-economic usefulness to my ideal enthusiasm because it concerns not my money here, but it concerns duties to the very, very unlucky German nation, which was defeated by the whole world in the biggest war of all times and was left by its friends.

Finally, the paternalism and the damaging of the people by delusive encouragement must be stopped; in any case the authorities should not burden aviation with such deceptions.

At the moment the financial situation of the Reich does not permit that, merely to make easier the possibility of existence to interested circles to use raw materials and objects without any use value since raw materials, fuels, etc., are in need for economically more important purposes and therefore a very uneconomical use is excluded.

This open statement about the economical facts seems to me more useful than to awaken hopes which have no chance of fulfilment because the power of the conditions of this time are altogether stronger than we are and our wishes and enthusiasm for aviation.

Some efforts for the future of aviation focus on the nationalization of the whole aviation and try to snatch it from the hands of the traders, the industry and the previous pioneers; after the short period of development that the airplane and the aviation have made this is neither fair nor useful. The state is not able to substitute the personal initiative of afore mentioned pioneers in this stage of development.

Others pursue the idea to found a mixed economic society in which all currently important aviation interests should unite; then only some big, efficient enterprisers would probably considered as members of this society.

In this mixed-economic society the state should be given overweight at any time by the fact that 51 of 100 rights to vote fall to the state.

Then this mixed economic society to which all industrial enterprises and airline enterprises should belong that want to do air transport should alone work in the field of air transport. All the other private effort should be excluded.

What is to be argued against it, arises for the expert by itself, apart from the fact, that serious industrial enterprises will hardly be found, which will bear the costs for tests and development in favour of a prevailing specification and supervision by the state.

Companies and well-founded individuals will always risk their capital if there is a chance to develop a new item, to find public recognition and to use this success in the form of advertisement for their remaining businesses or the own person. It is not absolutely necessary that the value created for aviation is immediately converted into cash. They will achieve more – as the experience has shown – if they are freed from state influence and business control and may have the hope to receive the potential success of their speculation. This situation one should also make possible everywhere in our future state until an enterprise is ripe for nationalization.

The speculative moment is a considerable stimulus, while it is lost during a nationalization or with a state enterprise since a state can not make such speculations because of its responsibility which it has – among others – to the parliament.

The German army administration has undertaken various attempts during the war, which looked similar to a beginning of a nationalized aviation; the purely aerotechnical result was not important.

However, even if this had created big aerotechnical successes, it would not deliver evidence that a nationalized aviation is more efficient.

Moreover, the military authority has had much more degrees of freedom regards the available means during the war than the state and every private individual or company has had, or has taken all thinkable freedoms under the conditions of war.

Money has played no role here and parliamentary control just as little.

If the German aviation would become nationalized under today's conditions then it would be only a question of time and the nationalized German aviation would be non-competitive compared to other countries and collapse in itself and then soon sold again to private enterprisers. I believe one would hardly find a buyer for the means of transportation made by the state.

Today the relations to foreign countries and its aviation maybe also not restrained by state monopolies, but the personal relations of experts must compensate here for the international state of the technical moments.

It is also required for a nationalization that the thing to be nationalised is so far developed that it has a certain surplus of its abilities and ranges of application, as for example the railway.

If the state keeps its current position regarding the nationalization of aviation to only nationalize if the thing itself is ascertaining profitability, then already the profitability questions will prevent the related consultations about nationalization.

One should impose to those who categorically demand the nationalization of air transport to create a profitability calculation with proofs about such an air transport, on this occasion also the question of the possibilities of the future technical advancement should be treated.

The most important factor for further advancement is the personal liability and responsibility of the single enterpriser, who must be liable with his capital, his business future and his personality so that the public trust in aviation is not endangered.

To achieve such a responsibility with a nationalized aviation is preliminary not possible.

It is also to be considered for Germany that we have not managed during the last 50 years in our highest national unity to really nationalize in Germany the post, the rail traffic, and even not the post stamp, although all controls, which would be necessary to protect the federal interests, could be organized with certainty on the ground.

Therefore it appears to me with consideration of the federal character of the German Reich, which it will also keep in the future if not all signs are sketchy, very doubtful to combine all federal interests in a nationalized German aviation.

Also for this reason the biggest chance of success has the free activity of the economic private forces in the free competition of a German and international air traffic.

One imagine the above suggested balancing of the German nationalized aviation within a frame of the interests of the international aviation with other states.

A nationalized German aviation in competition with the free French aviation, which worked up to now considerably fruitful on the international aviation, would always be in a disadvantage in technical regards.

If we were not allowed to participate in the international air transport with a nationalized German aviation or we were not competitive and consequently can not take part, then every standard of comparison for our own technical efficiency and advancement would be missing because in peace one can not shot down the comparative moments from the air.

The question of the airfields is to be judged differently; one will purposeful nationalize them, to keep the control of aviation and aviation itself in the own hand; one part of the state-owned airfields could be rented out to the industry, other parts or the surrounding and enclosed place could be arranged for sportive activities to make the preservation cheaper. With it the real sphere of activity of the means of aviation on the ground would be in the hand of the state.

What we need for the next future is that we will gain the trust of the public for the air transport by successful tests and further advancements.

Further we also need to utilise the available means of air transport in the best possible way for advancement and to exploit all possibilities of application. Moreover preparations are in full swing and a special publication will inform about the opportunities and the activity of the Reichsluftamt in this field in the next weeks.

August Euler

Appendix 13: Memorandum about the Practical Application of Aviation

The Undersecretary of the Reichsluftamt

Berlin W 8, 15 February 1919.

No. 1430/19

II. Part

The practical application of Aviation.

In the last paragraph of part I of my memorandum from 9 January 1919 No. 136/19 I have promised another publication which should treat the question how the available means of aviation from the war could be utilized for the advancement of aviation and how one could record the opportunities of application for avitaion.

Before I come to this problem, I send the following ahead:

Up to now the activity of the businessmen, engineers, tradesmen, the arrangements of the private individuals etc were exclusively directed – as far as they got in contact with transport – at the available means of transport, the railway schedules, the opportunity to drive with a car etc., so that the existing means of transportation and railway schedules etc., the telegraph, the teletyper and the telephone were the basis and precondition for the processing of the business transactions etc.

It was hardly thought about an execution of the business transactions by air transportation, especially not because the single interested parties was not given any means in its hands to calculate with the advantages of air transportation.

The procurement or supply of an airplane was connected with considerable time delays; mostly the railway or the automobile have had already fulfilled the task in question.

The location and distance of the next airfield was often not known.

The single potential buyers did not know, which preparations were necessary for the purpose of an aerial trip.

He was often hardly or completely unable to find out, if, where and what airplanes could be immediately provided for such an aerial trip.

During the last five years the whole aviation was militarily used and before 1914 it was not so developed in the civil sector that the single businessmen who was maybe interested in a aerial trip, could hope an airplane would become quick enough available to him for a necessary trip.

Now the opportunities are given for the fulfillment of such sudden interests in air transportation by the duplication of the means of aviation during the war, the airfields, hangars, and the other related preconditions for an organized aviation.

Now it is possible to bring the aircraft so into the sphere of business dispositions, that it steps into appearance at every minute and hourly, like the telephone, the telegraph, the car, the railway.

I count among the application opportunities of air transportation all those cases, where the railway, the car etc. with longer travel duration come into consideration only later or not at all because of lacking availability.

So the airplane should become a kind of "extra train" for a single or a few persons and be available always then if other means of transportation are not so soon available or automobiles are not fast enough with their average cruising speed.

Moreover, for the cases in which the time of the ending of a business negotiation can not be assigned at first without accelerating the negotiations itself, while on the other hand after its closing immediately a travel opportunity should be ready.

The acceleration of the business negotiations arises from the confrontation of the traffic speeds of railway, automobile and aircraft.

An automobile with 70 to 100 horse powers has an average travelling speed between 40 and 50 km, in special cases (car races with barred streets excluded) of about 60 km.

The airplane has an airspeed of 150 to 200 km and more per hour.

To grasp completely the opportunities of the use of aviation will be the most difficult question and major task.

It is a much wide-spread view that these opportunities are only low.

One is inclined to this view until now since one is probably not realizing that an aircraft enters the competition with other means of transportation or make any comparison because the most important condition of an intense air transport was missing, namely the supply with different airplane types at all locations and in association with the automobile transport from and to the airfield.

I try to explain with some examples which travel opportunities we can satisfy with the air transportation and for which purposes the airplane is more efficient than the other means of transportation on the ground.
1. Example: After one – by telephone conversation or teletype-writer prepared – stock market transaction which, nevertheless, could not be brought to the end because it seems to be essential to inspect written documents and calculations and to have a verbal consultation with experts, the likelihood exists to finish this trade by verbal consultation with the help of records on location under more favorable conditions. Since a second competitor exists who is pressing for a decision it can last only hours until the decision has to be made. Now the competitor can immediately fly to the place where the seller and the second competitor are, to bring the business there to a close what would probably not be possible with view on the existing railway schedule .
2. Example: The oldest member or head of a family becomes severely injured by an accident; one tells him that he should order his private things. For the regulation of his inheritance is an immediate personal discussion with his children, who live in Hamburg and Breslau, of great benefit and the own wish of the dying person. Also in this case the sons could use the airplane without problems to speak with the father before his death.
3. Example: A businessman who must travel in urgent matters to America can not reach the next ship which is going to America on the next day with the railway; however, he succeeds in reaching his steamboat with the airplane still in time, or also, if he has been late by rail in Hamburg he can catch up by airplane in Rotterdam. Consequently he wins maybe six or more days for his arrival in America.
4. Example: Two competitors intend both to close the same deal in Stockholm. One is already travelling with railway or steamboat, the other finds this out later and arrives at the destination by airplane still before his competitor and makes the deal.
5. Example: It is a necessary basic condition to provide an officially accredited signature for the completion of a business transaction. After a telephone call the signature is written out and some hours later delivered with a post airplane.
6. Example: The life rescue of a sick person depends on a quick operation which can occur only there and then by a specialized doctor. Every hour delay can bring the death to the sick person. This specialized doctor will use if he is promised with success a high sum for an immediate intervention the airplane to avoid to come a few hours too late.
7. Example: A great artist has arranged several guest performances at different locations which he can not do with the normal means of transportation. ¬
8. Example: At the general meeting of an industrial enterprise in Essen the personal presence of the Berlin branch manager is urgently demanded for a verbal report. The wish was made at 10 o'clock in the morning and can be already fulfilled at 2 o'clock in the afternoon, if the branch manager uses an airplane from of Berlin. The whole supervisory board does not need to remain until the next day and can make its decisions in the evening and travel home.
9. Example: For the hasty admission and sending of important photos for daily newspapers and illustrated journals the airplane might be used advantageously.
10. Example: In Nimmersatt a person was bitten by a mad dog. For the rescue is a protective inoculation within 12 hours necessary in an institute which is only located in certain towns. By rail the next town being in consideration is not to be reached anymore, an airplane can be used with the best success.
11. Example: In the morning the absence of one of the most important witnesses of defence arises at a court during the main negotiation. The missing witness can be brought by the interested party within a few hours to the negotiation, while, otherwise, by the postponement of the whole court and proof apparatus big costs and other circumstances cause heavy damages for the affected persons.
12. Example: An important machine part of the machine equipment of an Upper Silesian pumping station in an Upper Silesian mine becomes defective. It can not be replaced there and then immediately; the machine equipment was delivered by a Mannheim company. To prevent a days long stop of the vertical tunnel, perhaps its drowning, a spare part for the pumping machines can be brought by an airplane stationed in Mannheim together with an assembler of the factory within a few hours.
13. Example: During strike riots in the western coal areas immediate negotiations there and then are necessary with a member of the government from Berlin to prevent a growing and longer duration of the strike. Since it depends on hours in these cases the airplane will be the mean of transportation for the member of the government (or the union boss).
14. Example: For electoral agitations is it necessary that the main candidate of a party can speak at many places to the voters; he will be able to use an airplane for this purpose.
15. Example: Big newspapers, especially those which appear with a midday and evening edition, will use airplanes for practical and promotional reasons for the transport of their papers to neighbouring big towns, to bathing resorts etc.In this manner

for example the "BZ am Mittag" can arrive at 2 o'clock, the "8 Uhr Abendblatt" at 8 o'clock pm in Swinemünde.

...

[Remark of the author: August Euler brings eight more examples for the use of airplanes in the service of the police, the economy, over seas and transoceanic flights, or flights between bathing resorts, which should not be cited further at this point.]

...

If all the different water and land airfields, airships and airplanes of different types and in sufficient numbers are available then bigger and smaller trips can be made as pleasure trips in the air. The air passenger will make first a flight attempt of some rounds near the airfield in question. If he wins trust to aviation he will make a bigger aerial journey and finally also use the aerial mean of transportation for the purpose of his business interests.

For the rational exploitation of all these opportunities an airfield or airplane overview plan, maybe called "aerial travel plan", should be created, which is including all airfields and the airplanes available there, etc., the types, the loading opportunities, as well as the range of action and the airspeed of the same.

Such a plan would have to give additionally the distances between the airfields, so that the interested customer can get a reliable picture with this book within a few minutes about when he can probably arrive at his destination with the airplane; and if the arrival at this place can be made substantially earlier than with means of transportation on the ground.

A sheet of such a general plan is added as an example on the opposite page.

As suitable mean for the quicker promotion of a general competent judgement in the public about the use of aviation is maybe right, there should be added some school examples to the aerial travel plan to allow the check whether an aerial trip is faster than with the other means of transportation which go to the destination.

Then the aerial travel plan would be also suited for schools as a teaching book, while from this aerial travel plan tasks could be used by the teachers for the transport system. Such transport tasks are high demands for the pupils; moreover, they are an extremely interesting and instructive employment.

In some years if the so trained youth comes to the riper age, and also by the transfer of the interest in traffic woken up at school on the parents will by itself result in the whole population in the steady consideration of aerial travel opportunities or the relevant questions are dragged onto the area of the traffic arrangements of the whole population; moreover, however, the use of the aerial travel plan as textbook in schools will mean another support of aviation by the enlarged sales of the aerial travel plan.

Such an aerial travel plan will additionally include instructions for suitable travel clothes and behavioral rules during the aerial trip, also introduce the aerial traveller into the scientific peculiarities of an aerial trip.

The aerial travel plan is published in all newspapers, is put up on the railway-traffic offices, mayor offices and town halls.

He is to be received as a pocket timetable at all newsstands, t the railway stations and in the bookstores.

In the cases of the demonstrated examples the interested customer will immediately be able to recognise that suitable airplanes are located on the airfield of a certain place. Also, he can ascertain at hand of the given figures, how lang his aerial trip will last, and whether it brings him earlier to the destination than by rail.

He calls up the airfield that a specific type of airplane is to be made ready for launch and comes with an automobile to the airfield soon after. During the journey he orientates himself in his aerial travel plan about the airfield of the town of the destination of his journey and before the take-off he gives a related instruction that he should be fetched by the means of automobile at his destination or orders his business partner on the airfield.

The application opportunities for such a thought occasional air traffic are raised in many cases by the determination and naming of numerous auxiliary airfields, which must be usable for starting and landing only, without halls or technical arrangements. I imagine such auxilary airfields in particular near small towns which are hard to reach or not connected to the railway system. If an urgent need for travelling arises at a place because of the afore mentioned examples, then the interested person in question will call up only the nearest aviation station that he has to be fetched from the auxiliary landing field with an automobile. The ordered airplane will make a stopover on the auxiliary landing field and take on board the passenger for his aerial trip. There many other possibilities will present themselves because the use of the airplane for traffic and trade in the preceding measure will give many other opportunities which one had to renounce earlier because of the absence of suitable airfields, means of orientation, airlines and communications.

One will also soon recognize in which areas air traffic is demanded mostly or the biggest

A

B

C

D

E

F

G

H

I

K
usw.

Altenburg (Sachsen-Altenburg)

Einwohner	39976
Größe des Flugplatzes	0,725 × 1650
Bodenbeschaffenheit des Flugplatzes	Grasnarbe
Entfernung des Flugplatzes von der Stadt . . .	6,5 km

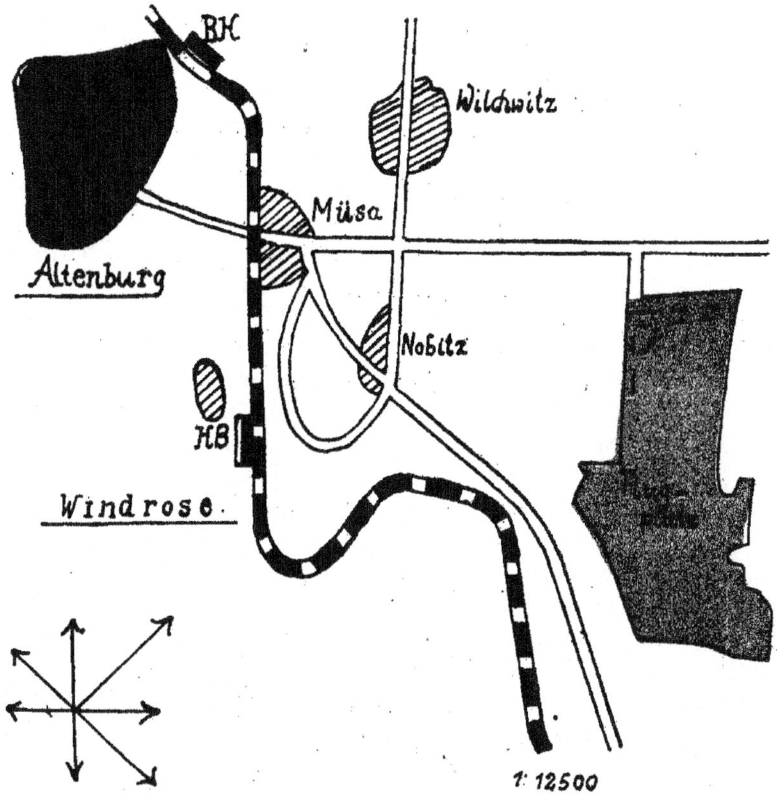

BH
Wilchwitz
Müsa
Altenburg
Nobitz
HB
Windrose
1: 12500

Bezeichnung der Luftfahrzeuge	Bezeichnung	Nutzlast kg	Stundengeschwindigkeit km	Aktionsradius km
Luftschiffe	Z	20000	90	5400 *)
Riesenflugzeug	R	2000	90	1000 *)
Großflugzeug	G	900	120	690 *)
Flugzeug mit 3 Sitzen . . .	—	220	130	550 *)
Flugzeug mit 2 Sitzen . . .	C, B	180	140	500 *)
Flugzeug mit 1 Sitz . . .	D	150	160	240 *)

Flughindernisse in der Nähe des Platzes: keine

*) Sämtliche Zahlen sind nur annähernde Beispiele und können keinen Anspruch auf Maßgeblichkeit erheben.

opportunities of the application of air traffic step into appearance.

I would particularly like to stress that it is not certain from the very beginning that the bigger traffic lies, for example, in the western industrial zones. It is easily possible that bigger interests in airlines exist in the eastern areas because the remaining traffic opportunities there are more unfavorably than in the west.

The ticket price can be settled for commercial purposes according to the object in question, like process fees of the lawyers.

They vary according to the distance, in relation to the considered liability and the risks under inclusion of the weather conditions etc.

Every aerial trip for commercial purposes would be negotiated accordingly, one will always soon find out at which price the customer would probably renounce to the flight.

Of course the price can be also set per km linear distance; what would have various other, maybe even more important reasons like those of an accordingly big benefit for itself.

The airline travelling would become unnecessary expensive, if the airplanes would return empty to their home bases after fulfillment of its travel purpose.

Therefore, they should not have a special home station but in this sense maybe to a part a flying domicile.

The airplane balance within the airfields can occur like the balance of the railway trucks.

The creation of a basic land and water airplane networks for the air traffic all over Germany is necessary; the latter should be in the hand of the state to allow a reliable control of the aviation.

The installations of the military Navy airfields, which should be utilized at the moment by the Reichsverwertungsamt, could be used immediately. I think it is better and more advantageous in the national total interest to use it for the here imagined air traffic than to knock it for cheap sale for other purposes.

In this manner the under war conditions exemplary and with big costs equipped military and navy airfields would be kept for future air traffic and the state, while they would only result in a little part of the earlier paid investments after an immediate liquidation and other utilization and later the parliament will maybe never again grant the means to create such suitable arrangements for air traffic.

The state should determine the value of the airfields in comparison to other currently possible utilizations in favour of the air traffic and with the so found value it should with reference to the unproductive costs for the administration of the airfield equipment in the next two years – either participate in the public air traffic or rent out the installations to airline companies or entrepreneurs based on the so found values.

The airfields in private property could be either bought by the state or be included in the airfield net also for the payment of a suitable rent to the airfield owners.

Every town and every place can have air- and landing fields.

They do not need to be locked under [certain] circumstances.

If a general interest of the state to install an airfield is not existing then the towns and locations have to carry the costs of the installation themselves to be connected to the air traffic net and to get the benefit of the above described faster business traffic.

The airfield question burdens the air traffic considerably with the expenses caused by the airfield.

If the expenses associated with the airfield are burdened exclusively to the air traffic , then air traffic will hardly be profitable.

Provisionally the air traffic on the airfields will still unwind for a long time particularly in the earliest morning hours in summer, namely in the time before 6 o'clock in the morning.

Under recognition of this fact it is also to be taken into consideration to create even lodging rooms for passengers and aerial travellers on the airfields because it depends substantially on the weather whether for example in summer an airplane flies away 3, 4, 5 or 6 o'clock in the morning, because fog, poor sight, heat compensation at sunrise are still playing an important role for the judgement of the beginning of the journey.

Therefore, airline passenger should be woken up only before the beginning of a bigger trip, actually, if the chance that can be flown in a half or one hour certainly exists.

The trust of the air passengers in aviation is in any case not raised by hour long standing around and waiting.

Therefore, on bigger airfields near big towns accommodation and restaurant possibilities must exist.

Furthermore it is necessary that additionally a lot of places, meadows and lakes, which are suitable for occasional landing of airplanes, are marked accordingly.

A regulation on the marking of such places should be remitted legally, so that one can recognize from the air easily at any time where an airplane can land without special danger.

If one imagines such emergency landing fields geographically in suitable distances distributed over Germany and made visible for pilots, so one could see in bright weather from the airplane in 2000 meters height 15 to 30 km to every direction,and can always judge if a suitable emergency landing field exists on the left, the right or straight ahead.

Quite a lot accidents which occur during the landing can be avoided by such an organization.

The trust of the pilot and the air passengers would be lifted considerably by the moment, that the eye always recognizes one or two emergency landing fields in certain distances.

The use of these meadows, fields and stubblefields occurs, since it concerns emergency landing fields rarely and therefore costs might hardly originate.

I can imagine that such signs for emergency landing fields are saying at the same time the place is not yet or is harvested, the place is a first class landing field, a landing ground of the second order etc. etc.

This can easily be brought to the attention of the flying audience by crosses, points and lines.

As well a regulation about the marking of all towns, villages and locations should be ordered by the law to allow the doubtless identification of the names of locations in flight and to make the navigation easier and secure.

The military interests in the field of aviation have to brought in balance with the civil interests.

In the coming peace the military can hardly exclusively demand the big airfields for itself and it would hardly touch the military interests if on one and the same airfield on one side the military installations would do their service while on the other side the starting and landing activities of the industry and the civil airlines occur or both parts work at the same time together; in particular if for common tasks not doubled work and doubled costs come up.

Places with a value of several millions would not be used exclusively for the activities of the military in peace times but could also be made serviceable and useful for public, economic, industrialy and trade interests in peace times.

Furthermore the airfields are to be considered for the opportunity that competitive events could occur on them which serve the breeding of future trade and traffic airplanes.

Here we have the precondition that such an airfield can harbor big masses of people.

The aviation offers currently only little perspectives for the future regarding sportive activities because one can probably surely say that until now only a few sportsmen existed who did only do aerial sport because of sportive enthusiasm, carrying their own costs.

All flight competitions in the years 1910, 1911, 1912 and 1913 were nearly exclusively outfitted by the industry or the air sportsmen in question and officers flew machines which were property of the industry or the army administration; in all cases they did neither own airfields nor aircraft hangars and mostly not even an airplane.

On big airfields the totalisator would have been a an appropriate tool to bind huge numbers of people with aero-sports events to the airfield and to use them on this way and by the payment of tickets for the carrying of the costs of the airfield.

Now I imagine the future air traffic – based on the enterprising spirit of of all interested persons – organized in the following manner:

All airlines, airship and airplane factories, flight engine factories, airfield owners, the state and the cities come together in a still to search common form of activity in a "Luftverkehrs-Versuchs-Gesellschaft Deutschlands" [Air Traffic Society of Germany].

The involved participate in profit and loss according to the amount of their contributions to the society. Contingents could be given for:

1. the airplane type,
2. the airships,
3. the airplanes,
4. the aircraft engines,
5. the air traffic personal,
6. the airfields,
7. the totalisator,
8. the air travel schedule,
9. the flight disctances,
10. the weather service,
11. the news service,
12. etc., etc.

Hereby I assume that the airship and aircraft industry different to the practice in war will develop more according to the American principle of division of labor and will distribute the production of different airplane types according to the different abilities of the factories.

I have the opinion that the industry should agree that one factory is only building Giant-, another only great airplanes, a third only 3-seaters, 2-seaters or post airplanes or airships etc.

So profitability can be achieved sooner than if a factory is building 10 and more different types and has to make the very different costly trials at the same time. An airplane for the imagined post traffic should be a lot cheaper than the price which was paid at last by the army administration.

Every new company should be incorporated into

the Luftverkehrs-Versuchs-Gesellschaft [Air Traffic Trial Society] if it can produce an airplane type which is suitable for air traffic and as soon as this type meets the requirements of the Reichsluftamt, has passed the examination of the type, was allowed for the air traffic and the company as such guarantees a specialized and expertise oriented participation.

The removal of unfit types will result from itself by the examination and solution of the tasks which were handed-over.

Airships and airplanes which are not often used or have little success and many accidents will be drawn back by this process like the unloved types.

The success of the competing different aircraft types and airships will benefit the development of the airplane and airship construction.

The yearly reports and the related publications will give a clear picture of the efficiency of the different companies and the whole air traffic.

The cooperation of all involved interested persons and moments occurs over the airfields of the state and the cities with steady mediation by the supervising state office.

The necessary supervision of the air traffic on the airfields will be made by organs of the state.

The check of the departure, landing and stopover is possible and sufficient.

It can be ordered for emergency landings that the airplane is not allowed to fly again away from the place of the emergency landing without the permission of the local, etc., authorities.

Every pilot has to be sworn in as duty office clerk under threat of stripping him off the pilot licence.

An organized aviation would not be a socialized aviation, it is in fact the opposite.

It would not be the monopoly of a single or a few companies but a competitive machine, in which every inventor, industrialist and able head can fully unfold his power.

Equally it would not be a Trust and also not a mixed economy society since influence, profit, loss and success results from the amount of free activity and initiative of every involved person.

Finance consortia would be avoided at first which would be of importance because this would very fast and soon call for socialization after a doubtful rentability or would give up again the newly founded air traffic or would sell the means of air transportation since the consumed capital would not yet be closely enough connected manual labour connected with aviation and the resulting responsibility.

Technology would have the most free imaginable opportunities of development.

Every involved participant would face the question of truth whether he could really contribute with his achievements in favour of the aviation in its greatness and in general since he faces the fact to be in competition with the remaining means of air traffic without any break and his performance would permanently depend on the judgment of all competitors and experts.

On this way individual influence can not result in the sale of the means of air traffic to the state, nevertheless it ensures the competitiveness and the public opinion is not misled by accidental successes when the air vehicle in question can compete under certain favorable conditions.

The flight competitions for the creation of suitable trade and traffic airplanes will be treated soon in a special chapter as well as the photographic sections, the signal and weather service, the insurances, the aviation equipment and finally the internationality of aviation.

If I summarize my considerations of the first – critical – part of my publication from the 9 January now and the content of this second available part so it becomes clear that the air traffic in its development to the trade air traffic can probably not provide a benefit in the next years.

Since the currently airplane types in use are principally developed the aircraft industry can evaluate if the air traffic will be profitable or a loss.

The private capital would probably be much easier enthusiastic for air traffic and decide to make the related big investments if one would see the first time airplanes and airships fly like we have seen in war.

The world would raise imaginable big capital with enthusiastic surprise to create the air traffic because it would not imagine all the pain, failures, dangers and costs which are connected with air traffic.

The military treatment of the here to consider moments in the last three years questioned the profitability even more.

Therefore only the question arises: does the state has an interest to keep pace in aviation with the remaining Kulturvölker [cultur nations]?

We should answer this question with "Yes" already for the reason that aviation with its ideal means of the future is more suited than any other mean to act as mediator of nations and politically balancing.

Also for us result ideal national values from aviation which are useful for all in the later future; air traffic and its enterpriser today can not carry alone the costs for this in today's economically bad times.

A subsidizing by the state with cash means will meet difficulties under the current dominating unpredictable economic conditions therefore I suggest that the Reich provides the available means of transport, airfields, hangars, workshops, etc. so far as it is owning them into the Luftverkehrs-Versuchs-Gesellschaft in a manner which equates the need instead of let the surplus army equipment sale out for other purposes.

Furthermore, all industrial enterprises which were involved in this pioneering developments in the trade air travel should make it a duty to themselves to put a certain number of airships and airplanes with service personal and pilots in aerial service and get well-measured subsidies by the state.

This is necessary since after the expected taxes on war profit and income the young aviation industry will only have left the brick stones and machine equipment and the capital available to the young industry from pre-war times will not be enough to keep it alive.

From anywhere the means for aviation must be taken because it is probably not possible over many years to take it from the earnings of the future air traffic.

So the state and the industry as well are facing the question: Should a German air traffic which is able to compete with other states called into life? If one is answering the question with yes, then there is no cheap way for the state because the industries of the other states work under the totally different conditions than our industry, in general they have the need of the whole world for their industrial exploitation and don't need by far not to carry the same burden as our industry.

However, if one says no to the question to create such an air traffic then nothing more remains as to leave the related interests of the state to the single private enterprises and enthusiasts with their insufficient means.

Seen from an international point of view then Germany would play a role in the realm of air which would make her defeat appear bigger then is really was if we look at the abilities of our nation.

August Euler

Appendix 14: Memormandum about the Internationality of Aviation

Berlin, 15 March 1919.

The Internationality of Aviation

Under the prevailing political relations the question suggests itself to make the aviation the trial balloon for the planned League of Nations.

In particular the aviation seems to be suitable for a League of Nation like beginning organisation. Therefore, the air should be made independent from state interests and are freed.

The aviation seems to be able to mean only a progress in the human culture if it can be regulated internationally; her legislation should be an international one. A national aviation also can not be profitable. The aviation should be controlled constitutionally and administered by national authorities. In the single parts of the countries, today still divided by national borders, authorities should be created which present the present national and international interests. As an example the international patent right can partly serve here, which is authoritative in the single countries and makes decisions for the for the judgement of relevant legal issues in all other countries, which are connected with the patent convention after internationally agreed international basic rules.

To explain closer this problem of a still provisionally figment of imagination I imagine the establishment of an international aviation commission, which has its main seat in one of the civilised nations of the world and establishes aviation authorities in all single states. It makes aviation independent of national demarcations and national laws and is exclusively working after instructions and arrangements of the international central authority.

In suitable periods international aviation congresses take place which would bring proposals for the perfection and improvement of the organizational and legislative measures and therefore guarantee a steady improvement of the international regulation of air traffic.

Which difficulties oppose the implementation of this thought under consideration of national reasons? In my opinion no big ones; since in the air the single states have not committed themselves yet, they can free themselves very easily from present arrangements about national aviation. Contracts, obligations and facilities do not exist in a form that they are mutually exluding each other by the state; the single states also have not to give up any traditional custom.

The practical aviation is ten years old, and if one subtracts the interruption by the war, only five years; already in consideration of the development of aviation experienced by nearly all living persons one should not close the internationally available free road for the latest achievements of technology in the air by national legislation. If we see that attempts of all states to head for a League of Nations with president Wilson, in whose draught contracts the considerations being considered here are already fixated here, so here the best views for the realization of the thought of the internationalization of the air come up for those people, who think in fact, that they must not live permanently in a border-defending state.

If, indeed, the League of Nations which we even have in mind today, was to be put in practice in the ideal view of president Wilson for the Earth, then one could probably state that this must be easy for the air.

The earlier position taken from England regarding aviation was repealed by the acceptance of the articles of the League of Nations; America has already committed herself by the Wilson program; Germany is in a situation from which one does not need to assume that she could come into conflict with the above idea; France has stood from the outset on the above-said position; since it initiated its earlier related international draft law with § 1 word-for-word: "The aviation is free, there are no borders in her."

However, the aviation also carries strength in itself to enforce a position as peace-keeping element; since if one considers the possibilities of future wars as they are recorded in the draught of the League of Nations contract, so then it arises even more, that aviation must be regulated internationally, to bring the air force as means of coercion in the hands of the League of Nations. If, for example, with the emergence of differences of opinions one member of the League of Nations is not complying to the decision of the League of Nations, the international air fleet would be able to bring the reluctant member to reason within hours. If one imagines all aviation means of the world used against a single country, then the possibilities to make a stand are rather low ones.

If a very big number of private and commercial airplanes can be converted into war tools after the breakout of different opinions and can arrive in the enemy foreign country within hours, then the internationalization of the aviation tools and a steady international supervision of the commercial fleets etc. are necessary if the League of Nations wants to win time for useful mediation in such cases.

Further it is to take into consideration, whether not, if an internationalization of the whole aviation is unachievable, the military aviation of all countries should be internationalized, in peace the control of the whole remaining civil air traffic implemented and an international military established and at the same time the League of Nations protected in the afore mentioned sense.

Technology and science will have perfected aviation soon so far that after human judgement after a few years every war can be prevented, if the use of aviation means is regulated internationally. Therefore, an aviation fleet, organised according to the right of the international League of Nations, should for this reason do the first mentioned work and should be the most efficient weapon of the League of Nations.

The internationally organized air-, commercial and League of Nations fleet would have an automatically establishing authority because of its reliability as being international and since an internationally organized aviation authority would get soon in every country a certain self-confidence with its internationality and not be inclined to obey the land to which the officials were related nationally before or are related. It is also not necessary to employ officials of the same state in each country. All officials of international aviation could be also explained as stateless persons and the internationality added as nationality to them or one could give them a constitutional position according to their international tasks, so that the organization of the international aviation with its administrative organs feels like a state over the other states and therefore a reliable authority's consciousness would be necessarily caused.

August Euler

Bibliography

- Fokker, A.H.G., und Gould, Bruce, *Der fliegende Holländer* – Das Leben des Fliegers und Flugzeugkonstrukteurs A.H.G. Fokker, Rascher & Cie, A.-G. Verlag, Zürich, Leipzig und Stuttgart, 1933.
- Heuss, Theodor, *Robert Bosch – Leben und Leistung*, Rainer Wunderlich Verlag, Hermann Leins, Tübingen, 4. Auflage 1946.
- Italiaander, Rolf, *Spiel und Lebensziel – Der Lebensweg des ersten deutschen Motorfliegers* Hans Grade, Gustav Weise Verlag, Berlin, 1939.
- Kronenwerth, Egon, *Der tolle Euler – Flugzeugführer Deutschland Nummer 1* – Erinnerungen von Egon Kronenwerth, Frankfurt a.M., Umschau Verlag, ohne Jahr, ISBN 3-524-88042-8.
- Supf, Peter, *Das Buch der deutschen Fluggeschichte, Vorzeit* – Wendezeit – Werdezeit, Verlagsanstalt Hermann Klemm AG, Berlin-Grunewald, Bd. 1 u. Bd. 2, 1936.
- Vetter, August, *Feldberg im Schwarzwald – Die Geschichte des höchsten Schwarzwaldberges*, der einstigen Vogteien Altglashütten, Bärental, Falkau und Neuglashütten sowie der Gemeinden Feldberg (Schwarzwald), Selbstverlag der Gemeinde Feldberg (Schwarzwald), 1982.

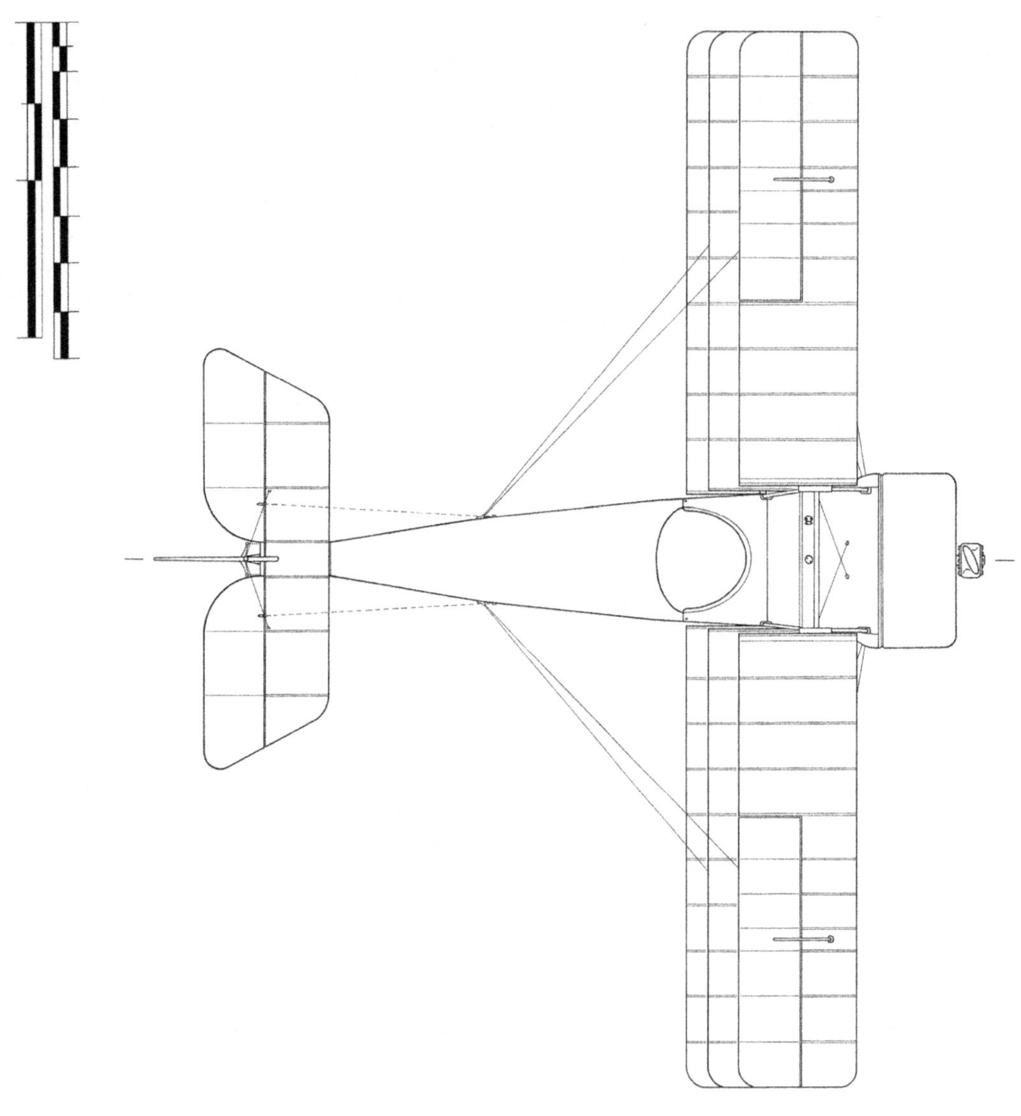

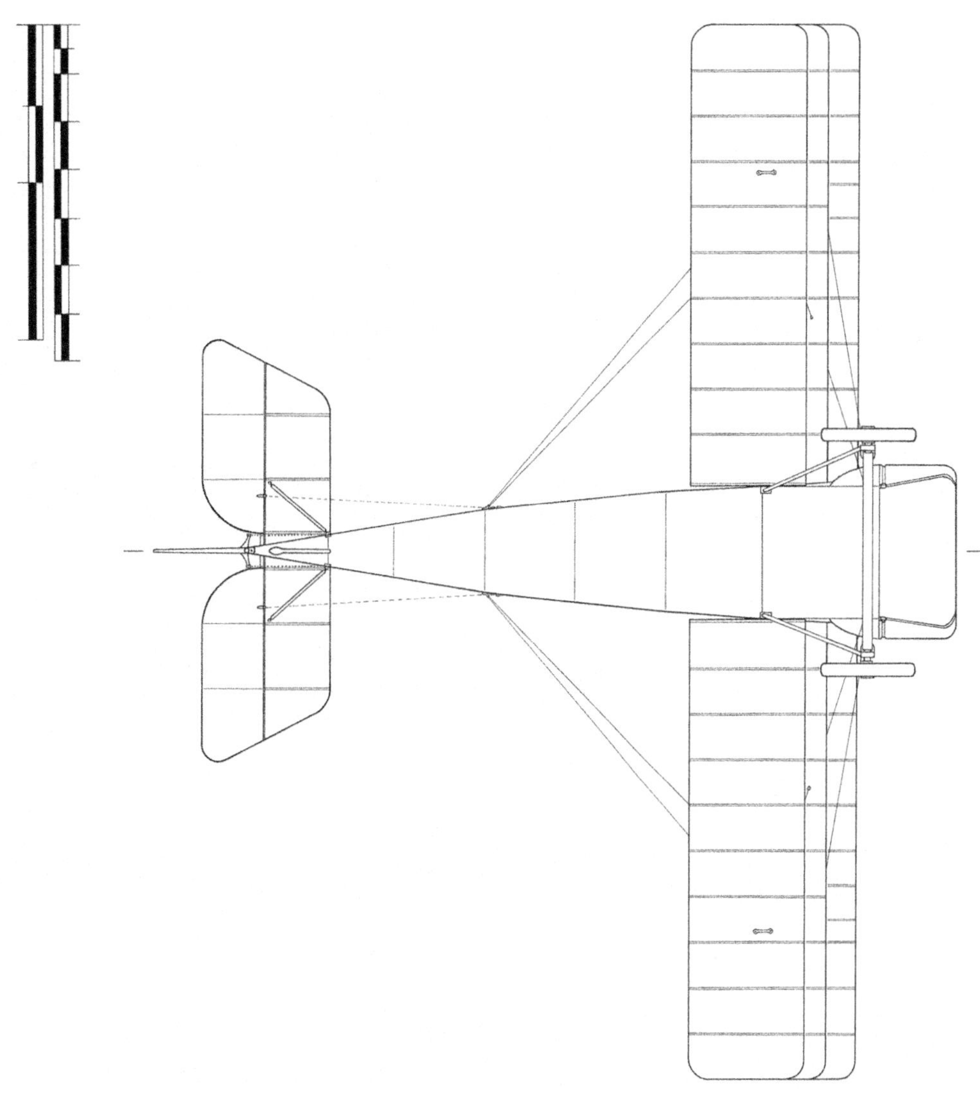

Euler D.R. 9

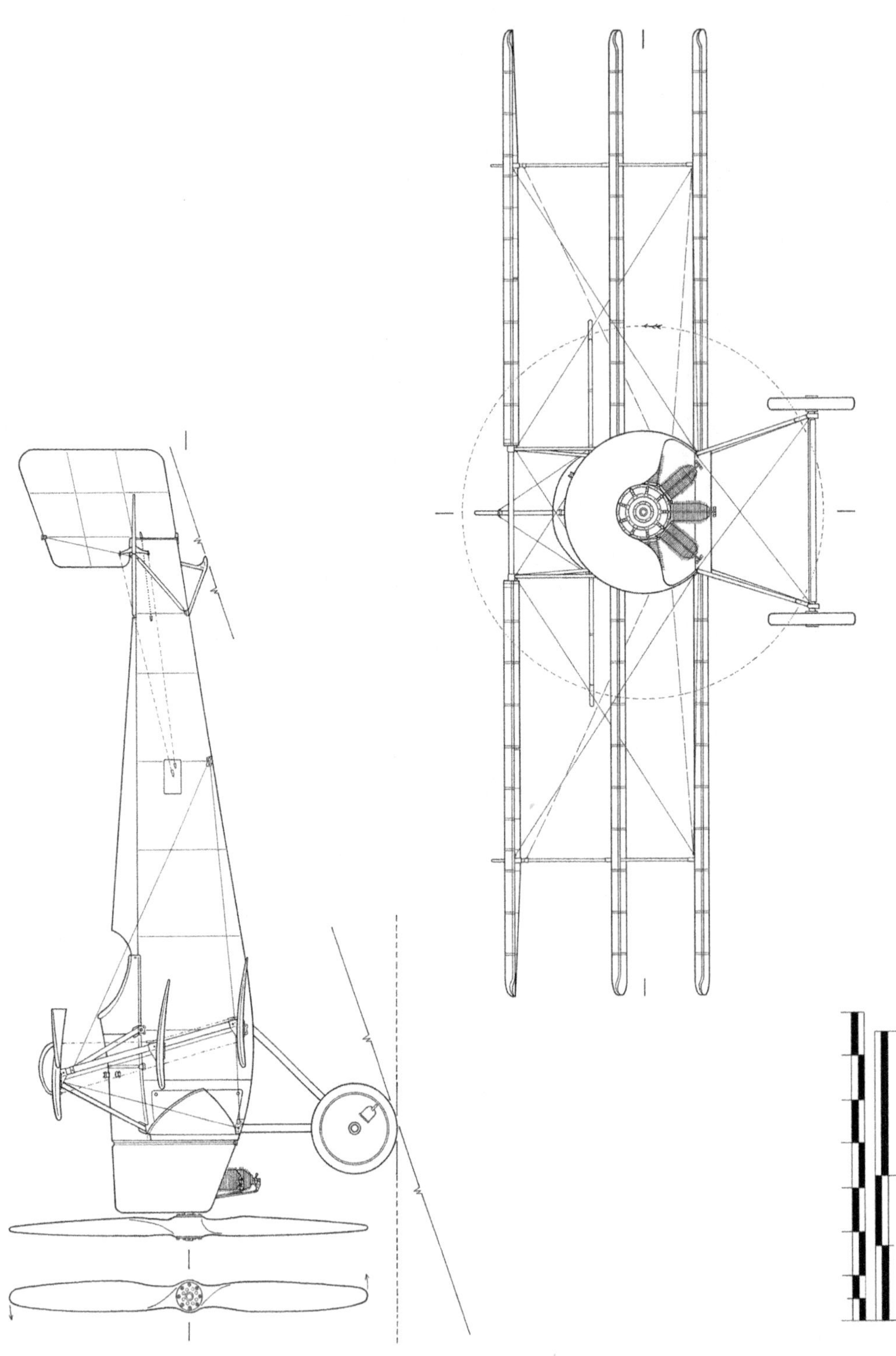

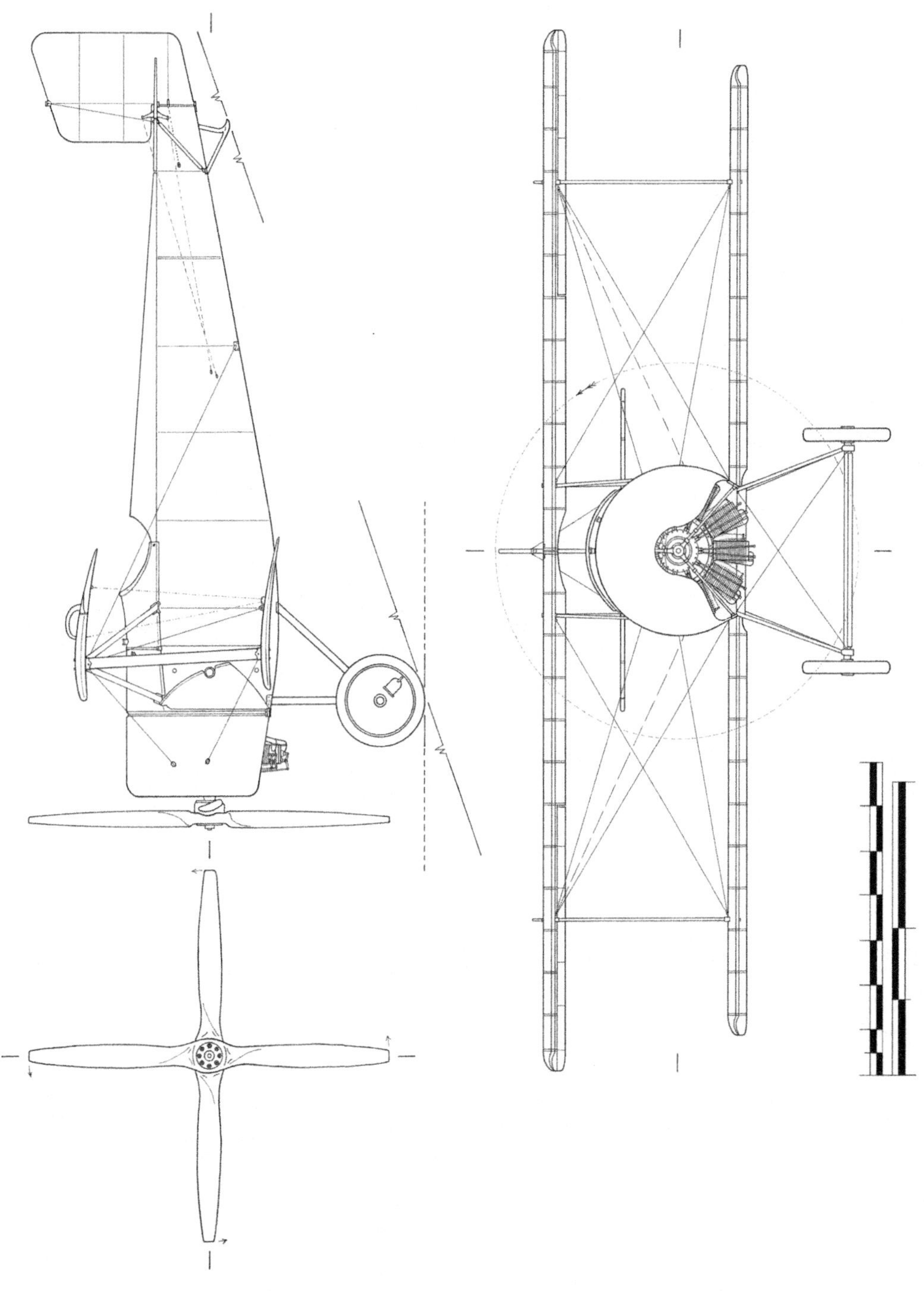

Euler D 6

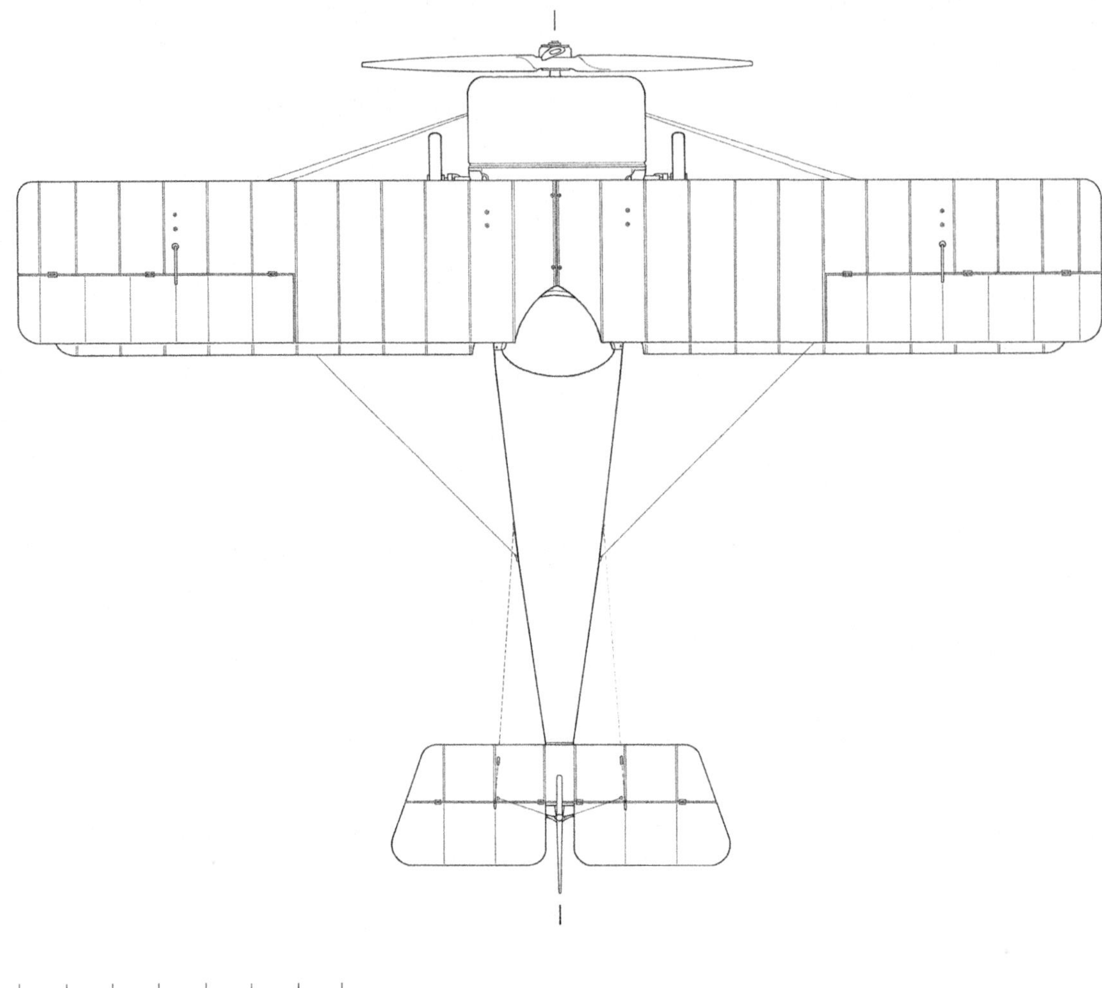

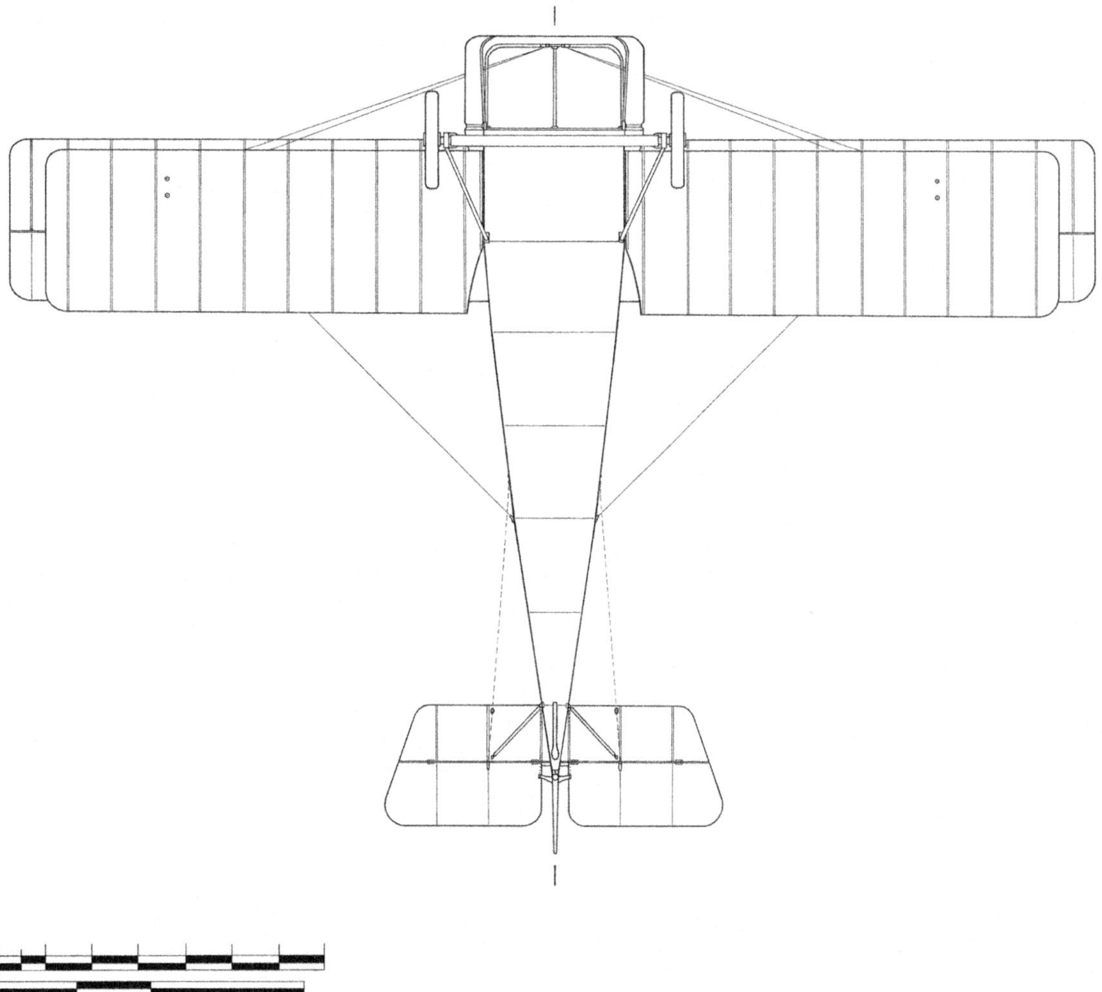

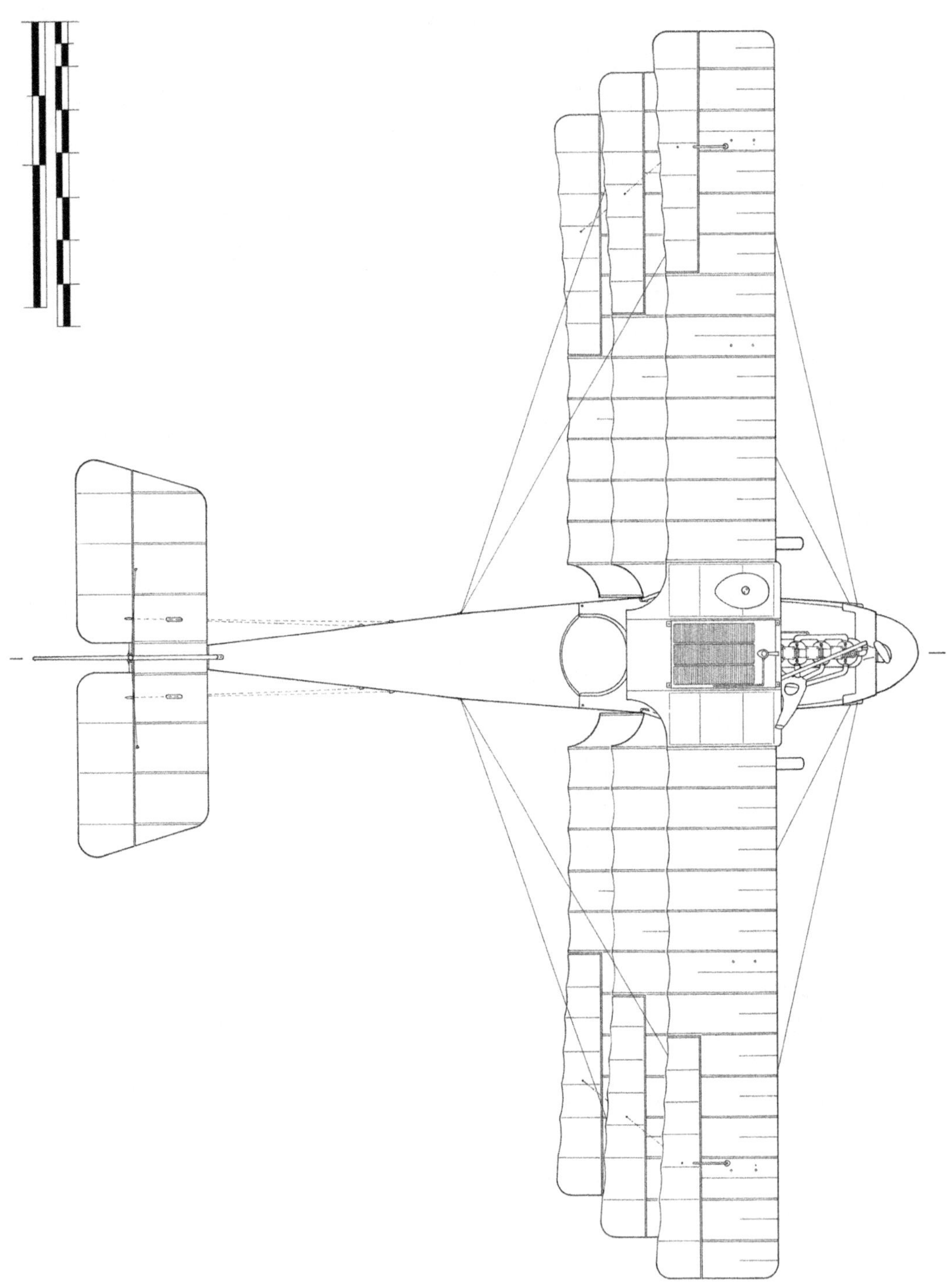

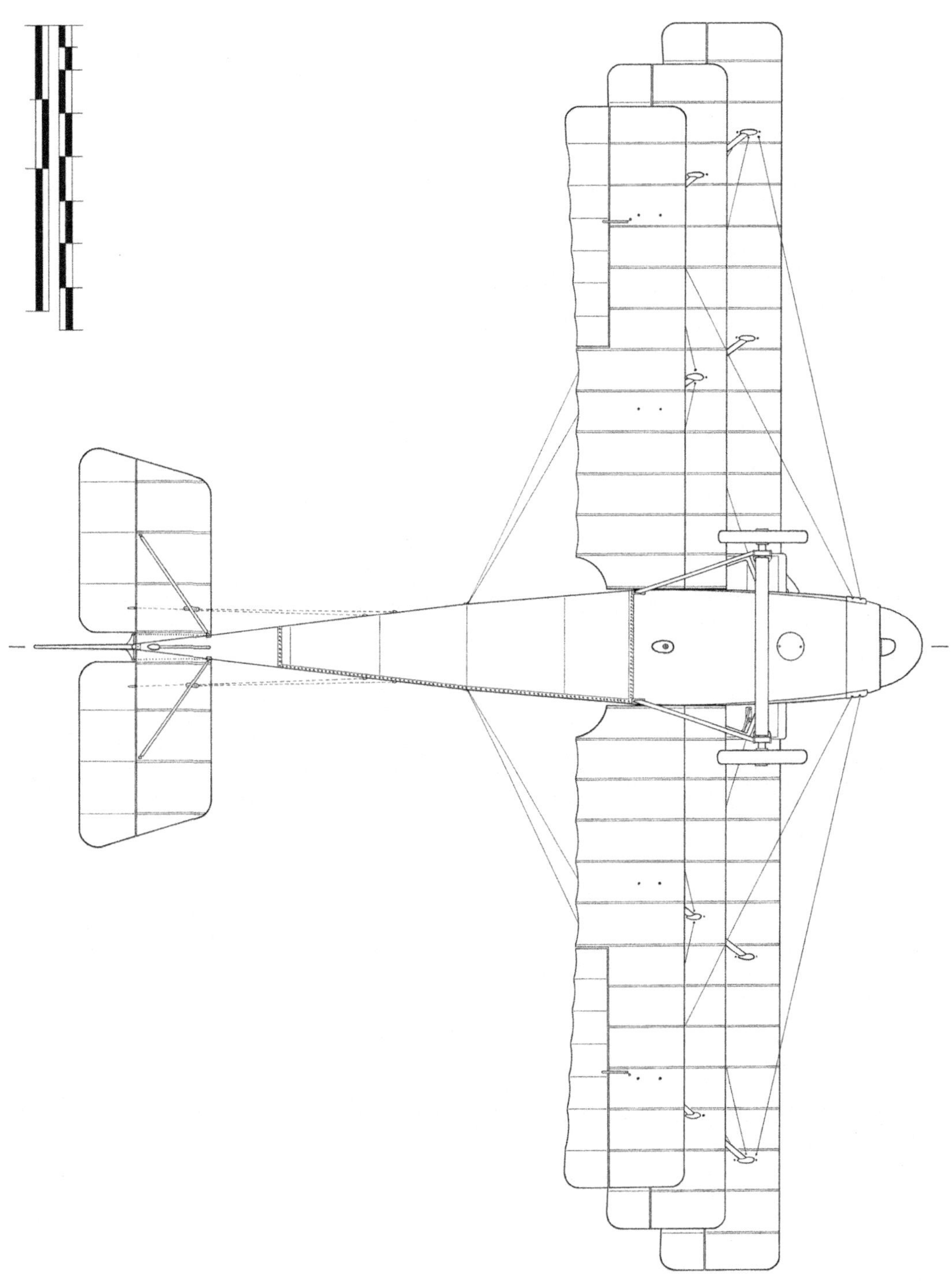

Euler D.R. 5

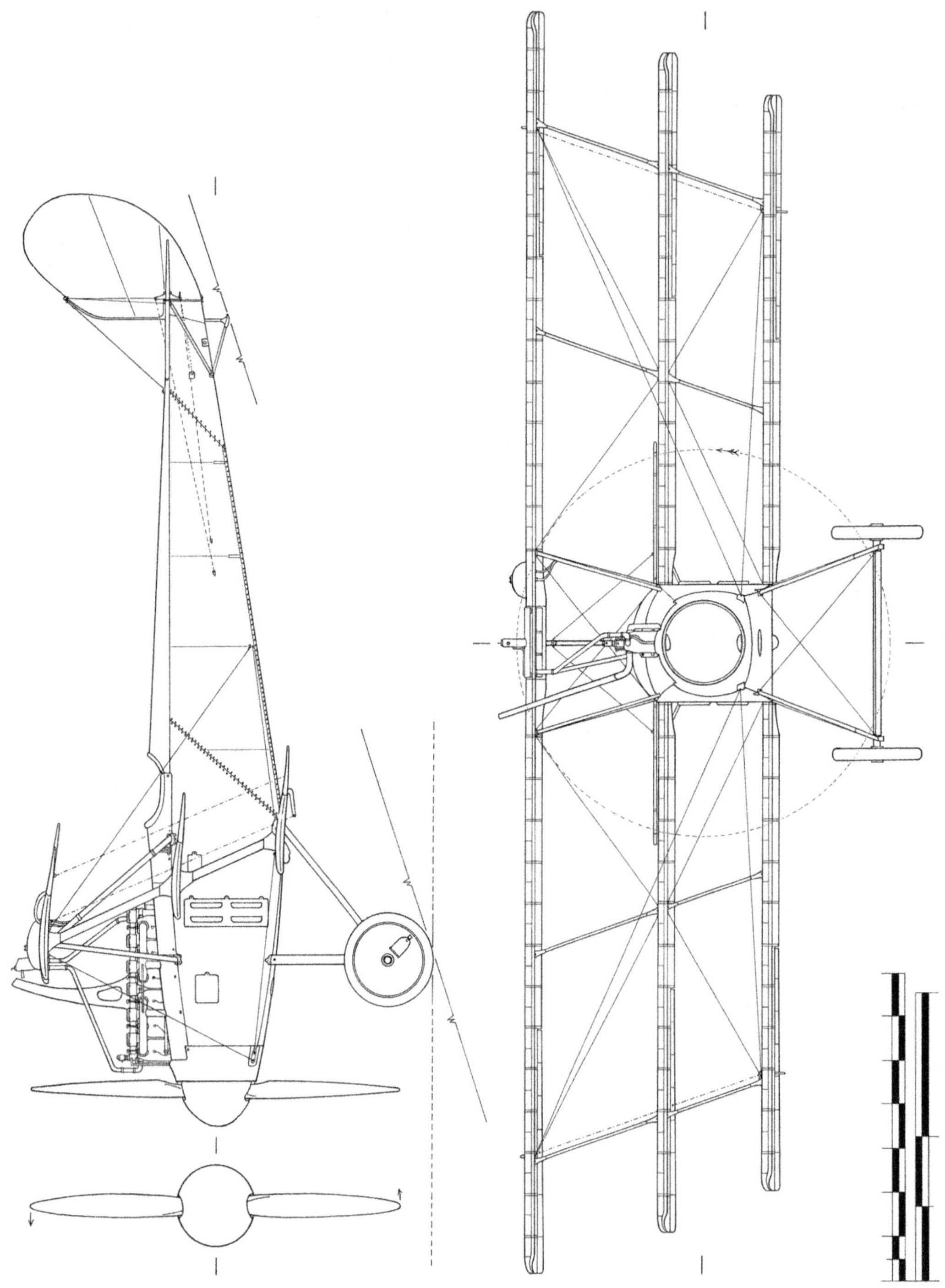

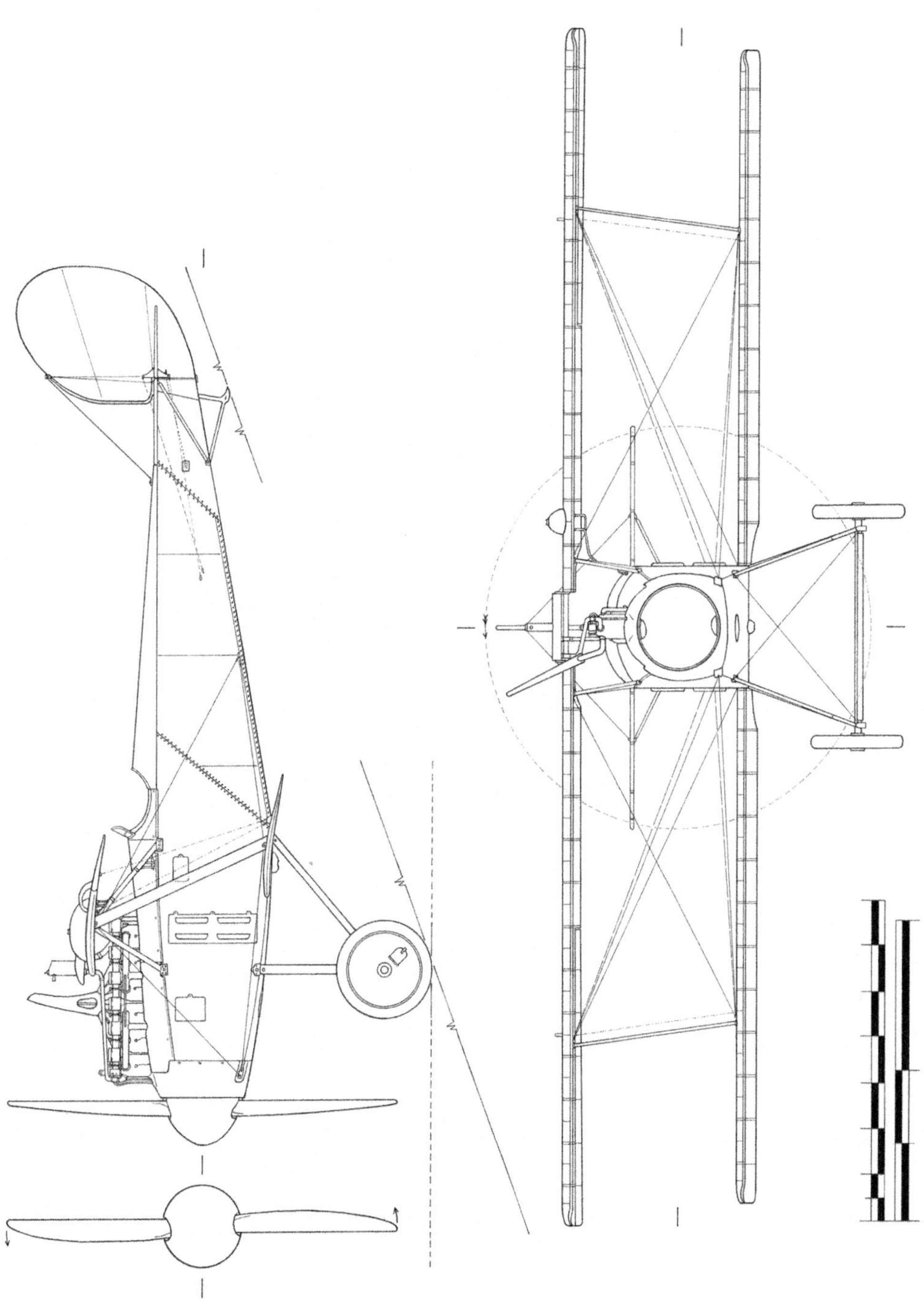

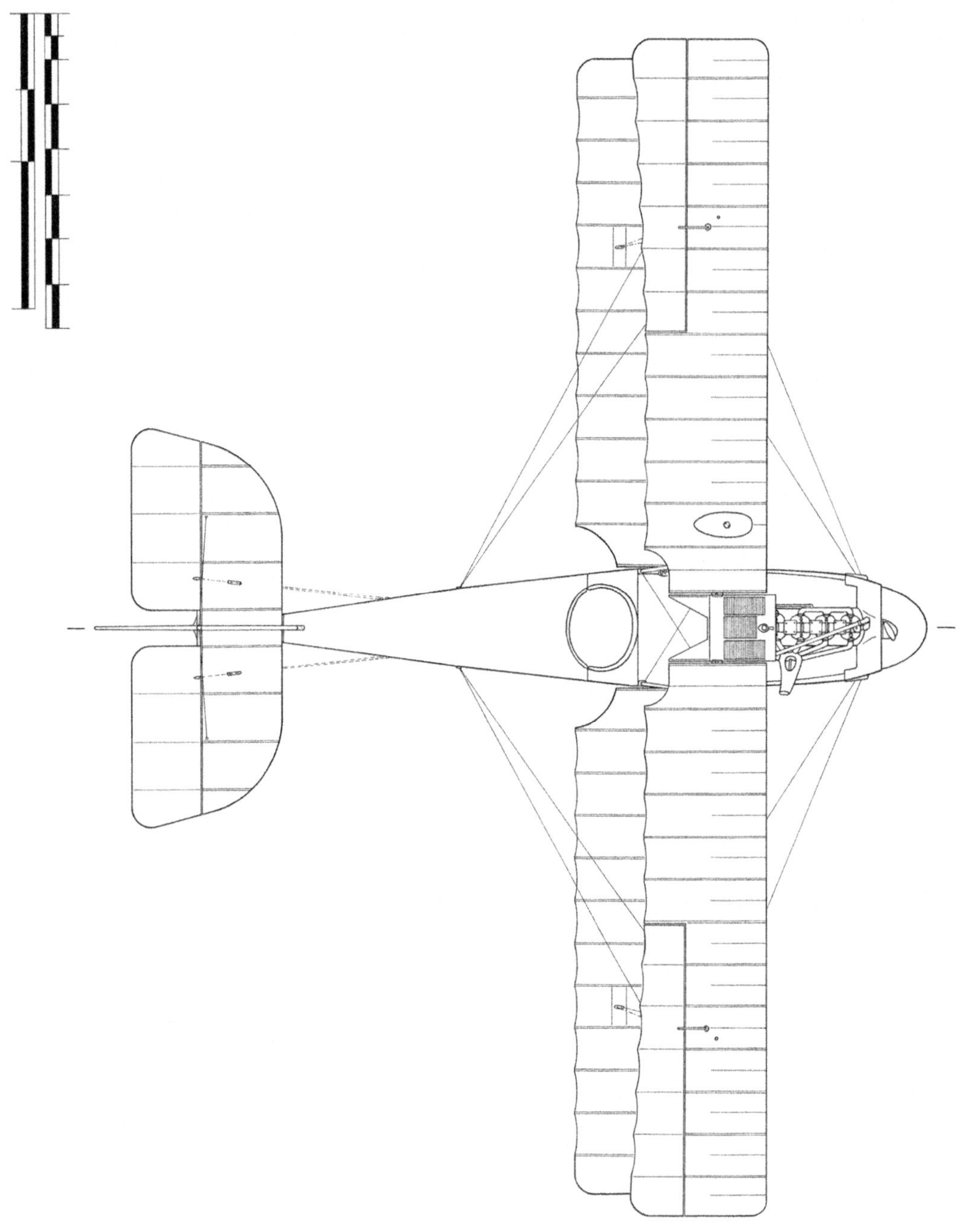

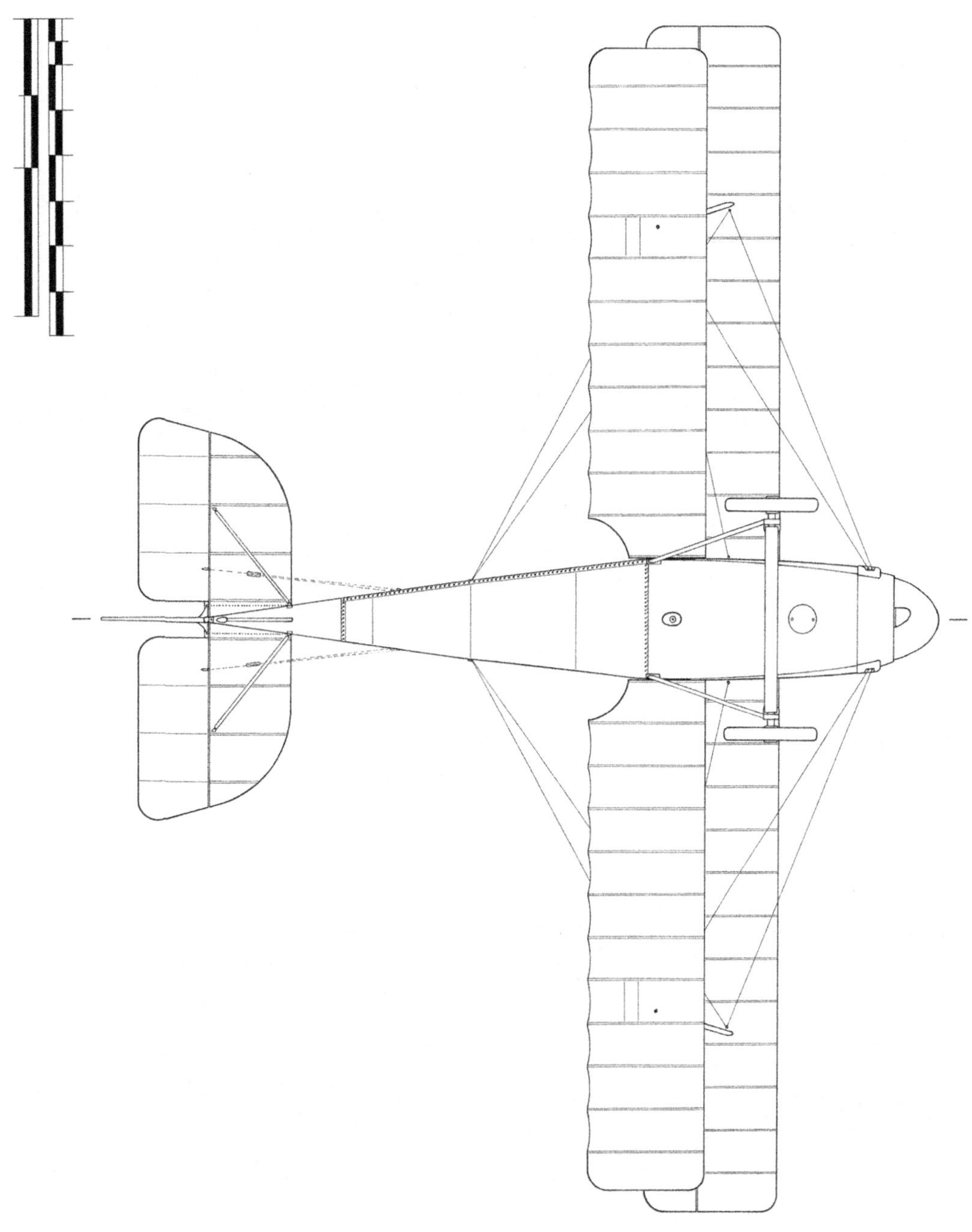

Above: Euler D II 274/16 with a massive Gotha WD14 marine number 1415. The Euler was used for training.

Above: Two Euler D II fighter-trainers with a massive Gotha WD14.

Printed in Great Britain
by Amazon